£7·95

Erik Arnold is ~~a~~ ~~member~~ ~~of~~ ~~the~~ ~~Science~~ ~~Policy~~ Research Unit, University ~~of~~ ~~Sussex,~~ ~~working~~ ~~on~~ ~~policy,~~ ~~skill~~ ~~and~~ employment aspects of technological change. Recent work includes studies of computer-aided design use in the UK and Europe, office automation, and the television industry.

Philip Bereano has been teaching technology and social policy at the University of Washington, Seattle, since 1974; previously, he was on the faculty at Cornell University. He has degrees in Engineering, Law, and Regional Planning, and is also an adjunct faculty member of the Women's Studies Programme at the University of Washington.

Christine Bose holds a Bachelor degree in Mathematics and a Doctorate ~~in~~ Sociology, and is currently an Assistant Professor of Sociology at the ~~State~~ University of New York at Albany, where she also served ~~as~~ Director of Women's Studies from 1978 to 1981. Prior to ~~that~~ ~~she~~ taught at the University of Washington. She has ~~published~~ articles on a number of issues related to women's ~~and~~ paid employment.

~~...~~ *Burr* graduated from the School of Independent Studies, ~~Lancaster~~ University, where her specialist subject was the social context ~~of~~ ~~science~~ and technology. In 1980 she began work for a PhD on ~~'Product~~ Innovation and the Female Consumer' at the Technology ~~Policy~~ Unit, University of Aston. She is currently employed as an ~~education~~ officer in the Consumer/Debt Education Unit at Birmingham ~~Consumer~~ Advice Centre.

~~Frances~~ *Evans* has a first degree in Sociology from the University of ~~Sussex~~ and has done graduate work on women's unemployment at the University of Kent. She is currently employed as a research officer by the National Health Service.

Wendy Faulkner is completing a PhD thesis at the Science Policy Research Unit, University of Sussex, on the links between academic and industrial research in the field of biotechnology. She was previously a member of the Brighton Women and Science Group which edited *Alice through the Microscope: The Power of Science over Women's Lives.*

Dot Griffiths teaches sociology to engineering students at Imperial College, London University, hence her interest in the position of women in engineering and science. She is a member of the British Society for Social Responsibility in Science, and is on the editorial collective of *Feminist Review.*

Anne Lloyd is a physicist with 15 years' experience in the computer industry. She was among the women who set up the Women in Computing group in London, and currently works in computer education.

Liz Newell has been actively involved in the women's movement for several years. She has worked in software support; as a programmer for a large computer manufacturer; and within the public sector. She is currently employed within the University of London.

Elkie Newman is based in London and has been an active campaigner on abortion, contraception and related issues both in Britain and internationally.

Elena Softley studied the effects of word processing upon secretarial and typing work as part of a PhD thesis at Manchester University. She is currently involved in producing training packages for people working with all forms of new technology.

SPRU Women and Technology Studies consists of researchers, based around the Science Policy Research Unit, Sussex University, some of whom are associated with the Women and Technical Change (WATCH) database held there. The exact composition of the group varies from project to project, but most of the present group were involved in producing *Microelectronics and Women's Employment in Britain*, published in 1982.

Nuala Swords-Isherwood worked in the Science Policy Research Unit, University of Sussex from 1974, publishing several articles on women and new technology. Since 1982, she has worked at the Technical Change Centre, London, on R&D management and innovation. She has three children.

Ann Whitehead is a social anthropologist and a feminist who has undertaken research in West Africa. She teaches at the University of Sussex and has a long-standing interest in issues affecting rural women. She is a member of the *Feminist Review* editorial collective.

Advisory Editors: John Irvine and Ian Miles

Smothered by Invention

Technology in Women's Lives

Edited by Wendy Faulkner
and Erik Arnold

Pluto Press

London and Sydney

First published in 1985 by Pluto Press Limited,
The Works, 105a Torriano Avenue, London NW5 2RX
and Pluto Press Australia Limited, PO Box 199, Leichhardt,
New South Wales 2040, Australia

Cover designed by Clive Challis A.Gr.R.

Photoset by Photobooks (Bristol) Limited
Printed in Great Britain by Guernsey Press, Guernsey, C.I.

British Library Cataloguing in Publication Data

Smothered by invention: technology in women's lives.
    1. Women—Social conditions 2. Science—Social aspects
    3. Technological inovations—Social aspects
    I. Faulkner, Wendy H Arnold, Erik
    305.4   HQ1154

ISBN 0 86104 737 0

Contents

Acknowledgements

Writing and editing this book has involved us all in undertaking a long and rather bumpy journey together. We are grateful for the efforts, help and forbearance of the other contributors, and hope that they, in turn, are grateful for ours! Richard Kuper, Jane Parkin, Ian Miles and John Irvine performed the unenviable task of editing the editors. In addition to others unnamed, Lynda Birke, Brian Easlea, Di Marquand and Kathy Overfield contributed to the conception of the book. For defects in its execution, however, we must be held solely responsible.

We are grateful to the British Association for the Advancement of Science, Pauline Marstrand and Frances Pinter for permission to use previously published material in chapter 10, parts of which first appeared in Nuala Swords-Isherwood, Christine Zmroczek and Flis Henwood, 'Technical change and its effect on employment opportunities for women', a paper given to Section X of the British Association for the Advancement of Science, Annual Meeting 22–6 August 1983; reprinted in Pauline Marstrand (ed.) *New Technology and the Future of Work and Skills*, London: Frances Pinter, 1983. We would also like to thank Jonathan Gershuny, Sandra Wallman and Associates and Gower Publishing for permission to reproduce figure 2 and Jonathan Gershuny for permission to reproduce figure 1.

Wendy Faulkner
Erik Arnold

several properties vary with distance their pressure in the
inner area of the gas cloud and smaller scale in their gas

Introduction

To talk about women and technology in the same breath seems strange, even incongruous. Technology is powerful, remote, incomprehensible, inhuman, scientific, expensive and – above all – *male*. What does it have to do with women?

Women probably invented it. At its broadest, technology is the science of how to make things – from food and shelter through medicines to spacecraft and electronics. In the distant past, women originated the agricultural technologies which freed our ancestors from dependence on gathering and hunting to eke out an existence. Agriculture marked a transformation for people from being dependent upon nature to trying to control it. Rapidly, however, technology also became a tool for controlling people. Today, by and large, women neither invent nor control the course of new technologies. Yet the shape of modern technology impinges on women's lives at every point – in paid work, medicine, housework, even in the intimacy of childbirth. This book attempts to trace some aspects of the male takeover of technology, and to show what these mean for women's lives.

Ultimately, the power of modern technology emanates from the powerful people in our society, and reinforces their power. As in other areas of our patriarchal and capitalist society, those with power are predominantly male. They are engineers and scientists; they are heads of the industrial, military and governmental organizations who make decisions about which types of techniques to develop and which to buy or sell. If modern technology has characteristics which are abhorrent to us, then realizing that technology is socially produced allows us to understand that things need not be as they are. Within the broad limits imposed by the 'laws of nature', we can change the shape of technology through social changes.

This book poses questions about technology in terms of its relation to women. However, it would be wrong to see this solely as a contribution to 'women's studies', important though these studies are. Precisely because men do dominate most of our social institutions, any analysis of technology which does not take gender into account runs the risk largely of analysing relations between men. Just as women have been hidden from history, so they have been hidden from economics, sociology and the host of other male-dominated ways of analyzing and understanding the world. The result of this omission is that most scholarly work fails to consider the often central significance of patriarchal dynamics in the shaping of social life. By focusing our attention on technology and women we hope to shed better light on its role and importance in society as a whole, as well as highlighting the particular relation between women and technology.

The need to understand – and transform – the social role of technology has become increasingly urgent. The burst of anger at the end of the 1960s about environmental pollution and resource depletion was not misplaced; nor have these problems gone away simply because it is now less fashionable to worry about them. The cynical use of technology to exploit and despoil the world which prompted the surge of environmental concern extends increasingly to the exploitation and degradation of people themselves, through 'progress' in pharmaceuticals, electronics and other technologies. As we believe this book shows, it is hard to avoid the conclusion that the particular shape of these technologies, and the social context in which they are used, is related to male control of both.

Nowhere is this more evident than in the field of military technology. The resurgence of peace movements around the world is a trenchant indictment of the suggestively penis-shaped technology bunkered by the major nations. Here, above all, we need to 'take the toys from the boys'. If the threat posed by male control of other technologies is not always so chillingly final, the need to democratize and redesign many of these 'toys' is nonetheless pressing.

Women have been active in both the environmental and peace movements of the last decades, and have generally taken male control of technology as read. But the women's liberation movement has not, until recently, given much consideration to the social role of technology or the general connection between the shaping of contemporary technology and oppression. (This is, perhaps, an important reflection of women's estrangement from it in the first place.) However, the relation between women and science has become a focus of feminist concern in recent years.[1] We now know a lot more about the reasons why so few girls go into science and the way in which women experience working as scientists. We also know that science has tended to view women in particularly oppressive and derogatory ways – in some instances contributing thereby to their very exclusion from it.

In so much as science plays an ideological role, then, it is clearly patriarchal. Technology, on the other hand, cannot be so simply characterized. There are fewer women actually doing technology than there are doing science, suggesting an even stronger patriarchal element in its social institutions. Perhaps this is because technology, even more than science, is about control. Perhaps, too, men have appropriated the controlling positions in technology precisely because they promise such enormous potential to influence things: if that power were held even equally by women, men could not derive such a large chunk of the benefits.

It was the diffusion of microelectronic technology and the recognition that this could have particularly dangerous consequences for women which prompted feminists to address the general relationship between technology and women's oppression. By the late 1970s, the social impact of microelectronics had become the subject of numerous research and review studies by trade unions, industrialists and academics, few of whom had previously considered the role of women, or patriarchy, in technological change. These studies drew on a number of analytical traditions concerned with the relationship between technology and production – or, more specifically, capitalist production.

The debate about the social effects of automation can be traced back at least to Norbert Wiener's *Cybernetics*, published in 1947, and was rapidly reflected in such fictional works as Kurt Vonnegut's famous first novel, *Player Piano*, published in 1951,[2] which explored the implications of computer-controlled manufacture using almost no labour. Worry about the effects of mechanization (as opposed to electronics-based automation) goes further back in popular culture: Fritz Lang's film *Metropolis* and Charlie Chaplin's *Modern Times* are classic examples.

There is also a relatively long-established tradition of looking at the social ramifications of science and technology within the Marxist analysis of capitalist society. The observation by Marx and Engels that 'The bourgeoisie cannot exist without constantly revolutionising the instruments of production, and thereby the relations of production, and with them the whole relations of society'[3] has played a key role in developing our understanding of the social roles of science and technology, and of the capitalist character of the powerful social relations surrounding these activities. In the last decade, this 'labour process' tradition of analyzing work, including the role of technological change in the management of work, has undergone something of a resurgence – due, in no small part, to the publication, in 1974, of Harry Braverman's book *Labour and Monopoly Capital*.[4] Analysis of the social aspects of science also underpins the thinking in this book. This tradition, associated most strongly with J.D. Bernal,[5] remains vigorously alive in the various radical science movements in Europe and North America,[6] as well as in various academic centres for the social studies of science.

Of course, there is also a long tradition of feminist social analysis. This has ranged from respectful suggestions that Marx and Engels might profitably have considered the 'woman question' a little more deeply, to a rich spectrum of radical feminist analysis which views patriarchal (not capitalist) power relations as the root source of social oppression. Five years ago we wrote an article with Lynda Birke about the implications of word processors for women's office work.[7] It became clear to us then that sex-blind labour process theory was as unequal to the task of explaining what was happening as were theories about patriarchy which did not take full account of the economic relationships between the people involved. We argued that, while it was in the interests of men to have secretaries as 'office wives', this conflicted with the interests of men in their economic roles as managers of companies concerned to reduce the number of secretarial and typing workers. None of the analytical traditions described here could cope on its own with this complex of conflicting interests.

In the past few years, these analytical traditions have begun to intermingle: people belonging to each are now struggling to deal with questions about women *and* technology *and* capitalism. We believe that out of this mixture will emerge new ways of thinking about ourselves and our society – ways of thinking which can form a basis for social and political change. We hope that this book provides a small contribution to that task. The fact that it has taken almost half a decade to find people to write, edit, rewrite, re-edit and finally publish this work with us illustrates, perhaps, not only our own difficulties in coming to grips with our subject, but also the difficulty of the subject itself.

Some people may be surprised to find men involved in writing this book. Some may even think it mistaken in terms of feminist practice. We acknowledge that it *is* an urgent political necessity for women to organize autonomously from men – both for conscious-ness-raising and for many types of political action. In our view, however, the production of this book falls into neither of these categories. Rather, it is intended as a 'linking' project – a resource which we hope will be useful to both the women's liberation movement and to other, sexually mixed, movements. As we have already indicated, it has become clear to us from our daily work in these fields that many problems in economics and science policy cannot be tackled as though patriarchy did not exist.

Whilst, for women, working with men potentially creates problems which are avoided by working with other women, we feel that male involvement in a project such as this book can be beneficial. One belief that we have inherited from the scientific tradition is that knowledge is, or should be, 'open' – that is, if something is knowable then in principle anyone can know it. This is not to deny that women can discover some things about the world more easily than men: far from it. Women are more likely to perceive the existence of patriarchal relations because it is more in their interest to do so. But patriarchy is about relations between women *and* men. It means that women and men have different experiences of the world, and these experiences will necessarily dictate the direction in which we look to make discoveries about the world. Equally, there is a need, when trying to understand aspects of women's oppression, to concentrate a fair amount of attention on men: after all, it is men who are the problem. Repeatedly, we – as editors – have found ourselves better able to understand questions dealt with in this book by bringing both female and male experiences to bear.

Our starting point is that women are largely absent from the powerful institutions which today shape technology. Women frequently use the technical products of technology; some are even involved in their construction, but extremely few are actively involved in their design. This fact is reflected in our choice of subjects for inclusion in the book. There are four sections. The first deals with technology as a body of knowledge. It looks at the social institutions in which the resultant techniques are designed, and so is concerned primarily with the exclusion of women from technology. The last three sections deal with technology as a group of techniques; they look at the impact of specific techniques women meet in three crucial areas of their lives – in reproduction, in the home and in paid employment. These chapters are more directly concerned with the alienation women feel from technology.

Women's alienation and exclusion from technology is a theme which recurs throughout the book and so merits a word here. On a very fundamental level, technology is alien to women because it relates to an 'other' world in which women have no part and so appears mystifying and frightening. Technology is also alienating to women in the sense that the goals embodied in it are not necessarily women's goals. This is most starkly illustrated by military technology – a subject which we were unable to include here and which, thankfully, is now being raised elsewhere.[8] But it is also evident in many of the techniques women meet routinely, where the lack of attention paid (in design) to women's needs is often glaring. Finally, the actual practice of technology is often alienating to women – demanding or at least encouraging traits which leave many women cold, and which offer little promise of a more socially aware practice. We believe that alienation and exclusion are two sides of the same coin: women are excluded from technology (partly) because they find it alienating, and they are alienated from technology because they are excluded. The technology we meet today is both cause and result of women's oppression.

We make no apology for failing to deal with every form of oppression or, indeed, for failing to deal with every way in which technology is involved in the oppression of women. We are aware that the articles included here have a predominantly First World bias. In part this is a reflection of the subject matter: the technology we are concerned with was created in the industrial capitalist countries. Those of us living in these countries are also effectively blinkered to the plight of Third World people and the price they have paid for our advances. However, it was not possible to deal with everything at once.

Our own introductory chapter, 'Smothered by invention: some thoughts on the masculinity of technology', is intended to provide a backcloth to the book, to make sense of its recurring themes of alienation and exclusion. We approached this task by identifying some important features of both patriarchal and capitalist social relations and have used this insight to explore the forces which together produced technological endeavour. The chapter is, necessarily, historical: we need to trace the origins of contemporary technology in order to understand how it has come to be more 'masculine' than previous technologies.

First we examine the rise of modern science. Only in the comparatively recent past have science and technology become socially interlinked. However, the scientists of the Renaissance played a large part in setting the tone of the technological endeavour. They had both a world view which was conducive to the invention of useful techniques and a burning commitment to the application of knowledge to the exploitation of the natural world. From the outset, this project was explicitly and exclusively male, but it was not new. Women had for centuries defied prevailing religious orthodoxy and engaged in empirical study of the natural world. Still, it was the male 'natural philosophers' who were able to forge alliances with the new holders of economic and social power who emerged as a result of the rise of Protestantism and the development of capitalism in Western Europe.

Capitalism changed the basis of economic production, vastly increasing opportunities for money-making through the introduction of new technologies into production processes. In the course of these changes, women increasingly lost out: it was men who laid claim to the resources upon which the appropriation of the material benefits of capitalism depended. They were able to do this by denying women access to ownership of capital – so few women were able to become capitalists – and by denying women, as workers, the means to bargain with capitalists for the better-paid and higher-status jobs. Critical amongst these is the ability to enter, and defend, jobs deemed 'skilled'. The application of technology to factory-based production tended to result in a deskilling process, in which work became increasingly fragmented and hierarchically organized. Capitalists' dependence on scarce skills was progressively decreased, whilst at the same time new and more skilled areas of work opened up. Women were (and are) peculiarly vulnerable to the deskilling and labour-displacing effects of technical change in the workplace. As men moved up the hierarchies and acquired new skills, so women tended to fill the spaces left behind.

Ultimately, the biggest space men left behind was the home, where women were increasingly relegated to perform all those servicing and production tasks which were not moved into the 'economic' sphere outside and which provided men – as husbands – with a source of unpaid, personal services. At the same time as women were being banished to the home (and, outside, to the lowest-paid and lowest-status jobs), engineering and the scientific and technical subjects were being integrated into the formal education systems of Western Europe and North America, and research and development departments were appearing in the technically innovative industries. Although women are no longer formally excluded from these activities, there has been no rush of women to enter them. Women have remained essentially on the receiving end of new technologies.

Chapter 2, 'The exclusion of women from technology', by Dot Griffiths, further explores how this came about, and makes particular reference to Britain. It begins by dispelling the idea that women don't do technology because they can't do technology. It then considers the history of women's exclusion: in particular, the decline of female craft skills; women's exclusion from the new skilled trades which developed during and after the Industrial Revolution, and their apparent absence from the ranks of the inventors/entrepreneurs of that period. There are, of course, even fewer women working in technology than in science. Dot Griffiths suggests that one reason for this is that technology, even more than science, is concerned with control – a singularly masculine trait in our society. Further, the major part of modern technological activity is funded for industry or war, both of which are male-dominated activities. The strength of this gender stereotyping is reflected in the development of school curricula in Britain, and in the fact that even though girls are no longer formally denied access to scientific and technical subjects at school, the odds are still against their making a cross-gender choice and opting for technology. Some of the difficulties involved in this choice are explored in a survey of women engineering students at Imperial College, London University. Finally, the chapter addresses the alienation of women from modern technology and asks whether their exclusion from it is in any way a function of its nature.

Chapter 3, 'Women in British engineering' by Nuala Swords-Isherwood, further explores the situation of women in British engineering. Britain has the lowest representation of women among professional engineers of any industrialized country. The essential features of the engineering industry in Britain, as elsewhere, are that women are concentrated in office jobs, semi-skilled operative jobs (such as assembly) and unskilled support jobs. Although in the last decade there has been some increase in the proportion of women in skilled engineering jobs, and in training for this work, the absolute levels remain derisory – especially among technician (as opposed to professional) engineers and craft workers. The author shows that even relatively enlightened policies designed to encourage women into these male bastions have had only minimal impact.

Again, stereotyped notions of what is appropriate work for women are clearly very powerful in shaping the attitudes of both schoolgirls and their potential industrial employers. More particularly, it is assumed that girls will not enjoy engineering because it is 'too dirty' or because 'women would not be strong enough'. Such assumptions are typically shelved when economic contingencies – or *man*power shortages – demand, as during the world wars and at the present time in Britain, where women are now seen as a possible solution to shortages of engineers. Few would argue today that women are incapable of doing skilled engineering work, but in practice women who attempt to do so are rarely taken seriously. Traditional prejudices abound in the engineering industry and serve, for example, to exclude women from the managerial roles normally open to professional engineers. More imaginative and far-reaching programmes of positive action are required if this situation is to change.

The next chapter, 'Medical technology and the right to heal', looks at an area of technological skill which was dominated by women for many centuries: healing. Here, Wendy Faulkner describes the protracted and at times bloody battle surrounding the rise of the exclusively male medical profession. The result of these battles was the virtual elimination of women lay healers from Western Europe and the spawning of modern medical technology. The medical men made technical intervention the hallmark of their practice. They called on the prestige of modern (masculine) science to legitimize their new role as healers, even though the healing powers of the 'wise women' whom they sought to displace were, at least until the twentieth century, much more effective and empirically based than their own. As healing became progressively institutionalized, the healing process was transformed in a way which gave doctors an unprecedented degree of authority over both those they healed and other healers. Women lost autonomous control over their own health.

The division of labour within modern health-care systems is also profoundly unequal, and that inequality is built in no small part on the fact that women and men health workers have significantly different relationships to medical technology. That technology is now based on a powerful body of scientific and technical knowledge, but women – be they health workers or patients – have very little control over either the shape of the technology or the use of specific techniques which emanate from it.

The male takeover of healing has profound implications for women's health throughout the world. Doctors' right to determine whether women are ill, and how they should be treated, has become an important aspect of patriarchal control over women. This is of direct relevance to the next section of this book, which considers some of the techniques women encounter as a result of their particular biological role in reproduction. There is now a great deal of legitimate concern about the possible impact of recent developments in reproductive technology, such as *in vitro* fertilization and artificial insemination to produce so-called 'test-tube babies'. Jalna Hanmer and others have explored some of the possibilities this, and related, lines of technological development could involve.[9] This book concentrates on the two groups of technologies which women routinely encounter in the course of having babies and in contraception.

In chapter 5, 'Managers and labourers: women's attitudes to reproductive technology' Frances Evans addresses the controversy about routine technological intervention in hospital deliveries. She describes the results of a recent survey of women who have given birth in British hospitals which show that women have apparently contradictory attitudes towards their experiences of the medical management of pregnancy and childbirth. On the one hand, many had great trust in the doctors they met, and saw access to medical technology as a basic right of women during pregnancy and labour. On the other hand, they deeply resented the way they were treated at ante-natal clinics and during their deliveries, feeling that they had minimal control over the care they received. They were, in short, more disturbed by the social relations within which medical technology is organized than with its use *per se*.

In order to understand these social relations, Frances Evans examines the political processes surrounding the management of pregnancy and childbirth. She argues that women's ambivalence about doctors and their technology is a product both of men's having assumed the role of managers in childbirth, and of the confused and confusing picture of pregnancy and motherhood which accompanied this change. Finally, she considers how women's experiences of the use of technology in pregnancy and childbirth match up with various political strategies which address this issue.

In contrast to childbirth, contraception has become a medical province only in the last few decades. Indeed, traditional methods of birth control have only relatively recently been superseded by new techniques. One of the most critical factors here has been the sudden fear of a world population explosion, and the ideology of population control which was fuelled by that fear.

In chapter 6, 'Who controls birth control?', Elkie Newman looks at the development of new, mass-produced birth-control methods and their subsequent promotion worldwide. She points out that while on one level family planning has given some women more control over their fertility, it is also, on another level, a highly developed means of oppression. Population reduction, especially in the Third World, is an international priority: the politics of women's right to choose do not enter into it. The author outlines various birth-control methods available and shows that, although it is now feasible for women to decide how many children they will have, this potential has not been realized. Women suffer a range of abuses in the hands of the professionals involved in the development and promotion of birth-prevention methods. Every stage of the process – from research into new methods to their testing and sale – affects and imposes on women. Women must organize politically if they are to regain control over their own fertility.

Reproduction, and its social organization, have always been a pivotal feature of women's lives – precisely because of their central role in it. In patriarchal societies, this has been used as a justification for extending women's role in childcare and excluding women from other productive activities. Thus, with the development of industrial capitalism, *house*work – work which was not sucked into the money economy – was left in the home for women to perform, unpaid, along with childcare; men appropriated the greater material benefits of productive work outside the home. In the new money economy a new, industrial capitalist ruling class appeared, but in the home the rulers remained the same: male dominance continued unchallenged. Housework, however, has undergone a number of changes since the Industrial Revolution, as has every form of paid work outside the home. In the latter area, the application of science and technology to production has played a vital, indeed a central role, while in the case of women's domestic labour this role has been less direct and obvious. The nature of this relationship is addressed in the next section of the book.

Chapter 7, 'Housework and the appliance of science', by Erik Arnold and Lesley Burr, deals with the creation of housewifery as a separate feminine sphere during the Industrial Revolution, and with the subsequent application of quasi-scientific notions of efficiency to housework. It examines some of the economic and ideological changes which facilitated the construction of housework as a feminine activity, and the processes by which it was increasingly deskilled and devalued during the nineteenth century. The number of tasks actually involved in housework gradually decreased, leaving something of a domestic void. This was, in effect, filled by the efforts of the domestic science and home economics movements which, through the promulgation of domestic science education, encouraged the adoption of rising standards (and, therefore, expectations) for housework. In doing so, these movements paved the way for the so-called appliance revolution of the twentieth century.

It is commonly assumed that new domestic techniques such as appliances have eliminated much of the work remaining in the home, saved time and generally lightened the housewife's workload. In chapter 8, 'Kitchen technology and the liberation of women from housework', Phil Bereano, Christine Bose and Erik Arnold explore these assumptions with reference to four distinct groups of domestic techniques: utilities, appliances, convenience foods and services. The available evidence is patchy, but overall there appears to have been no decrease in the amount of time women spent on tasks which we would now define as housework during the first half of this century, even though urbanization removed some tasks from the home. New household technologies helped to maintain the number of hours required for housework, partly because they were accompanied by increasingly high standards of efficiency and partly because of the effects of some modern 'conveniences'. Since the 1960s, the time spent on housework has tended to decline, but the effect of modern domestic technology is negligible compared with factors such as family size and women's employment rates. In general, the sexual division of labour within the household has been little altered by either technical change or women's re-entry into paid work. Furthermore, the expansion of services outside the home has reinforced the sexual division of labour in society. The authors conclude by arguing that we cannot rely on technology to liberate women from housework. Rather, political intervention is needed to redefine the social relations of marriage and the nuclear family so as to challenge the assumption that housework is women's work.

The final section of the book addresses women's relationship to modern technology in the workplace. It deals with women's paid work which, as the two previous chapters indicate, takes place substantially outside the home in industrialized countries. In the Third World, however, the physical boundaries between women's paid and unpaid work are not as distinct. Much of the work which both women and men do has not entered the money economy. There are parallels between the changes taking place in the Third World today and those which accompanied the development of capitalism and, later on, industrialization in Western Europe. In both cases, changes in technique have accompanied increases in productivity and the drawing of production into the money economy. The difference is that the technologies which are so transforming Third World production originate largely from the industrial countries. Indeed, technology transfer is often a central part of 'development' strategies. Because of the particular connection between Third World economies and international capitalism, this process tends itself to create a relation of dependence between rich and poor nations. The fate of women in this process is often overlooked. This is the subject of chapter 9, 'The Green Revolution and women's work in the Third World', by Ann Whitehead.

The Green Revolution was a major technical innovation intended to solve the problem of hunger in the Third World by enabling all farmers – large and small alike – to increase their production of food crops. In the event, the larger farming enterprises benefited disproportionately; they were able to mechanize production and purchase additional land while many smaller farmers were forced to sell up and join the landless labourers. The implications of this for rural women varied, depending on the particular sexual division of labour and the social relations (especially within marriage and the family) surrounding the allocation of work and resources. In general, burdens of unpaid 'family' labour increased in intensity, whilst the amount of casual wage labour available to women either decreased or disappeared. The mechanization which accompanied the Green Revolution tended to exacerbate this. While the tasks which women perform as part of family labour have largely not been mechanized, tasks which were previously undertaken for money have, once mechanized, almost invariably become the preserve of men – irrespective of the initial gender designation of the tasks.

Wage labour in the Third World, as in developed countries, involves a pronounced sexual hierarchy in which women are subordinate to men. There is a powerful tendency for this male dominance to be reinforced when technology changes. The sexual division of labour may change, but for the most part women lose out in terms of skill, security and financial rewards. Thus, industrial companies frequently benefit from the lower cost and greater subservience of female employees, who are easily dispensable when production needs change. This has recently become particularly apparent in the production of microelectronic components in South East Asia.[10]

The revolution in electronics which has taken place during the last four decades has had a profound and pervasive effect on work, as well as producing a seemingly limitless number of new high-technology products. The three remaining chapters of the book deal with various aspects of this new technology as it affects women in the industrial labour force. This is, of course, by no means the only type of technological change with which working women are confronted. However, it is one of the few areas in which research has been done.

Chapter 10, 'Microelectronics and the jobs women do', by the SPRU Women and Technology Studies group, starts by outlining some of the patriarchal constraints imposed on women's employment opportunities and pay, such as the 'problem' of combining paid and household work and the consequent predominance of women in part-time jobs. Using data from Britain, the authors explode some of the myths surrounding women's paid employment. They argue that the particular jobs women hold and the status attached to these jobs make them especially vulnerable to the job-degrading and labour-displacing effects of technical change. Microelectronics, in particular, tends to displace jobs at the bottom of organizational hierarchies, where women are concentrated, whilst creating new, more technical jobs higher up. Men are more likely to enter these jobs, if only because they have the requisite training, so the overall effect of new technology is likely to be a reduction of women's job opportunities relative to men's. Evidence of the specific impact on clerical work, sales and distribution, banking and finance, manufacturing and the 'caring professions' (such as nursing and teaching) suggests that the effects of microelectronics will be fairly uniform across all sectors of the economy. The authors conclude by indicating some of the policies which would lessen the constraints facing working women.

They argue that only when these are removed will women become involved in the design of new machines and derive an equal share of the benefits of technological change.

Chapter 11, 'Word processing: new opportunities for women office workers?', by Elena Softley, examines the specific effects of word processors, an application of microelectronic technology which threatens the most female-dominated of all occupations – secretarial and typing work. The office provides a prime target for the introduction of labour-saving technology because it remains highly labour intensive. However, word processing cannot be treated as just another labour-saving technology because it affects a specifically female area of work. Elena Softley looks at the historical relationship between technical change and the sexual division of labour in offices. The differentiation between secretarial and typing roles highlights the different influences of capitalism and patriarchy in office social relations. The continued diffusion of word processing is likely to alter these social relations. Introducing word processors into typing pools saves labour, fragments tasks, raises the intensity of work and increases managerial control over typists' work. Secretaries' workloads also increase with word processing, but – contrary to manufacturers' claims – new technology has not generally enabled secretaries to move into non-routine managerial work. Indeed, there appear to be few opportunities for women to gain significant new skills as a result of the introduction of word processors, although the unionization of clerical workers is increasing. There are signs that men are entering this traditionally female stronghold, but there is nothing to suggest that women will succeed in entering traditionally male office jobs.

One of the most vital areas within electronics technology is computing, especially computer programming. Although not originally a male occupation, programming was taken over by men during the post-war period, when computing really became an industry in its own right. Anne Lloyd and Liz Newell are both computer programmers and in chapter 12, 'Women and computers', they discuss the work and experience of women in that field.

Despite the widely held belief that the new computer industry provides opportunity for all, women are concentrated at the bottom levels of the increasingly structured hierarchy among computing jobs. Women's re-entry into programming is a relatively recent occurrence associated, at least in part, with a recent fragmentation and stratification of this work and a consequent reduction in its level of perceived skill and status. As in older industries, men seem more able than women to claim high status and pay for the jobs they do. Both the assumption that computing work demands technical and mathematical training and the dense barrier of jargon which is associated with computers have effectively been used to bar women from the field. In the authors' experience, work in computing – especially at the higher levels – can be both challenging and enjoyable. However, it is difficult to break into the charmed circle of male cameraderie which surrounds computers. Many men become so hooked on computers that they find it more satisfying to interact with them than with other people. The authors suggest that women are less likely to become obsessed with technology in this way, and that this is another strong reason why women should be involved in computing.

Their conclusions are ones which are echoed throughout this book. Quite apart from considerations of equal opportunity, we need more women in the controlling positions in which technology is designed in order to transform it into a less alienating, more socially beneficial and, perhaps, even liberating force.

1. Smothered by invention: the masculinity of technology

Erik Arnold and Wendy Faulkner

Ours is a technological age. Our politicians boast of technological achievements; our military planners flex technological muscle; our scientists apply their knowledge to generating technology; our industrialists manufacture a continuous stream of new technology-based products, and we bask in the reflected glory of what we are pleased to call technological *progress*. Technology enjoys the prestige of science and the combined power of industry and the state. If technology sometimes appears to be an irresistible social force, that must surely be because the most powerful elements in society line up behind it and have an interest in it.

The social institutions of technology are, like most institutions in society, dominated by men. They constitute perhaps the most powerful of all social-interest groups in our patriarchal society. But technology has become an obvious and dynamic social force only during the past two centuries or so and under a particular form of economic organization: industrial capitalism. If we want to understand how and why technology is so important in our lives, we need to explore these two fundamental types of social organization – patriarchy and capitalism – which underlie it.

This chapter seeks to examine how technology has acquired its current importance and why it now seems to offer us such a masculine face. Subsequent chapters focus on some more detailed aspects of the story, but here we intend simply to provide backdrop to the later chapters. We paint on a very large canvas, so our brush-strokes must be correspondingly broad.

We start by explaining what we mean by 'technology' and by 'patriarchy' before examining in greater detail the workings of the latter. Then we consider the rise of science and capitalism, each of which spurred in rather different ways the development of modern technology. We point out that men appropriated the vital sources of power in both, and we use this perspective to explain how women came to be smothered by the resulting invention of technology. Finally, we return to the idea that technology is a social thing and that – for that very reason – it is neither alien nor immutable but can be changed through social actions.

Technology and patriarchy

'Women constitute half the world's population, perform nearly two-thirds of its work-hours, receive one-tenth of the world's income, and own less than one hundredth of the world's property', according to the 1980 United Nations Report.[1] Men collectively have better living standards than do women. Examples of matriarchal societies exist, but in most countries today men, not women, hold the greater social, economic and political power and derive the greater benefits from society's produce. Because men control social, economic and political structures and institutions their strength tends to be perpetuated.

This, broadly, is what we mean by patriarchy. To many, the term is more mystifying than enlightening – suggesting either the relations between women and men which characterize feudal societies or a rather historical and non-material phenomenon associated with the 'psychic' make up of men. In an attempt to clarify the term, Heidi Hartmann has defined patriarchy as

> a set of social relations between men which have a material base, and which, though hierarchical, establish or create interdependence and solidarity among men that enable them to dominate women. . . . In the hierarchy of patriarchy, all men, whatever their rank in the patriarchy, are bought off by being able to control at least some women.[2]

This definition is useful because it recognizes the material benefits to be gained from the oppression of women. It also emphasizes that patriarchal relations, within which women are oppressed, operate between men as well as between women and men: they encompass *all* of society. Thus, although today capitalist men may exploit working men and white men may oppress black men, all are united in their dominance over women. But this definition does not explain *why* it is women, and not men, who are at the bottom of the pile, or how women are kept there.

In order to answer these questions we need first to examine the structure of social life. There are two pivotal activities in any society, and these Frederick Engels described as the 'production and reproduction of immediate life', meaning:

> On the one side, the production of the means of existence, of food, clothing, and shelter and the tools necessary for that production; on the other side the production of human beings themselves, the propagation of the species. The social organization under which people of a particular historical epoch live is determined by both kinds of production.[3]

The ways in which reproduction and production are organized vary enormously from culture to culture. In all cultures, however, there is a division of labour organized to some extent along sexual lines. And this sexual division of labour usually implies a sexual hierarchy. Although women and men may be mutually inter-dependent in terms of the contribution they make to social welfare, they are rarely equal in terms of the control they have over the way society is organized.

Most people acknowledge the importance of both production and reproduction in shaping social power relations, but their relative importance is often hotly contended.[4] Those schooled in the Marxist tradition often view the material basis of women's oppression in somewhat narrow, economic terms. Engels himself thought that capitalism would emancipate women by sucking them into the waged labour force on the same terms as men. Here, the mode of production (capitalism) is considered fundamental: power relations are therefore reduced to a question of cash. Sexual inequality, even in the acute sexual division of labour found in advanced capitalist society, is seen primarily as a hangover from feudal times which will, in time, disappear; the oppression of women is relegated to the realm of ideology.

We reject this line of thinking for two reasons. First, we believe the mode of reproduction – the ways in which childbearing and rearing are organized – to be itself material in nature, and not solely ideological. Concern principally with formal economic categories (capital, labour, profit, and so on) is inherently sex blind and sexist: it cannot see, let alone explain, the power relations most affecting women, because these operate substantially outside the money economy. Second, the power relations generated by the modes of reproduction and production do not necessarily coincide or work together. In the case of capitalist societies, for example, the interests of particular men as capitalists, or as workers, occasionally conflict with the interests of *all* men in dominating women.

We do, however, agree with Marx and Engels that a crucial role was played by the emerging capitalist mode of production in creating and shaping what we now call technology.

While the words 'technology' and 'technique' are often used rather loosely, we need to distinguish between them rather carefully here. *A technique is a way of making or doing something: a particular product or a particular process.* In all societies the tasks associated with the production of things (and in some cases the reproduction of people) have been made easier by the invention of specific techniques – from simple objects like bowls and hoes to more complex things like jet engines. *Technology encompasses the knowledge that goes into creating techniques.* The use of herbal remedies, for example, implies some knowledge of the effects of plants or plant extracts on the body and of techniques for growing and harvesting plants. Such knowledge is not given: it results from social processes of experimentation and communication. Knowledge may also be used as a *social* tool in the course of power struggles. For instance, where special institutions such as universities, professional societies and company research laboratories are established to advance technology, power relations operate to manage or control the access of 'outsiders' to that knowledge. These conditions in turn affect the type of knowledge which becomes embodied in specific techniques.

Technology, then, encompasses the social relations involved in creating, changing and sharing (or not sharing) knowledge about techniques. Nowadays, technology is generally thought of as something modern, industrial and highly sophisticated. Indeed, the *Oxford English Dictionary* defines technology as 'the science of the industrial arts', implicitly locating technology in the industrial capitalism of Europe and North America. Of course, all pre- or non-industrial societies have developed some technology. However, that of the industrial capitalist period in which we live is substantively different from that of earlier times. Furthermore, it has become internationally pervasive. For these reasons, this book is primarily concerned with the technologies and techniques which emerged during and since the transition to industrial capitalism, and hence focuses on the social relations generated in this transition.

Technology is central to the immense productive dynamism of capitalism, as Marx and Engels perceived, but it is also more than this: it is a vital aspect of modern patriarchy. It enables men to exercise unprecedented domination over the natural world and over society. In the capitalist period, more than in any previous epoch, technology has excluded and alienated women; it has become *masculine*.

Biology, gender and power

Women and men make disproportionate contributions to the propagation of the species, and this simple biological difference has several implications. Most obviously, it takes time to carry, bear and suckle children – time which men (and women not immediately involved in reproduction) may spend doing other things. In practice, the biological division of labour has provided men with a rationale for excluding women from certain areas of productive activity, and often for extending the time women spend in childrearing beyond that which is biologically necessary. While different patriarchies allocate tasks among the sexes in a range of possible ways, childrearing is the only activity which is universally performed by women.

Another feature of patriarchal societies is that women are also universally devalued. Those tasks which in the sexual division of labour fall to women are generally given low social status, whilst those which men claim as their own are invariably elevated in social esteem, irrespective of their nature or their social usefulness:

In every known society, the male's need for achievement can be recognised. Men may cook or weave or dress dolls or hunt humming birds, but if such activities are appropriate activities of men, then the whole society, men and women alike, votes them important. . . . Hence may be found the relationship between maleness and pride; that is a need for prestige that will outstrip the prestige which is accorded to any woman. [5]

The 'prestige which is accorded to any woman' is, of course, that associated with her ability to bear and suckle children. It appears that having an inflated pride in their achievements is one way in which men can make up, psychologically, for the fact that their only biologically significant contribution to reproduction is confined to conception, and that even this contribution is fraught with insecurity.

Insecurity is a general feature of oppressors' relationship to those they oppress. As Ruth Wallsgrove explains:

> In controlling someone else, you cut yourself off from that person; in imposing your definition of that person on her/him as a limitation, you lose your ability to see what that person actually is. The price all oppressors pay for their power is losing any understanding of the oppressed.[6]

When something is not understood it assumes a mysterious quality and becomes potentially frightening, and when that something is also oppressed, it may strike back. It would seem that as well as envying women's procreative powers, men also fear them. Things female are thus not only devalued but also demeaned, ridiculed and often despised.

Men's fear of women extends to the realm of sex and sexuality, where it is expressed in various forms of sexual violence. Rape, and the threat of rape, is a very potent means of ensuring the submission and subordination of women. Indirectly, sexual slavery and female prostitution fulfil the same purpose. Lesbianism is widely vilified and suppressed: it is a token both of women's sexual independence from men and of their sexual prowess. Male homosexuality, on the other hand, is usually repudiated for slightly different reasons: it is feminine and thus to be despised. It is also seen by men as a form of treason. The common bond which unites men in a patriarchy is their power to dominate women: males are bonded together by a common material interest in controlling women, not by love.

Critically, men benefit by controlling the work women do. The form of male control varies, but in industrial capitalist societies it hinges on the institution of monogamous heterosexual marriage. This serves not only to restrict women's sexuality but also to deny them access to essential productive resources – a job that pays a living wage, for example. Women's generally lower wages can lead to financial dependence on men and this, together with the extreme isolation of the modern home, serves further to enforce an emotional dependence – couched though this usually is in terms of romantic love. The nuclear family in which women (and, as individuals, men) are thus caged provides men with unpaid personal and sexual servicing as of right. It also provides them with a very effective means of controlling reproduction.

The labour women expend in childbearing and rearing also benefits men, because children can bring social and economic rewards. Characteristically, children in rural societies are an important source of farm labour. They contribute to the standard of living of the family, especially of the male head, and provide a form of insurance against old age and ill health. But even when children are not an economic asset, they still tend to confer prestige on their father – particularly if they are boys – not least because children are taken as a token of his sexual potency. Under these circumstances, a father will generally want to be sure that children born of 'his' woman were 'seeded' by him. The very fact that men can never be completely sure on this point reinforces their need to secure property rights over women's bodies, for example in marriage. Men's interest in guaranteeing the paternity of their children, combined with primogeniture – inheritance of all property by the first-born son – has promoted a cult of bridal virginity in many places. In Britain, as in other European countries, this cult of virginity and chastity has been reinforced since medieval and renaissance times by mockery of cuckolds – men whose wives succeed in sleeping with other men.

Men also benefit from controlling reproduction in another less direct but equally crucial way. Unlike the fruits of economic production, those of sexual reproduction grow up to be social persons or, more specifically, gendered persons – feminine females and masculine males. Girls are taught to conform to social norms of femininity just as boys are taught to be masculine. Behavioural and psychological differences between women and men result, therefore, from a process of socialization or gendering in which the expectation of male power and female subordination is itself reproduced from generation to generation.

According to Sandra Harding and others, the broad limits of

infants' socialization are established within the first three years of life. In the earliest stage of this 'psychological birth', infants learn to distinguish themselves from the person who first takes care of them. They come to recognize themselves as separate social individuals with desires and needs which may conflict with those of their initial nurturer. Of course in patriarchal societies, this traumatic and bewildering separation is almost invariably experienced with a woman, not a man. So,

> the person from whom we first individuate ourselves both devalues herself and is perceived as devalued, and this shows up both in the different quality of mothering given to infant boys and infant girls and in the different *experience* which male and female infants have of becoming a person.[7]

The 'other' from which all young children have to separate themselves includes their mother, on whom they are so intimately dependent in early life. But this separation is likely to be more extreme for boys than for girls.

Childrearing, perhaps more than any other activity, demands altruism and concern for the welfare of others. Consequently the qualities which boys in patriarchal societies have to learn to devalue usually include those associated with caring. The progression to masculinity involves a conflict which operates right through adult life.

> Thus infant boys' psychological birth in families with our division of labour by gender produces men who will be excessively rationalistic, who will need to dominate not only others but also their feelings, their physical bodies, and other bodies – nature – in general. . . . It produces misogyny and male bonding as prototypes of appropriate social relations with others perceived to be respectively unlike and like themselves.[8]

Of course, boys never fully succeed in 'mastering' their emotions. Rather they tend to become emotional 'cripples', unable to deal with their own (devalued) caring qualities. In contrast, little girls are not encouraged to reject quite so squarely the nurturance and altruism of their mothers, and they tend to remain emotionally close to other women. Indeed, emotions are generally far less repressed, more close to the surface in women than in men. Thus the psychological and behavioral traits socialized into girls equip them to perform the childcaring role expected of them in adult life and not to compete in the hierarchies men have created.

These processes take place within a specific sexual division of labour. There is no inevitability about patriarchy – either psychologically or biologically. Nor is it necessary to explain patriarchy in terms of particular avarice or inadequacy on the part of individual men. The biological differences between the sexes establish *limits* on the ways in which societies organize themselves: they constrain human behaviour rather than determine it. The differences are material – men are unable to give birth or suckle young – but the constraints they place on human behaviour are also very loose. There is no biological reason why men should not share in most aspects of childrearing, and there is no biological reason why women should not share in the designing of our social relations. Indeed, if social roles were changed in this way, we would expect a qualitative change in the psychological characteristics laid down in infancy.

As the recent rebirth of feminism indicates, there is considerable room for manoeuvre, even within the confines of capitalist patriarchy. But here, as elsewhere, the social barriers to women's liberation are enormous. It is to these barriers that we now turn, and in particular to the part played by modern science.

Science: the masculine endeavour

Modern western science, or natural philosophy as it was initially called, was born in the tumult of seventeenth-century Europe. Its arrival was marked in Britain by the establishment in 1662 of the Royal Society, the first official organization of the natural philosophers. Its members devoted much of their energy to recruiting new – and specifically male – supporters to their cause, while also seeking to identify themselves with the throne, the source of power in the contemporary society. Henry Oldenberg, secretary to the Society, announced in 1664 that its aim was to 'raise a Masculine Philosophy . . . Whereby the Mind of Man may be ennobled with the knowledge of solid Truths'.

Unlike the older philosophy it replaced, the new philosophy was active with respect to the natural world: solid truths were to be derived by a combination of experimentation and reason rather than by passive observation and contemplation. Francis Bacon, the celebrated proponent of the new philosophy, explained the reasons for this new methodology: men (and he meant *men*) were not on 'such familiar terms with nature that, in response to casual and perfunctory salutation, she would condescend to unveil for us her mysteries and bestow on us her blessings'. Rather, 'the secrets of nature reveal themselves more readily under the vexations of art than when they go their own ways'. Thus, Bacon appealed to the 'true sons of knowledge' to turn their 'united forces against the Nature of things, to storm and occupy her castles and strongholds'.[9]

The use of sexual metaphor here is not coincidental. Nature was traditionally associated with women. It was also viewed as mysterious, creative, and therefore potentially threatening. Natural philosophy offered men a way of overcoming this threat – by 'penetrating' nature's inner mysteries, 'making her subserve our purposes' and thereby achieving the 'Empire of man over Nature'. The implied *rape* of nature has chilling parallels. At the time when Bacon urged men 'to bind [Nature] to your service and make her your slave'[10] there had been an upsurge in woman-hating or misogyny in Europe. Many women already possessed considerable knowledge of nature's workings and to this extent probably *were* more in touch with nature than men. During the witch hunts of the late fifteenth to early seventeenth centuries, thousands of these 'wise women' were purged, their 'castles and strongholds' quite literally stormed and occupied. The witch trials had shown men (and women) that women's 'secrets' could be 'unveiled', or torn out, in the form of confessions. Indeed, the Nature on which the natural philosophers were to build their Empire included women.

So how did this masculine philosophy arise? The roots are highly complex, but Lynn White has argued that the Judaeo-Christian tradition was the ideal seedbed for modern scientific values, precisely because it made a clear distinction between *man* and the rest of nature.[11] Most other religions view people as part of nature rather than as standing above it. Similarly, many other gods were made in the image of woman. Even in medieval Europe popular religious practice contained much woman worship and naturalistic ritual. However, in creating man first and woman as an afterthought to be 'an help meet to him', the Judaeo-Christian God runs truer to modern patriarchal form.

In this respect, the Christian church adopted many pre-Christian and, from the late thirteenth century onwards, especially Aristotelian ideas. Women were viewed as carnal, more 'base' than men. Indeed, this explained Eve's leading role in the fall of *man*. Contrary to today's orthodoxy, women were considered sexually voracious, providing both continual temptation to 'purer' men and a potential source of mockery of men's lesser sexual staying-power. Men's search for God, therefore, involved chastity: abjuring all things base and female. The Greek philosophers believed that only men were capable of pure and abstract thought – which they esteemed highly. Women, precisely because of their lower position in the natural hierarchy, were deemed intellectually inferior to men.

These views were reflected in Aristotelian ideas about nature and the cosmos. Heaven was seen as perfect, male, immutable – a fit place for God the Father; earth was corrupt, female, changeable – the very pit of the universe, the natural place for all things heavy and inferior. The church added to the Aristotelian cosmology by invoking the presence of 'spirits' and 'unseen hands' to explain natural phenomena. Their view of the universe was essentially organic, requiring continual intervention by God. In sharp contrast, the new philosophy sought to cast all spirits out of nature and establish a more mechanistic world picture. Where the Christian organic view required continual intervention by God in the universe, the new philosophers relegated God to the role of cosmic clockmaker: creating nature perfect and setting it in motion without the need for further intervention (except for the purposes of biblical and other holy miracles, of course).

But the natural philosophers were not the only group to challenge the orthodoxy of the church and Aristotelian thought. The magic which the wise women were accused of practising was also active with respect to the natural world. Indeed, as Barbara Ehrenreich and Deirdre English point out, the witch was empirical in her methods:

> She relied on her senses rather than faith or doctrine, she believed in trial and error, cause and effect. Her attitude was

not religiously passive, but actively enquiring. . . . In short,
her magic was the science of the time.[12]

This revelation is typically omitted from standard histories of
science. The medieval scientists are often mentioned, as is the
predominantly male hermetic magical tradition of the sixteenth
century. It, too, sought power over nature, although through the
individual magician's strength of imagination and command of
the spirits abounding in nature, rather than by his acting directly
upon it. However, the tradition of the wise women predated both
of these groups. By the time the natural philosophers were
beginning to organize themselves, the church had virtually silenced
any female claim to a 'new' philosophy, and while the natural
philosophers were themselves as disdainful as the wise women of
the church's anti-empiricism, they were never subjected to the
same campaign of terror.

Perhaps because of its pagan and Aristotelian elements, the
enclosed and inward-looking world of the medieval Catholic
church did not produce the western science which Lynn White
ascribes to the Christian tradition. The Catholics did not, for the
most part, presume to explain the mysterious workings of the
natural world. In the event, it was the new and individualistic
Christianity of the Reformation which proved the better seedbed
for the growth of modern science. Protestantism was not fundamentally anti-empirical; it legitimized the natural philosophers'
search for 'solid truths' and, significantly, gave them licence to
interfere with nature.[13] Where the Catholic God regulated
Christian society though custom and a divinely ordained social
hierarchy (in which social class was determined by birth and,
hence, kings ruled by 'divine right'), the new Protestant God dealt
directly with the individual and with the individual's conscience.
Thus, Protestantism made everybody theoretically equal before
God. This ethos was seized upon by the new philosophers, many of
whom were active in the new religious movements: it meant they
need no longer defer to the authority of the priests.

It should be remembered that both the development in Europe
of a natural science based on experimentation and calculation and
the rise of Protestantism took place alongside the emergence of a
new economic order based on capitalist relations of production. It

is far beyond the scope of this chapter to map out in detail the complex of social and economic factors which contributed to these great transformations. The decay in the narrow framework of medieval life – structured, as it was, in every respect by the feudal system – took place over centuries. Certain features, however, bear mention because they illuminate the historical relationship between science and technology.[14]

The first of these is the importance of the great explorers – Marco Polo, Vasco da Gama, Christopher Columbus and others – in stimulating and reflecting a new outward-looking and often piratical adventurism in the courts of medieval Europe. During the thirteenth century contact with the Arab world prompted a revival of learning in numerous disciplines, including medicine and astronomy, as well as opening new opportunities for the accumulation of wealth by trade. Improvements in navigation at the end of the fifteenth century brought the possibility of using open-sea routes (rather than the more restricted coastal routes) to reach new markets – including the 'New World' of the Americas – and saw the increasing affluence of maritime nations such as Britain. Navigation was also a major stimulus to medieval science: by bringing new information, maps and products, as well as opportunities for invention, it provided applications for science, which had previously been a wholly scholarly activity. Similarly, the increasing importance of mining (especially for precious metals) and warfare stimulated the building of applicable bodies of knowledge in chemistry, metallurgy and mechanics.

Where the medieval scientists had tended to be generalists, the new natural philosophers were extremely focused in their concerns. Their work was geared explicitly to solving the pressing technical problems of the day and so to producing practical inventions which would be of use to the new ruling powers. In physics, this change was reflected by the shift in focus from the cosmological concerns of Copernicus, Tycho Brahe and Galileo to the more earthly interests of Newton in mechanics.

The second important feature of this period was the increasing influence of the traders and artisans, who were often important sources of wealth for their monarchs. By cutting the divinely ordained feudal ties between people, Protestantism provided a religious and ideological background which effectively gave this emerging merchant capitalist class permission to go about its economic business. The mechanization of nature and of cosmology, implying as it did the relaxation of God's hold on (and support for) the established social hierarchy, provided a powerful justification for the economic exploitation of the world; the traders and artisans increasingly provided the means – in the form of new techniques – for so profiting.

Natural philosophy also held out the promise of providing techniques for the economic exploitation of the world. Although contemporary scientists in fact made little direct contribution to the great innovations of the seventeenth and eighteenth centuries, the technical inventions of the artisans and traders in this period often increased the scope for scientific enquiry, which in turn yielded discoveries with practical applications in industry. The combination of mechanical force and latent heat embodied in the steam engine, for example, attracted the attention of scientists, who subsequently explained its action by producing a unified theory of energy. Steam power also prompted the discovery of laws of gases, following on from earlier experiments with air and vacuums, which themselves were linked with perhaps the most notable scientific contribution of the eighteenth century – the founding of chemistry.

The late eighteenth century was to see an unprecedented social mixing of scientists with the early engineers and manufacturers – notably in the new industrial centres of the Midlands and Scotland. The rise of manufacturing in these areas brought a shift in power and influence away from the London of the monarchy and Parliament and towards the rising industrial areas. This, in turn, was reflected in a movement of the centres of scientific teaching in Britain away from Oxford, Cambridge and London and towards the growing cities of the Midlands, North of England and Scotland. The late eighteenth century was, then, in the words of J.D. Bernal,

> a period of dynamic equilibrium of technics [sic] and science, a transition between a period in which science had more to learn from industry than to give it and one where industry came to be based almost entirely on science.[15]

In the course of the nineteenth century, science and technology became increasingly interrelated activities both as institutions – as governments and private companies began consciously to invest in research and development programmes – and as bodies of knowledge, as sustained technical innovation became increasingly dependent on specialized scientific information. Eventually, whole new science-based industries – notably chemicals and electricals – emerged; these were to become dominant features of twentieth-century industrial economies.

From the outset, the natural philosophers actively aligned themselves with the new political as well as economic order. In Britain, many members of the Royal Society had strong personal ties with the post-Civil War Parliament. Gresham College, Oxford, for example, was founded in 1579 through the bequest of Sir Thomas Gresham, a successful London merchant, financial agent to the Crown, and the founder of the Royal Exchange. Gresham College was the first centre of science teaching in Britain and the original meeting place of the Royal Society.[16] The alliance of the new philosophers with the new political order of the time was probably the most important reason for their ascendancy over the Hermetic magic tradition.

In contrast, all women were excluded from this alliance. The men who rose to power in seventeenth-century Europe rejected only those aspects of their Aristotelian and Christian heritage which were restrictive to them in their own new endeavours. The theoretical equality of all before the Protestant God was rarely, in practice, extended to women. Many of the early Protestant groups embraced the misogyny contained in the Hebrew (Old Testament) tradition, and for a while the practice of witch hunting continued under Protestant direction – in some places, such as John Knox's Scotland, with even more ferocity than before. In science, of course, sexual equality was not even a theory. The implicit belief in women's carnal ties with nature, and the explicit belief in women's intellectual inferiority to men, were retained when so much other 'superstition and ignorance' was discarded.

Brian Easlea has argued that another major driving force of science, and specifically its exclusion of women and female traditions of knowledge, stems from a continuation of the masculine endeavour to out-do women's reproductive abilities.[17] Bacon and his contemporaries promoted those most noble causes: the 'Relief of Man's [sic] Estate' and the 'Greater Glory of God'. Underlying these pursuits was a powerful vision of masculine achievement borrowed from the early explorers and adventurers: to boldly go where no man has gone before; potentially to rule the world. Contrary to Bacon's claims, scientific endeavour has often tended to plunder rather than glorify or relieve the natural and social world. The resulting unnatural 'miracles' now threaten to culminate in the destruction of all life by nuclear holocaust. At the very least, by divesting nature of its mysterious and creative powers, the natural philosophers 'made it possible to exploit nature in a mood of indifference to the feelings of natural objects'.[18] In so far as science has resulted in a rape of nature, this is an appalling indictment of male insecurity.

In order to dominate nature, men had to make it 'other' – in much the same way as women become 'other' to young boys as they grow up. Such implied conflict was reflected in the broader philosophical debates of the seventeenth century. With the help of Descartes, something of a compromise with God was eventually struck as the now familiar dichotomies – of mind (the 'rational soul') and body, reason and emotion – were added to the older distinction between man and nature. Needless to say these splits embodied huge moral judgements. Cartesian ideas underpinned the requirement for 'excessively rationalistic' men capable of exercising control over nature, the body, emotions – and, on every count, women. In this context the exclusion of women from the new philosophy could easily be justified. John Glanville, himself a member of the Royal Society, argued that science, and thus progress, would be impeded where 'the *Affections* wear the breeches; and the Female rules'.[19]

Science, masculine from its beginnings, has involved both the male appropriation of methods for acquiring knowledge and the creation of a new male hierarchy to administer and improve upon that knowledge. This pattern is epitomized in the male takeover of healing, which started with the bloody period of the witch hunts and resulted in the rise of a powerful medical profession siding firmly with the established male authorities. Ultimately science, including medical science, provided men with new means of controlling women. The moral crusade of the witch trials – to protect society from women – was, in the so-called 'enlightened' nineteenth century, turned into a moral crusade to protect women from themselves. The contemporary practice of sexual surgery for women deemed 'over-sexed' or who aspired to enter the masculine spheres of life was only slightly less punitive than the older forms of witch hunting. More persistent and effective, however, has been the wide credence given to scientific theories about the sexes which, although they have changed in form over the years, have consistently tried to tell women what is and is not natural behaviour.[20]

Capitalism: the new power base

Capitalism in Western Europe can be split into two distinct but overlapping phases: *mercantile* capitalism, characterized by the accumulation of wealth through buying, selling and transporting goods and raw materials, and *industrial* capitalism, characterized by factory production. The science we know today only really took off with the full development of industrial capitalism in Western Europe.

Paralleling the evolution of capitalism in trade and manufacture was a long, slow and uneven process of change in agriculture. This involved the gradual enclosure of commons, the introduction of new techniques and the eventual evolution of capitalist farming as we currently know it: a farm represents an opportunity for capital investment on a par with a factory and involves no more social ties between employers and employees than exist in modern industry. The growth of the cities with industrialization and the changes in agriculture were mutually reinforcing. The cities provided growing opportunities to switch land from subsistence farming to exploiting cash crops for sale to the industrial population. While enclosure of commons and agricultural mechanization (such as Jethro Tull's seed drill) tended to push poorer people off the land, industrial development also tended to pull them into the cities.

The Industrial Revolution in Britain is normally thought of as having taken place between 1750 and 1850. While these dates are necessarily arbitrary, by the end of those 100 years a largely rural nation had been transformed so that approximately half of its population lived in the growing urban centres where new factories offered the more secure, and usually the most lucrative, employment. Nations which industrialized later looked on capitalist

England both as an example and as a threat as cheap English goods – especially textiles – flooded the European markets in the early nineteenth century.

Some of the earlier industries grew out of the practice and techniques of cottage industry in rural areas. The textiles industry, which was the major growth sector in the first years of the Industrial Revolution in Britain, was the first of these newer types of industry to invade the towns and to set up alongside the established artisan trades. After agriculture, textiles were the largest source of employment in eighteenth-century England. The growing city and colonial markets combining with the difficulty of controlling workers (who were scattered among rural cottages) provided important incentives to the development of the first factories in that industry. As mechanization of production brought a dramatic decline in prices, domestic demand for textile goods was able to rise and English producers captured important export markets such as France and Germany.

According to Marx, capitalism was the first truly 'economic' mode of production in that with it society became organized around the exchange of money: what he called the 'cash nexus'.[21] This contrasted with the greater importance of barter and the exchange of responsibilities in earlier, feudal society. Here family members farmed some of the time on land granted to them by the local landlord and some of the time on the lord's land. In return, the lord ensured that his farmers and their families were protected and fed, even in times of famine. As Britain made the slow transition into capitalism, the whole web of social responsibilities which tied feudal society together was torn apart and replaced by a new pattern of 'free enterprise' and 'free labour'. These institutions were free precisely because they were irresponsible: formally, capitalists and workers owed each other nothing. Their relationship consisted of the purchase of labour power and the handing over of hard cash. Where, previously, wealth had come through the ownership of land and the opportunities this gave for the appropriation of agricultural surplus in the form of rent, capitalist enterprise provided an alternative way to accumulate wealth, through access to sufficiently large sums of money or capital to start a business. The patriarchy of pre-capitalist times influenced this change: just as a male-dominated aristocracy had, for the most part, controlled the ownership of land, so the new economic power base of capitalist enterprise came to be controlled by men.

It is not always realized, especially by those of us living in the industrialized world, just how much the sexual division of labour has changed in form over the years, or just how prominent women's work is in some other societies. Agriculture, for example, was probably invented by women, as were many of the tools required; to this day, agricultural labour is undertaken primarily by women in many parts of the Third World.[22] In seventeenth-century British agriculture, women worked sometimes inter-changeably with other family members (especially at harvest time) and sometimes on their own. Dairying was often undertaken exclusively by women. Similarly, in textile production, women tended to prepare and spin the fibres while men wove. Other areas of family industry – notably brewing, baking and healing – were the province of women, with skills and tools passing from mother to daughter.

The sexual division of labour practised in the household was often reproduced in trade. Most alehouses in seventeenth-century London, for example, were owned and run by women. Generally, however, women worked alongside men. The records of some 500 guilds remain, and of these only five did not admit women on an equal basis with men. Marriage was the most common entry route into guild membership, husbands and wives having equal rights and responsibilities as business partners. Equally, however, women – whether married or not – could set up as *femmes soles*, a status which allowed them to conduct business and employ apprentices. Neither marriage nor motherhood appears to have interfered with women's work. While there are no official statistics for the eighteenth century to guide us, we may get an impression of the extensiveness of women's work (at least in London) from a contemporary list of 86 couples in the sessions papers of the Old Bailey: in only one case did the wife not have an occupation in her own right. Even middle-class women are recorded as having been actively involved in finance and business.[23]

The guilds were set up by people in trade to keep secret the details of their craft techniques and to establish a monopoly. This allowed prices to be controlled and tended to protect the incomes of guild members. Unlike the modern craft skills employed in industry, the old crafts related to the whole process of manufacture – from raw materials to finished product. There was a division of labour within society – butchers, bakers, candle-stick makers and so on – but not within businesses. This meant that anyone possessing craft knowledge could set up in business alone. It also meant that her or his techniques were limited to those relevant to production in small quantities and to those requiring no more capital than one person could amass in an age when usury (the lending of money at interest) was a crime as well as a sin.

By the end of the eighteenth century usury began to become an accepted fact of business life, and successive Acts of Parliament progressively decriminalized it, in line with the needs of the emerging capitalist classes. This promoted the formation of larger and larger businesses. The opening up of new markets overseas (partly through colonization) stimulated expansion and provided seemingly endless sources of raw materials for British manufacturers.

It was when the importance of craft knowledge waned and capital replaced land as the basis for accumulating wealth that women increasingly lost out. The business partnership of marriage appears previously to have been relatively equitable. For example, widows usually retained tenancy of land or inherited their husbands' trade in preference to any sons. For the most part, laws relating to labour and property did not differentiate between women and men. This probably resulted from the egalitarian traditions enshrined in Anglo-Saxon law. At some point in the transition to the cash economy and the development of large-scale enterprise, however, a more restrictive dogma intervened. But change was slow.

The earliest evidence of women being paid less than men for agricultural work dates from the mid-sixteenth century. By the end of the seventeenth century, most of the guilds had moved into male hands; even brewing had become a masculine trade. In 1795, provision for the poor and unemployed first allocated financial responsibility for dependent children to men (a responsibility which previously lay with the mother). By that time it was virtually impossible for women to trade on their own account, and by the end of the nineteenth century the entry of women apprentices into the crafts had all but disappeared. Retailing was the only business which remained open to women.[24]

Women were, almost without exception, denied access to capital at the time when this was becoming an essential prerequisite for remaining in business: ownership of means of production became a right reserved for men. English common law, dating from medieval times, distinguished between real property (freehold land) and personal property (everything else). At marriage, the husband became the legal owner of all his wife's personal property but not of any real property she owned. He controlled any income from her land; but he could not dispose of her land without consent; should he die before her, she resumed control over it. While this arrangement clearly benefited men, it provided some safeguards for land-owning women when land was the major source of wealth. However, capital was personal rather than real property. As married women had no separate legal identity from their husbands with respect to personal property, they were effectively barred from capitalist entrepreneurship in their own right. Only in 1882 did it become possible for married women to hold personal property, by which time the expectation that women should enter business had virtually disappeared.

Men's legal control of personal property was reflected in the power relations operating within the family. This is especially clear in the development of the textiles industry. There had always been an imbalance in productivity between fibre preparation and spinning (which were tasks traditionally done by women and children) and weaving (which was normally a male activity). This imbalance was aggravated by Kay's invention of the fly shuttle in 1737, which further increased weavers' productivity. In the old cottage organization of the textiles industry, it took several women and children to provide enough raw materials for one male weaver. The pressures pushing people off the land in the eighteenth century, however, made textile production an increasingly attractive full-time alternative to agricultural work, where previously it had been a part-time activity taking place alongside work on the land. It therefore became necessary to balance the output of the women and children with the needs of the weaver. Rather than changing the sexual division of labour, 'female' types of work were put out to be done by non-family members. On these occasions it was the male head of household who paid the out-workers and sold any surplus. Some enterprising individuals went on to put out weaving as well as fibre preparation and spinning. It was only at this point, when a delicate balancing act, intended to secure an adequate supply of raw materials to weavers, turned into a more conscious form of capitalism, that the traditional sexual division of labour began to break down: as putting out occupied more of weavers' time, so their wives took up the loom at home.[25]

As the productive process moved out of the home, it appears to have been regarded as natural for men to act first as the external economic representatives of their families and later in other roles of authority. In the early factories, whole families were initially recruited and paid as a unit, transferring male authority in the home directly to the factory. The increasing mechanization and scale of production in the factories, however, gradually ended this practice of employing family labour. Men's authority over their own families was translated over time into male dominance in the supervisory jobs, where they exercised authority over an un-differentiated mass of individually paid women and children operatives. Again, some women were allowed to weave as men moved into the new positions of authority.

We can see the development of capitalism as a process whereby men used their traditional hold on property and their authority inside the family as a basis for beginning to operate in the economy outside it. Capitalism, in other words, was essentially a male creation, and as men began to migrate into the controlling roles – both as capitalists and as workers – within the new industrial enterprises, so women filled the spaces they left behind. This reflects precisely Heidi Hartman's concept of patriarchy as discussed earlier: there is a hierarchy among men, but one important source of male solidarity is the ability to dominate at least some women.

Ultimately the biggest space men left behind was the home itself. Only some of the tasks which had previously been performed in the household entered the economic mode of production. The remainder, those associated with the production of goods and services for immediate consumption by family members, continued to be unpaid and, along with the rearing of children, became the sole prerogative of women – enshrined as 'housework'. This, of course, provided men with personal servicing whilst, at the same time, reinforcing their claim to economic power. Still, the shift of women back to the home took place over nearly two centuries. In the meantime, men developed new and subtle means of controlling women's labour power outside it.

Women fill the empty spaces

The factory as the hallmark of industrial capitalism, as opposed to pre-capitalist and mercantile capitalist forms of economic organization, emerged in the latter part of the eighteenth century. It was a social innovation rather than a technical one. By housing workers in one place – often no more than a shed equipped with the relevant craft tools – capitalists were able to supervise their workers to an unprecedented extent, ensuring that they worked the agreed number of hours and that they were prevented from embezzling raw materials for their own use.

Factory-based production allowed the capitalists to reorganize work and split the production of any one item into a sequence of discrete operations. The contemporary economist and advocate of the new system, Adam Smith, analyzed the factory manufacture of pins, and showed how much more productive it was to have workers specialize in one aspect of manufacture rather than to have each one perform the whole operation from start to finish:

> The great increase in the quantity of work, which, in consequence of the division of labour, the same number of people are capable of performing, is owing to three different circumstances: first, to the increasing dexterity in every particular workman [sic]; secondly, to the saving of time, which is commonly lost in passing from one species of work to another; and lastly, to the invention of a great number of machines which facilitate and abridge labour, and enable one man [sic] to do the work of many.[26]

In this way, the social division of labour of the earlier trades was replaced in factories by a detail or technical division of labour. What Smith did not point out was that this had the effect of making workers dependent on capitalists. Under a detail division of labour, workers knew about only part of the process involved in manufacturing a commodity. Thus, while a competent pin-maker could always leave the employ of a capitalist and set up in business alone, someone specialized only in putting heads onto pins could not.[27]

Equally, under a detail division of labour, workers' interests were opposed not only to those of the capitalist but also, potentially, to those of other workers when it came to negotiating wages. Charles Babbage, writing half a century after Smith, described the advantage of this for capitalists:

> The master manufacturer, by dividing the work to be executed into different processes, each one requiring different degrees of skill or force, can purchase exactly that precise quantity of both which is necessary for each process; whereas, if the whole work were executed by one workman [sic], that person must possess sufficient skill to perform the most difficult, and sufficient strength to execute the most laborious, of the operations into which the work is divided.[28]

This realization was probably one of the factors which ended the practice of employing whole families in the early factories in favour of taking on individual workers. In any case, it was not long before wages were paid to individuals, irrespective of their family ties. Although this helped undermine some of fathers' earlier authority in the family, it also opened the way to men seeking wage increases independently of, and often in opposition to, their womenfolk.

The problem with the new capitalist system was, for Marx, that it constituted a form of systematized exploitation. Society was divided between those who owned means of production – land, machinery, factories – and those who did not. Those who did were, in principle, able to appropriate the labour power of those who did not. They did this by paying employees only part of the value of the goods they created during their working day, retaining the balance or surplus value, which they could either take out as profits or reinvest in the business. As a result, the interests of these two classes – workers and capitalists – were fundamentally opposed. Individually, capitalists might or might not be monsters, set on grinding the faces of the workers into the dirt, but all were obliged to exploit their workers in this way, to a greater or lesser extent. Capitalism was a kind of game in which the individual capitalists had either to eat or be eaten. They needed to keep wages as low as possible in order to stay competitive, which they did by offering lower-priced, higher-quality or new types of goods on the market. And they needed profits, partly to finance these efforts and partly to make their firms grow, for with size came power – especially the power to dominate markets and buy out other capitalists. In effect, capitalists had to fight a war on two fronts: they had to struggle with their own workers over the appropriation of surplus value, for profits, and they had to compete with other capitalists for control over markets.

It was these conflicts which produced the scientific and technological dynamism of modern capitalism. The imperative for capitalists to gain control over markets provided an enormous stimulus to the development of new products and processes, and in creating these techniques the interests of individual capitalists were mutually opposed. But all capitalists had a common interest in new techniques which increased their control over workers within the factory. As Adam Smith realized, the division of labour in a factory encouraged the 'invention of a great number of machines', which in turn affected the division of labour and the skills required of particular workers. Factory-based production went through an evolution from a system of supervised *manu*-facture (from the Latin *manus*, hand) to what Marx called *machino*facture, where water and steam were used as energy sources to replace human power. Power-using machines were constructed in such a way that tools were literally taken out of the hands of workers and fitted to the 'business end' of the machines. The worker was then left to control the new machine. Eventually, machines began to be built which actually embodied aspects of the knowledge used by workers in controlling previous generations of machines. These automatic or self-acting machines removed even the control of the machinery from the hands of the workers, leaving them simply in attendance on it. Where machines had originally been the servants of factory workers, the workers now found themselves the servants of the machines or, in many cases, out of a job.

Labour usually accounts for a large part of production costs, but this is not the only reason why capitalists should want to replace workers with machines. Machines, unlike human labourers, do not talk back, need rest breaks or demand for themselves a portion of the profits they produce. As mill-owner Andrew Ure, a contemporary of Marx, said: 'when capital enlists science into her [sic] service, the refractory hand of labour will always be taught docility.'[29] Thus Nasmyth, for example, invented his steamhammer at a time (1851) when his workers (who previously sledge-hammered iron by hand) were on strike, and halved the number of men he employed.[30]

In practice, the most 'refractory' workers tend to be those with scarce skills. Less-skilled workers are generally more plentiful, cheaper to employ, and altogether less troublesome. Capitalists therefore have a particular interest in introducing machines which specifically reduce their dependence on scarce skills. Mechanization both strengthens the control of capitalists over production and allows them to exploit Babbage's principle, discussed earlier.

One effect of this has been the process of deskilling, which operates continually in industrial capitalism. The quality of the labour required by employers is lowered as an accompaniment to technical change in the production process. Paradoxically, the design and production of the automated machinery responsible for this deskilling process is itself very highly skilled work. Hence, the process of deskilling work at one level in the manufacturing hierarchy implies the creation of new, skilled, technical work at higher levels.

Like Nasmyth, many of the early factory owners themselves designed the techniques used in their factories. But during the nineteenth century machine building became the business of a separate and specialist trade and, in some cases, of separate engineering departments. While the early inventions of the Industrial Revolution were based on a great deal of art and precious little science, their innovation or commercialization required access to capital. Thus, even in those cases where inventions were made by women, their commercial exploitation necessarily fell into the hands of men. Competition between capital goods producers has played a vital part in shaping both the character of techniques used in production and the psychology of the engineers who produce them. Like other producers, machine builders have to compete to supply goods which best satisfy the desires of their buyers. Machine users are interested in machines which produce the maximum possible output in return for the minimum possible input and which weaken the control of their workers over their work. Hence, machine builders compete to supply deskilling or labour-displacing machinery. This is the background against which the modern engineering profession arose.

Just as the inventive function of the capitalist entrepreneur has been split off into engineering, so the control of the firm (or more specifically of workers) has tended to pass to specialist management. Historically, in fact, management is an offshoot of engineering, having been established as a separate intellectual discipline only in the early twentieth century. However, both arose as agents of the capitalists within firms.[31] Nowhere is the relationship between management and engineering made more clear than in the writing of F.W. Taylor published in the early years of this century. Based on his experience as an engineer and as a manager, Taylor wrote a systematic account of existing 'good' management practice, which he called 'scientific management'.[32] He argued that 'management' was a combination of methods for appropriating engineering knowledge and specifying in detail how work was to be done. Ideally, he wrote, management should, first, control and monopolize knowledge about the productive process; second, decide how work is to be done, permitting no worker initiative whatsoever and, third, use its monopoly of knowledge to control every step of the labour process.[33]

Informed by Taylor's principles, we may think of the modern capitalist firm as a pyramid with a few managers and engineers at the top and many supposedly less skilled people further down the hierarchy. The drive of much capitalist technical change seems to be to suck knowledge about the production process towards the top, where managers and engineers (including, in effect, engineers in capital goods firms) transform this knowledge into machinery and instructions, which are passed down the pyramid, in the process deskilling or displacing some jobs. The pyramid is, of course, hierarchical in terms of control, status and pay, with the tasks associated with the conception of the production process located near the top of the pyramid and those associated with execution concentrated nearer the bottom. Techniques continually change, and work is continually reorganized as knowledge about production is embodied into machines and work organization. At the lower levels, workers are displaced or become increasingly interchangeable as a result of deskilling, thereby reducing the reliance of the entrepreneur on their individual co-operation. At the same time, newer and more skilled jobs are created higher in the hierarchy.

Needless to say, as the detail division of labour deepened, it became increasingly sexual in nature: men tended to move into the upper reaches of the hierarchy, leaving women (as well as children) to fill the spaces left behind. During the Industrial Revolution, women had entered factory work, notably the textile mills, in their hordes. They came first from agriculture, where mechanization tended to displace women rather than men, and from domestic service and the so-called unskilled trades. As piece-work began to dry up, both women and men domestic textile workers, and their children, were increasingly obliged to follow into the factories. Thus, of the 288,700 textile workers employed in 1835, 47 per cent were women and 15 per cent were children under the age of 13.[34] As production was progressively mechanized and the tradition of family labour disappeared, men tended to move from supervising their children to supervising the new machines. In some instances the introduction of new techniques actually opened up opportunities for women. But in the longer term women's work was progressively deskilled. Women became both cheaper to employ and easier to displace. Significantly for the capitalists, women were 'taught docility' rather better than men, and this made women especially dependent on the capitalists for employment.

The peculiar vulnerability of women's work to the deskilling and labour-displacing effects of technical change reflects the operation of patriarchal relations in the new workplace. While skill sounds as if it is something which can be measured in some objective way, in practice it is not. Workers and management effectively negotiate about skill descriptions just as they negotiate about wages. Many of our modern trade unions have their roots in the earlier guilds, which had of course been substantially taken over by men by the late seventeenth century. Male workers were therefore in a stronger position to protect their craft skills than were women. Even where women were also organized, their 'brothers' tended to claim higher status and pay for the tasks they themselves performed. Skills increasingly became a masculine prerogative, and many skilled occupations became exclusively male – for example, compositing in the printing industry. Capitalist assaults on such monopolies of skill therefore represented a threat not only to the economic power of their holders but also to their masculinity. (These battles are now being re-enacted in parts of the printing industry, especially the newspaper industry, with the application of microelectronics to compositing.)[35] Women's paid work was increasingly devalued, just as other things female are devalued, and in many instances this has resulted in women's work being deemed unskilled when equivalent work done by men is described as semi-skilled or even skilled.[36]

Of course male workers were also deskilled by technical change but, taken over society as a whole, not as much. The now traditional equation of women with unskilled work is the result of a process by which men were effectively bought off through being allowed to move up the hierarchy created by capitalist production and, at the same time, gaining more control over women's labour power. In this way, male workers as well as the male capitalists benefited from women's learned 'docility'. But the battles which took place on the shop floor were only one part of the eventual exclusion of women from paid work and from jobs which paid a living wage.

As the nineteenth century progressed, single women without children began to dominate the female part of the labour force. In 1851, only a quarter of all married women were employed, and by 1911 the proportion had dropped to one in 10.[37] The remainder were relegated to the home, unpaid 'housework' being the fastest-growing area of work for women at the time. Childrearing became a much more lengthy process as protective legislation progressively eroded the use of child labour in the factories and as the period for which children were considered dependants increased. Of course, not all families could afford to forgo the wage brought in by the mother and wife, but as the middle-class ideal of enforced 'leisure' for women began to percolate through to the working class, so men began to demand a family wage for themselves.[38]

At the same time, the association of women with the home was increasingly reflected in the type of jobs women held. By 1841, two-thirds of women in paid work were employed in domestic service.

The remainder worked in the cotton mills, dressmaking and millinery, agriculture, laundry occupations and teaching (in that order).[39] This increasingly acute sexual division of labour in paid work made it more and more unlikely that women and men would do equivalent work. Apart from agriculture, factory work was the only area of women's paid employment in which men were also numerous. For a while, women in factory work were actually better off in terms of pay and hours than women in most other areas of paid work, these being female dominated, and so less likely to attract decent wages. As industrialization ran its course, however, women's pay decreased relative to men's, even in those industries where women still worked alongside men. In modern production processes women are largely confined to the bottom of the hierarchy, operating or assembling the machines men design.

Women on the receiving end

Marx rightly perceived that science and technology became tools of the new capitalist class in their struggle with workers. But he failed to notice that the new capitalists were also men and that, because of the new economic role of technology, capitalist technology is more inherently masculine than any previous technologies. Just as there were institutional mechanisms, in the form of property laws and male authority within the family, which allowed men to dominate the new capitalist economy, so there are mechanisms which tend to keep men in control within the rapidly changing hierarchies in capitalist firms. Technology is one of the most important of these mechanisms. It operates through male control of the deskilling process, through male domination of the technical and scientific skills which lead to the creation of new products and, above all, through male control of the institutions through which technology is produced and reproduced.

Typically, in the early years of an industry's history, there is a need for new technical skills. The difficulty of finding appropriately skilled people reinforces the drive for entrepreneurs to develop deskilling techniques, but the creation of new industries with associated needs for new skills is an important reason why the populations of the industrialized countries have not been deskilled into unemployed ignorance. Indeed, the very opposite is the case: over the last century we have, as a population, become increasingly literate in the 'science of the industrial arts'. Governments nowadays assume responsibility for generating much of the technology (in the form of skills as well as research) on which new techniques are based. School education is now compulsory to the age of at least 16 in most industrialized countries and usually includes some grounding in science if not in technical skills. Further, the number of technical and scientific courses available in further and higher education has multiplied prodigiously. We are constantly being reminded that, even in times of high unemployment, industry needs people trained in highly specialized technical fields. But despite this perceived need, and the existence of equal opportunities legislation in almost all western countries, the number of women entering technical work remains pitifully small.

It was in the last half of the nineteenth century that technical change began to acquire an increasingly scientific basis, especially in the emerging chemical and electrical industries. While the historical association of engineering with the early capitalist entrepreneurs effectively barred women from entering this profession, the maleness of science also operated to exclude women from the new sources of invention. In this way, women were denied access to the new skills and knowledge created by the technological dynamism of capitalism. If women entered the new and increasingly research-based industries at all, they came in, and typically stayed, at the bottom of the hierarchy, where they were involved in the execution of tasks laid down by management rather than in their conception.

This pattern is now being reproduced all over the world, including those Third World countries already plundered by the colonial conquests of nations which, like Britain, industrialized early on. The capitalists' division of labour has now assumed international proportions with, in some cases, different components of the same product being manufactured in different countries – often (and still in line with the Babbage principle) because of differences in wage levels. In the Third World, as elsewhere, women employed in factories often assemble products but play no part in designing them. The larger number of Third World women, however, are involved primarily in rural production for which they are increasingly expected to use techniques developed by men who live thousands of miles away. Of course the specific character of patriarchal relations varies enormously across the world, but in general new techniques tend to benefit men rather than women – partly because they are based on western models. As the more powerful men in Third World countries embark on their own institutionalization of science and engineering, there are signs that women will simply find themselves at the bottom of this new hierarchy.[40]

Clearly the net result of men's domination of the invention of new products is that women have only negligible control over the development and character of technical change. But the exclusion of women from the design of technology also has the incidental effect of producing techniques which are appropriate to male needs and male bodies, not to female ones. Even when techniques are intended to be used by women – as, for example, are most contraceptives and domestic appliances – it is clear that women's needs and priorities are not incorporated into the design process. Understandably, this has given rise to demands for a reorientation of research programmes, more stringent testing, and so on. Yet it is difficult to imagine how this kind of consumer pressure can be effective unless many more women are able to influence the technological power base of modern industrial society by understanding and entering the institutions of science and engineering. This is most obviously true in the area of design. How can women's needs be reflected in the design of products unless women are involved in design processes?

Of course, until relatively recent times, women were simply excluded from membership of the key institutions like the Royal Society. But in the last 100 years it has proved very difficult for even these institutions to hold out against the isolated but determined woman entrant. The question is: why did the trickle of women into technical areas never turn into a flood? Clearly, part of the answer lies in the way in which little girls are taught to be feminine and to reject male roles. This socialization continues from their first waking moments, through school and into adult life. As we have already noted, science itself has contributed to this process. Now the masculinity of technology and its institutions is protected more by persuasion than by coercion.

Other reasons why girls (and women) reject technology concern the way in which men approach scientific and technological work, and the ugly fruits of that labour. As many women actually involved in science and engineering will attest, women are far less likely than men to conceive of 'pure' science and technology: this implies a degree of detachment from the living world (human and otherwise) with which few women are comfortable. Women are also less likely to become hooked on the 'gee-whizzery' of technology.[41] The qualities of pure detachment and technical excitement appropriate to current science and technology are qualities which little boys, not little girls, tend to develop – as a means of learning to dominate their 'feminine' emotions, and as an outlet for them. These qualities are alien and alienating to women. They are also very disturbing in a world constantly menaced by a high-technology version of Armageddon.

So what of the future? Are women destined to remain on the receiving end of a masculine technology? We hope not. More particularly, we believe that technology can itself be transformed into something more liberatory than it has so far proved. Doubtless the further entry of women into science and engineering will help. Today, women need as many technical skills as they can amass. But as long as there are oppressive power relations in society, these will be built into the overall pattern of technological development and so shape the individual techniques which emerge. While a greater presence of women in the relevant institutions might well do much to humanize technology, the fact that technology and techniques tend to reflect the interests of those who advance them means that there is also a need to democratize these technological institutions and to dismantle men's hierarchies. Precisely because technology is socially created, the values of caring and of nurturance which so desperately need to be embodied into it can appear only as a result of social intervention. Technology need not be alien or inhuman, and surely not all of it is, but if we want a liberatory technology then we will have to make it ourselves.

2. The exclusion of women from technology[1]

Dot Griffiths

I work at Imperial College, University of London, which is arguably the premier technological institution in Britain. It has over 200 teaching posts in engineering subjects, of which six are held by women. In 1983–84 only about 10 per cent of the engineering students were female, yet its record is better than that of many other colleges: in 1978 only 6 per cent of all British engineering students were female. And at the craft as opposed to professional level, the entry of women is currently even lower: 0.3 per cent of apprentices are women.

The task of this chapter is to ask why. Why are there so few women in technology in Britain? How are women excluded from technology? What implications does this exclusion have for women's experience of and relationship to technology?

I begin by discussing, and dismissing, the old familiar argument that 'women don't do technology because they can't do technology'. I then consider how the exclusion of women has developed through history, and how it is presently maintained. This in turn leads to a discussion of the experiences of women who do enter technology. The chapter concludes by asking how fundamental the exclusion of women from technology is. The discussion focuses on Britain, the country where the Industrial Revolution began and where the contemporary exclusion of women from technology is probably most extensive. The arguments which are made, however, apply only with differences of detail to all major industrial nations.

Justifying the exclusion

The under-representation of women in technology is often explained by reference to differences in cognitive ability between the sexes. Women, it is argued, excel at tasks involving verbal skills whilst men excel at those involving spatial skills – that is, they can visualize and mentally manipulate objects in three dimensions. It is further argued that spatial ability is important in mathematical performance. Since maths is crucial in engineering and many technical trades, the under-representation of women is said to be a consequence of their relatively poorer performance at tasks involving spatial skills.[2]

The biological arguments take two forms: the evolutionary argument, which seeks to explain *why* sex differences in cognitive abilities evolved, and the proximate argument which seeks to explain *how*, by what biological mechanisms, these differences are expressed. The evolutionary explanations start by pointing out that, biologically speaking, we are still effectively a gatherer-hunter species, our cultural evolution having proceeded much faster than biological evolution. In a gatherer-hunter society there is usually a clear division of labour between the sexes: women carry the major responsibility for childrearing and make the major contribution to the diet through their gathering activities while men travel farther afield to hunt and are responsible for group defence.

Male superiority in spatial ability is supposed to derive from this social division of labour. Better spatial ability confers an advantage in the activities of hunting and fighting; its possession thus improves the bearer's chances of survival and reproduction. Gradually, and in this way, spatial ability will have been selectively developed in men. Different selection pressures apply to women. Female verbal superiority is suggested to be a consequence of women's caring activities, which provide children with an appropriate environment within which to acquire language.[3]

Three mechanisms have been proposed to explain sex differences in cognitive abilities. The first suggests that there are brain differences between men and women. The two halves, or hemispheres, of the brain carry out different functions; speech, for example, is located in the left hemisphere. Psychologists use the term lateralization to describe this division of function between the hemispheres. However, while some researchers suggest that male spatial skills are a consequence of the greater bi-laterality of brain function in males, others argue the opposite![4] The second explanation suggests that spatial ability is inherited, probably via a sex-linked recessive gene (thus favouring its expression in males).[5] The third explanation is hormonal, the suggestion being that female and male hormones differentially affect cognitive functioning.[6]

None of these ideas withstands critical scrutiny. The evolutionary arguments are very weak given the extreme scarcity of information about social organization left by a fragmented fossil record. No one has satisfactorily explained how the selection pressure might have operated, for children can acquire language under very adverse conditions. Theories of the laterality of brain function, as well as the genetic and hormonal explanations have all been criticized on their own terms.[7] In practice, sex differences in cognitive abilities do not appear to be universal: in Eskimo societies, for example, both sexes perform spatially orientated tasks equally well.[8] Moreover, the actual differences in the performance of women and men in tests of cognitive ability are much smaller than one might expect given the conclusions drawn from them. The 'scores' of most women and most men fall within a common range. Sex differences in tests of spatial ability are certainly not large enough to account for the differential representation of women and men in engineering. If female entry into engineering was based on the distribution of spatial ability alone then the ratio of women to men would be 2:3 rather than 1:300.[9]

Finally, ability differences are not consistent over time. Girls perform at least as well as boys at spatial and mathematical tasks until adolescence. Only then does their performance deteriorate and give rise to adult sex differences in spatial skills. There are probably several reasons for this deterioration. Confidence and self-assurance have both been identified as important for success in mathematics, but both are against the norm of sex-stereotyped female behaviour. When girls are socialized to be independent and assertive they perform much better on spatial ability tests.[10]

As we shall see later, there is considerable evidence that girls at adolescence turn away from science and mathematics because they identify them as male. In short, from adolescence onwards, there are educational, psychological and sociological pressures discouraging female achievement in spatial and mathematical skills, and hence women's participation in technology.[11]

Generating the exclusion
Women are credited with a whole range of the earliest technical

inventions – pots, utensils, textiles, fire – developments which made a major contribution to the social evolution of humanity.[12] Now, however, women are largely excluded from the processes of invention and innovation and from the acquisition of technical skills. How did this change come about? When did women get pushed out of technology?

Prior to the Industrial Revolution women had more opportunities to acquire technical skills than they have today. This was partly because families supplied far more of their own needs for food, drink, clothing and utensils than they do now and partly because manufacture was largely organized on a domestic basis: home and work were one location. Women could acquire skills, at least under some circumstances. Daughters acted as assistants to their fathers, a wife assisted her husband in his trade and widows were allowed, if not expected, to carry on their husband's business on his death. Moreover, certain trades were entirely female. Handspinning was a female skill (hence the term spinster): in the woollen industry women were employed in every activity, undertook apprenticeships and were admitted to membership of the craft guilds; the silk industry was almost entirely under female control (although there was no guild of silkwomen.)[13]

All this changed between the seventeenth and nineteenth centuries. Home and paid work became separated as manufacture moved into factories. At the same time, craft skills were challenged by the introduction of machines, and new skills emerged from the impetus of the many inventions and technical developments, which marked the Industrial Revolution.

The factory system itself arose through changes in the organization of production, changes initiated in the textiles industry, which set the pattern for the future development of female occupation and skills.[14] Spinning was one of the first textile processes to be mechanized, not least because it took the work of several spinsters to keep one male weaver busy. However, the substitution of machine for hand spinning took place at an uneven pace in different parts of the country. The first machines (such as the spinning jenny) were small and cheap, and were often bought by spinsters and used in the home. Later machines (such as the mule) were heavier, more costly and demanded different operating skills – skills which became a male monopoly.

After the appearance of the mule in 1779, women spinners were soon superseded. By 1768, jenny spinning in the cottages was over. Heavier machines required the strength of men and spinning on the mule quickly became highly skilled work monopolised by a new class of men spinners.[15]

This pattern was to become familiar across a range of industries. The harnessing of the bleaching properties of chlorine heralded the decline of the independent female bleacher and the rise of the factory-based male chemical bleacher:

> It was inconceivable . . . that the woman who had successfully managed a bleaching business in the fields around her home should adopt the new methods and set up a chemical bleaching factory. She had neither training nor capital for such an enterprise, nor were there means of her acquiring either.[16]

In brewing, also a predominantly female trade, a monopoly over production was granted to a few large brewers, supposedly for the convenience of excise collection. This led to the exclusion of the majority of small female brewsters.[17]

The movement of manufacture out of the home denied women even the limited opportunity to assist their husbands and fathers. But more important for our discussion of women's exclusion from technology today was their exclusion from the new skilled trades which developed under the impetus of the Industrial Revolution. The previous male domination of technical skills (such as carpentry and iron working) translated into a male monopoly of the new skills of patternmaker, iron founder, turner, fitter, wheelwright, and so on. These key technical trades were male dominated from the very beginning and largely remain so. In this way, the Industrial Revolution and the rise of factory-based manufacture resulted in a more rigid division of society along gender lines, and the women who became industrial labourers found themselves working in the least skilled jobs, for the lowest pay.

Women were also being excluded from technology at another level during this period. Today, technological innovation is a highly organized activity which usually involves significant expenditure and is undertaken by professional technical and scientific staff who are employed in large industrial and governmental organizations. In the eighteenth century, however, there was a much closer relationship between invention and entrepreneurship. Typically an individual would have an idea for an invention and would either put up the capital to exploit the idea or seek a wealthy partner.

In order to participate in the inventive activity of the Industrial Revolution both ideas and capital were thus needed. The 1882 Married Women's Property Act gave women legal possession and control of any personal property (including capital) independently of their husbands. By that time, however, the growth in the scale of industry, and in the amount of capital needed to engage in viable production, together with the removal of industry from the home meant that only in exceptional circumstances did women act as entrepreneurs in their own right. Two widowed female members of the Darby family, for example, ran the family business at Coalbrookdale in Shropshire, the valley in which Abraham Darby began using coke to smelt iron: a development which heralded the Industrial Revolution in Britain. The Darbys were Quakers, a religious sect which has always maintained greater equality of opportunity between the sexes. (Notwithstanding this, the section of the award-winning museum at Coalbrookdale which discusses these women is entitled 'Petticoat Management'!).

At the same time as women were being excluded from entrepreneurship they were also denied access to education, and specifically to the theoretical grounding in mathematics and mechanics upon which so many of the contemporary inventions and innovations were based. As business activities expanded and were moved out of the home, middle-class men increasingly left their wives to a life of enforced leisure. This change in social roles was soon reflected in the education given to daughters and sons, girls learning 'accomplishments' (such as fancy needlework and piano-playing) whilst boys received an academic education. Accomplishments, it need hardly be said, were not the most appropriate foundation for participation in the world of the inventor-entrepreneur.

Again, some women escaped these constraints and made important contributions. Mary Somerville was a very distinguished mathematician, and to Lady Lovelace belongs much of the credit for early ideas on computer programming. Mozans has reviewed American women's roles in invention. 'What particularly arrests one's attention . . . is not only the large number of inventions made by women, but also the very wide range of devices which they embrace'.[18] History has forgotten or distorted many of these contributions. The cotton gin, for example, 'one of the most useful and important of American inventions', was invented not by Eli Whitney but by his employer Catherine L. Green. Whitney's name is on the patent because 'so opposed was public opinion to woman's having a part in mechanical occupation that she would have exposed herself to general ridicule and to loss of position in society' had her name appeared.[19]

From the mid-nineteenth century onwards, middle-class women began earnestly to seek access to higher education and the professions. Their struggle did not extend to technology: middle-class women did not beat a path to the door of engineering education. Importantly though, neither did their brothers – at least not in Britain, the home of the Industrial Revolution. Here the cultural élite have always been anti-industrial, with the consequence that formal engineering education was very slow to emerge. (Even science was hardly taught at boys public schools, and its availability was negligible at girls schools.) Engineering schools were established at Cambridge and the two London colleges – University and King's – in the mid 1800s, but there were very few graduates. Even in the 1920s, only about 200 engineering degrees a year were being awarded. (Imperial College alone now awards twice this number every year).[20]

Such a background as this renders the achievements of Hertha Ayrton all the more remarkable. Mrs Ayrton was probably alone amongst women of her generation in becoming involved in engineering. In 1899 she became the first woman member of the Institution of Electrical Engineers, and in 1901 she almost became the first woman to read a paper to the Royal Society. She had been allowed to demonstrate her experiments on a ladies' night but, 'they apparently did not yet feel able to proceed to the length of allowing a woman to read a paper at one of their meetings . . . so a compromise with tradition was effected when Professor Perry FRS read a paper written by Hertha Ayrton'.[21] Only a few women followed her example, although the inter-war period witnessed a number of important developments for women engineers. For example, in 1921 Letitia Chitty (later to join the staff of Imperial College) became the first woman to be awarded first-class honours in the Mechanical Sciences Tripos at Cambridge; in 1922 Margaret Partridge set up a large-scale electrical contracting firm in Exeter, and in 1926 the Women's Engineering Society was formed.[22]

The dominant attitude towards these pioneers, however, is probably summed up by the cartoon opposite, taken from the Imperial College magazine of November 1927.

Hertha Ayrton, Letitia Chitty and the others were exceptions to a male rule. The two world wars facilitated other exceptions. In both periods women were allowed to take over men's jobs in engineering, munitions and other areas . . . but only for the duration of the war. Women were again excluded when the men came home expecting their jobs back. (The American film *Rosie the Riveter* provides a compelling account of what this meant to five of these women.)

Maintaining the exclusion

So far I have considered some of the ways in which women came to be excluded from modern technology. Now we must consider how this exclusion is maintained, for today most scientists and almost all engineers, engineering technicians and craft workers are men. The particular pattern of gender (and class and racial) divisions which developed about the time of the Industrial Revolution persists today. For when a girl or woman chooses to become involved in technology, either as a skilled worker or as a graduate engineer, she is opting to pursue a particularly 'masculine' path. Furthermore, the difficulty of making such a choice has been reinforced – until very recently at least – by differences in the school curricula thought appropriate for girls and boys, and by the consequent under-resourcing of mathematics and science teaching for girls. To all of this must be added female under-achievement, particularly in mathematics and science.

Technology as masculine
Sex stereotyping involves treating females differently as a result of socially received beliefs and practices about what are appropriate feminine and masculine behaviours, interests and attributes. In all societies there are patterns of

From *The Phoenix*, magazine of Imperial College, Vol. XII, No. 6, November 1927.

typically feminine or masculine behaviour into which girls and boys are socialized and to which women and men largely conform. However, wide variation occurs between societies as to which activities are defined as feminine and masculine.[23] In advanced industrial societies, technology and the physical sciences are both seen as masculine pursuits, and they are embedded in a complex of masculine activities.

War, industry and, increasingly, commerce are all major stimuli for technological development. Almost half of Britain's Research and Development (R&D) budget is funded from industrial sources. The state supports most other R&D activities, and a staggering 55 per cent of the British government's R&D budget is spent on defence. War and industry institutionalize the masculine personality attributes of competition, assertion, aggression and dominance; all are key values in these activities. There is, therefore, little for girls and women to identify with in any of these activities or their related technical inputs. Both the technical craft apprentice and the undergraduate engineer enter a strongly masculine defined world.

This masculinity of technology affects the exclusion of women both actively and passively. Passively, girls and women turn away from technology as a consequence of its sex-stereotyped definition as an activity appropriate for men. Actively, girls and women opt out of technology because they reject its goals and values: the development, for example, of weapons of destruction, of boring and dehumanizing work processes and products designed with artificial obsolescence in mind. Modern technology has become symbolic of male domination. Technology, far more than science (in which women are better represented), is about control. Harnessing nature to serve *man*'s needs, exploiting natural resources, diverting the flow of rivers, manipulating the physical world – all of these are controlling activities. And in our world, control and domination are masculine prerogatives.[24] While the shape of rockets is, no doubt, based on sound aerodynamic principles, the phallic symbolism is hard to ignore. . . .

The school curriculum Sex-role socialization begins, quite literally at birth. It is the 'pink for a girl, blue for a boy' syndrome. Girls are socialized to be *sub*ordinate; they are to be dependent, nurturing, emotional, intuitive and person-oriented. Their social role is to be wives and mothers, servicers and carers of men and children. Work outside the home must always be secondary to this primary role. Boys, in contrast, are socialized into *super*ordination. They are to be dominant, assertive, aggressive, and object-oriented. Facts not intuition, maths not poetry, objects not people, control not caring: these are the elements of male sex-role socialization.

Education plays an important part in all of this. And it does so at two levels: formally, through the reflection of sex-role stereotyping in the school curriculum, and informally through classroom practice and interaction. In the eighteenth and nineteenth centuries, middle-class education was divided along gender lines. When formal working-class education began after the 1870 Education Act, it was little different. From the very earliest, education for working-class girls emphasized domestic and housewifely skills. The 'Regulations for Secondary Schools' published in 1909 demanded practical housewifery for girls and woodwork and metalwork for boys, demands reflecting their respective future roles as domestic servants and housewives and as low-grade industrial fodder.

These curricula differences changed little through the 1920s and 1930s. Science and mathematics teaching for middle-class girls was undervalued and under-resourced, whilst few working-class girls had the opportunity to acquire any non-domestic, technically-based, practical skills. (Technology as such has never been taught in British Schools.) The Second World War demonstrated even more clearly than the 1914–18 conflict the range of work women *could* do, if only given the opportunity. Yet neither the 1944 Education Act (a major educational reform) nor the Crowther Report in 1959 recognized this. Crowther suggested that it was sound educational policy to take account of 'natural' interests, and that the curriculum should 'respect' the different roles that [women and men] play'. The Newsom Report, a few years later, again argued that children should 'be educated according to ability and social role. Thus, girls should be educated in terms of their main social function – which is to make for themselves, their children and their husbands, a secure and suitable home and to be mothers.' Throughout the 1960s, and until the 1975 Sex Discrimination Act, overt sex stereotyping in the curriculum continued.[25]

The consequent underprovision of science and mathematics teaching for girls and their exclusion from male craft lessons have seriously impaired women's entry into technology.[26] Aptitude in science and mathematics is the entry qualification for academic engineering courses, as is aptitude in craft skills for technical trades. Denying girls the opportunity to develop these abilities through the school curriculum means that sex-role stereotyping is an important mechanism by which their exclusion from technology has been maintained. Now, of course, such gross stereotyping is outlawed – but not, one suspects, banished – in Britain. For example, removing the barriers which prevent girls taking metal-work and actively encouraging girls to choose it are rather different acts. In a society which is so deeply divided by gender, long-held attitudes about the appropriate curricula for girls and boys cannot simply be legislated away.

A cross-gender choice In order even to consider entering a craft apprenticeship or an engineering course, a young woman must usually have studied mathematics, physics and often technical drawing at school. In Britain, the choice of subject is made at the early age of 13 or 14, when pupils are prepared for the public examinations taken at the minimum school leaving age of 16. In England and Wales (there are regional variants) these examinations are called General Certificate of Education (GCE) 'O' Levels. At the age of 18 a further set of examinations, 'A' Levels, may be taken, normally in a maximum of three or four subjects. Entry into British higher education is usually dependent upon performance in these examinations. As Table 2.1 illustrates, many girls drop out of the technical and scientific subjects at the point at which they are given a choice.

There is a wealth of evidence to suggest that girls and boys understand and act upon the *image* of school subjects. I have already argued that technology and the physical sciences are defined as male-appropriate activities; this view is upheld in a recent study in which schoolchildren of both sexes classified physics, chemistry, maths and woodwork as male and cookery as female.[27] In the same study, the male/technical/scientific subjects were also seen as difficult, complex and intellect-based, and girls showed less interest in them than boys. This difference of interests

Table 2.1 Numbers of boys and girls as candidates for GCE O Level and A Level, 1978

Examination & subject	Boys	Girls	Girls as % of boys
O level			
Mathematics	165,632	126,125	76
Chemistry	79,550	43,851	55
Physics	116,710	34,024	29
Technical drawing	50,862	1,532	3
A level			
Pure & applied mathematics	38,228	11,543	30
Chemistry	27,755	11,896	43
Physics	37,484	8,121	22
Technical drawing	3,020	46	1.5

Source: Department of Education: *Statistics of Education*, Vol. 2.

develops quite early. The 'Girls Into Science and Technology Project' (a recent interventionist project based in Manchester to encourage more girls to enter science) found differences in the scientific interest of girls and boys at age 11, although there was little difference at this age, in their level of scientific knowledge. When asked to write essays,

> Most of the boys chose 'how cars work' or 'rockets and space travel' but these topics were very unpopular with the girls. Girls predominantly chose 'the human body'; 'birds near my home'; 'seeds' or 'pond life'.[28]

The boys also had greater experience of tinkering – using tools, taking things apart and mending them, playing with constructional toys – experiences which, later, both predispose them more positively toward technical craft subjects and allow them to approach these subjects more confidently.

Such differences of interest are amplified by the pressures of adolescence, that complex and confusing transition from childhood to adulthood marked both by the physical changes associated with puberty and by the onset of adult sexual and social roles. This is the period when girls and boys begin to anticipate their future roles as women and men. And, as the fashion manufacturers and the pop industry know only too well, it is a period of intense peer-group pressure for conformity. It is also the time when the 'tomboy' has to hang up her jeans and put on her bra and tights (cross-gender behaviour in boys is crushed much earlier on and is anyway much less tolerated).

It is at this emotional crossroads that a girl has to choose whether to pursue technology. Most, as we have seen, do not. To choose technology means choosing – consciously or otherwise – to be different. It means choosing to enter an area in which there will be a conflict between subject choice and the girl's growing awareness of the requirements of femininity. It also means choosing an area in which there are unlikely to be role models; that is, the example of other women who have entered technology and succeeded. Girls in single-sex schools are more protected from the conflicts of a cross-gender choice and are therefore more likely to choose physical science subjects.[29]

The pressures of adolescence, together with girls' disinclination and lack of opportunity to take 'male' craft subjects, mean that very few girls who leave school at 16 are in a position to seek a technical craft apprenticeship even if they want to. Since girls also receive little careers information about such opportunities, their very sparse representation among craft apprentices is not difficult to explain. Similarly, the swing away from science (especially physical sciences) and maths among more academically inclined girls between the ages of 16 and 18 means that engineering is not an option open to many of them if (and when) they decide to apply to university. The early specialization encouraged in the British school system serves further to reduce the range of girls' subsequent choices. Subject preferences expressed at 13 can structure a pupil's entire future and girls probably lose out more than boys as a result of this. Whereas a science-based choice at this stage does not prevent subsequent entry into non-science subjects, a non-science bias effectively prevents subsequent entry into both science and engineering.

It should be stressed that those girls who do persevere in

mathematics and the physical sciences generally do slightly better at their exams than do the boys. Further, the percentage of women admitted into degree courses is slightly higher than the percentage of women applicants, suggesting that those who do apply are highly regarded as candidates.[30] These observations in no way diminish the relevance of the pressures referred to above; rather, they reflect the high levels of motivation required of girls and young women wishing to pursue an interest in science or technology.

It has been suggested that the female swing away from science and maths is a consequence of girls' believing them to be more difficult than other subjects and so wishing to avoid them.[31] Studies of classroom interactions shed some light on this question. Carol Dweck and her co-workers found that whereas boys were rewarded for good work, girls were rewarded for good behaviour. Conversely, boys were chastized for poor behaviour and girls for poor performance. Teachers attributed poor performance in boys to a lack of motivation (poor behaviour) whilst in girls it was attributed to a lack of ability. The authors of this study suggest that girls thus learn to attribute their difficulties to a lack of ability. This 'learned helplessness' means that they will be less willing to struggle with subjects – notably science and maths – which they perceive to be difficult.[32]

Such arguments also explain why girls' performance in science and mathematics declines as they progress through secondary school. Far from reflecting a biologically based sex difference, this decline reflects and is a consequence of socially induced differences. Girls and boys develop and internalize different beliefs about their abilities, beliefs which all too often are reinforced by their teachers.[33] They learn not only that different subjects are appropriate for them, but also that it doesn't do for them to have too much ability. Komorovsky has shown both that boys don't like clever women, and that girls are aware of this. Since both sexes acknowledge physical science as difficult, the conclusion is obvious. Girls learn to underachieve and to develop what Horner has called 'a fear of success'.[34]

Policing the exclusion

Two American sociologists, Zuckerman and Cole, have suggested that women who enter science face a trio of obstacles. First, they must overcome the recognition that science is male; then they are faced with a lower evaluation of their scientific abilities, and, finally, they encounter discrimination. Women who dare to enter technology face all of these barriers, and more – if only because technology is an even more masculine activity than science. Hostility to their entry is consequently greater.[35]

The conflict between femininity and subject choice which deters girls from technical and physical science subjects at school is magnified several times over when it comes to technical apprenticeships. To choose to become a foundry worker, a metal worker, a patternmaker, an electrician, a welder, or any of the other skilled craft trades, is to choose to be very different indeed at age 16. All of these trades involve a whole range of attributes which are conventionally unfeminine: tool handling, operating potentially dangerous machines, lifting, sometimes getting dirty, and so on. And as we have seen, the curriculum of sex-role socialization pushes girls firmly away from the informal skill acquisition which underwrites entry into and achievement in the manual trades.

Women's relegation to the low-status, low-paid and low-skilled jobs in the engineering industry means that their participation in practical shop-floor work is seen as very undesirable. The female apprentice has to be prepared to enter an almost totally male world. It is a world in which women are allowed only two roles – sexual object (the nude calendar, the pin-up photograph) and domestic support (girlfriend, wife, mother). There is no room for a woman as co-worker, colleague or boss. The girl who makes this choice is likely to feel isolated. She will probably also be seen as a threat to her peers and supervisors who, not knowing how to respond to her, may resort to ridicule and belittlement. Because she is trying to do something which, by definition, is not women's work, it will be said that *clearly* she can't do the job as well as a man, can't be serious about doing it, can't be a 'proper woman' for wanting to do it, and so on. In the face of all these barriers, I find it surprising not that only 0.3 per cent of craft apprentices are women, but that there are so many.

It is, of course, now illegal to discriminate *overtly* against women in any field, and the Engineering Industry Training Board is very anxious to encourage more female apprentices (see chapter 3). What fate awaits those women who make this choice? In a small survey which I undertook in collaboration with the Women in Science and Technology Group at Imperial College, women engineering students were asked about various aspects of their experiences as women engineers.

We asked the women in our sample what kind of encouragement and discouragement they had received in applying to do an engineering degree course, and from whom. Roughly one-fifth of the respondents had received only positive encouragement; the remainder had been discouraged. The most common argument put forward to dissuade them from engineering was the difficulty of combining a career with a family (a problem which, in practice, faces every mother in paid employment). Other reasons were the reluctance of shop-floor workers to work with women engineers; the inappropriateness of engineering as a job for a woman; that engineering is a dirty (read unfeminine) job, and that men don't like to see women in traditionally male jobs. The discouragement had come from, in order: both male and female friends (peer-group pressure), male teachers and fathers.

We also asked these women whether they had faced any particular difficulties once on the course. A lack of assumed background knowledge was the problem experienced most frequently. Also fairly common were feelings of isolation and the belief that they weren't respected by their fellow students. To a lesser extent they felt that they had to perform better than their

Table 2.2 Distribution of female engineering students: Imperial College 1983–84

Department	Percentage female
Aeronautics	5
Chemical engineering	15
Civil engineering	14
Electrical engineering	9
Mechanical engineering	7
Mineral resources engineering	2

Source: Imperial College, 1984.

male colleagues if they were to be taken seriously by the male staff, and that they were treated overpolitely. Overall our sample gave us little doubt that the women felt themselves to be less than equal to their male colleagues.

Being a student engineer, however, is arguably less difficult than what follows. At Imperial College a significant proportion of engineering undergraduates are sponsored: that is, they are taken on by companies as student apprentices, spend a year with the company before coming to college and return to it each long vacation. About half of the women in our sample were sponsored and a further one-third had attempted to get sponsorship. Their comments are interesting:

> The companies wanted to be thoroughly convinced that I wanted to be an engineer. One company was surprised that I appeared to know something about what I was letting myself in for. Another company tested me by suggesting that I wouldn't like certain aspects of the training: getting dirty, not being liked, etc.

> With one company the interviewer was blatantly rude to me on the grounds that it was ridiculous that a woman should want to be an engineer. At the second company I encountered a patronizing/derisory interviewer who again put me off. Hence I did not apply for further interviews at other organizations.

> They wanted to know why I wanted to do it: very difficult to answer, in fact an unfair question because most boys couldn't have answered it, but they were never asked. Also they wanted to know if I had a motorbike, etc. However, most engineers are trying to reject the 'mechanic' image. *Totally unfair.* I don't know why I did engineering really so I suppose that I didn't give too good an impression, but then how many men do? They wanted to know if I wanted to get dirty – how many of them wear suits and have nails longer than mine?

> I was always asked about how I viewed women in engineering as it was relatively uncommon, but most seemed keen to show that they wanted more women. Probably being female helped slightly as some firms want a token woman.

My guess is that while most large companies are now sufficiently concerned about their public image to want to recruit a few women engineers, traditional prejudices intervene when it comes to their promotion. Working *for* a woman engineer is very different from working *with* a woman engineer. Once in industry, 'she who dares' is going to face problems of juggling career and family, of not being taken seriously, of being a threat to male colleagues and of being excluded from the camaraderie of male colleagues and the all-too-influential old boy network. In addition, most engineers enter management at some point in their careers. If women engineers make this transition then yet more problems await them.[36] British engineering is a man's world and it isn't very keen to go co-ed.

A fundamental exclusion?

There are a number of ways in which it is possible for women to relate to technology: they can be *generators* of technology, the engineers and scientists who conceive of new technical developments; they can be *constructors* of technology, the skilled and semi-skilled craft workers who actually build the machines, roads and rockets; they can be *assemblers* of technology, the unskilled workers who, for example, assist in the manufacture of technological components, and they can be *consumers* of technology, using cars, trains, hair dryers, fridges, telephones, and so on. For the most part, women are neither the generators nor the constructors of technology; some are assemblers, and all are consumers. The main focus of women's relationship to technology (as many chapters of this book illustrate) is therefore as its (largely) passive recipients.

In contrast, men's relationship to technology is generally more active, encompassing all of the possibilities outlined above. And, in my view, this imbalance in women's and men's relationship to technology underlies women's present alienation from it.

Most women do not understand technology and are a little afraid of it. While many women know how to drive a car, or use a sewing machine, microwave oven or stereo, fewer women than men will attempt to repair a car if it breaks down. Yet there really isn't anything very difficult involved in car repair or car maintenance. Many men manage to perform both of these activities without any special training, so why is it that they somehow acquire these and similar skills and women do not? There are, I believe, two reasons. First, because technology is a male activity it is socially appropriate and acceptable for them to acquire such skills and, second, they have the confidence to do so. Boys are no more born with spanners in their hands than girls are born with knitting needles: both have these sex-appropriate technologies thrust upon them at an early age. The tinkering with objects described earlier predisposes boys towards things technical, regardless of whether they will later become accountants, engineers, clerks or bus conductors. Most men are thus spared the crisis of confidence which any woman must overcome if she is to service her car herself. I realise, of course, that there are a large number of men who are unable to tell the difference between the boot and the engine, can't change a tyre and don't know what's happening when they change gear. Nevertheless, a great many more women believe they can't do or understand these things. And even when they try to, they are often held back: 'Here, let me do that', or 'I'll do it, it's quicker . . .'

This lack of technical understanding and associated lack of confidence is another aspect of women's subordination in our society. Women are subordinated because they have to depend on men as the generators and constructors of technology and, consequently, defer to male technical experts. They are subordinated by their lack of understanding of this important and powerful type of knowledge, mystified by its complexity and alienated by its masculine values and goals. Nevertheless, more women are entering technology, and this raises the question of whether (and how) they will affect both technology itself and women's relation to it.

These are not easy questions to answer. Partly the answers depend on the level at which women enter. More women working as constructors of technology, for example, could have a demonstration effect which might increase women's confidence in relating to technology. Partly too, answers will depend on the number of women entering. It is logical to assume that as more women enter technology so women in general will grow more technically confident, and the cross-gender conflict will be lessened, but the exact numbers needed to create this effect is less clear.

The more important question, however, is the potential impact of women on the goals and values of technology. It could be argued that the impact of greater female participation will be a reorientation of these goals and values in a more feminine direction. Women as generators of technology would bring to, say, product and process design, a different view of the world. Women may be less willing than their male peers to sex-stereotype the user of a product or to accept the socially oppressive technology, for instance by assuming that a process should be made economic by using women workers at lower rates of pay.

Put so simply, this is, however, too crude an analysis, for it ignores the broader web of economic, social and political relationships in which technology is embedded. Technologists do not choose the technologies they generate and construct. Such decisions are made elsewhere: in the Ministry of Defence, the Home Office, in company boardrooms, and so on. And these decisions are made in line with the interests of war, industry and commerce. Changing the values of technology away from competition, aggression and control will not happen simply as a result of changing the technologists (unless, by any lucky but improbable chance, they were unanimous in their opposition to these values). Technology is competitive, aggressive and controlling because it is generated in a social context which is itself characterized by these values. Changing these values must thus be a part of a broader struggle. A similar argument applies to the objectives of technology. While more women engineers might introduce a more humane dimension into engineering, simply increasing their numbers will not in itself reorient defence R&D or give rise to less dehumanizing work processes or to products with a greater social utility. (Thus, while I welcomed 1984 as Women Into Science and Engineering Year, I cannot be too optimistic about its longer-term effects.)

Changing the direction of technology is a long-term project involving a radical restructuring of the social order. Technology is both capitalist and male-dominated. And they are not just male interests which predominate in technology but particular male interests. Class *and* gender divisions are involved in the exclusion and alienation of women from technology. To win back for women a role in the generation and construction of technology thus involves a challenge to them both.

3. Women in British engineering

Nuala Swords-Isherwood

The number of women working in engineering is notoriously low. In Britain, however, official bodies are beginning to recognize that specific policies are required if this situation is to be redressed, and some attempts have been made to encourage women into this male preserve. As early as 1969, for example, the Institution of Civil Engineers established a working party on the role of women in engineering in response to 1969 being declared Women in Engineering Year by Shirley Williams, then Secretary of State for Education and Science. The effectiveness of these efforts may, perhaps, best be judged by the fact that the Equal Opportunities Commission and the British Engineering Council later found it necessary to designate 1984 as Women Into Science and Engineering (WISE) year.

To a large extent, it has been Britain's relative shortage of skilled engineering craft workers, technicians and graduate engineers which has prompted these developments, rather than a new concern on the part of government with women's job opportunities. Despite increasing levels of unemployment, many firms still say that they suffer from a severe shortage of time-served, skilled engineering workers, even if they do not all recognize a need for more highly qualified engineers and technologists. All this was noted by the Finniston Committee when it inquired into the requirements of the British engineering industry for skilled personnel in 1980. Among the recommendations of the Finniston Report, *Engineering Our Future*, was that efforts should be made to attract more women into engineering, since engineers were effectively recruited from only half the population.[1] This concern has since been taken up by the British Engineering Industry Training Board, itself increasingly conscious of the need to meet the spirit, not merely the letter, of the equal rights legislation passed in the mid 1970s.

Discussions of the position of women in engineering tend to focus on the higher echelons of graduate professional engineers, but women are also under-represented amongst technicians and skilled and semi-skilled craft workers. Although there has been progress in recent years, the rate of change has so far been slow, especially in the last two fields. Traditional prejudices abound and typically these are modified only when economic necessity or convenience dictates.

This chapter seeks to address these issues. It is divided into four sections. The first outlines where women work in the British engineering industry and discusses their participation in training courses and programmes. The second considers the impact of recent moves to encourage women into engineering. The third looks at the forces shaping attitudes to female entrants in the engineering industry. The final section considers what it is actually like for women to work in that industry.

The material presented here is limited to Britain, but the picture is similar in many industrialized countries with relatively well-established engineering industries. One special feature, however, bears mention: the relatively low status of engineering in Britain compared with most other countries. This reflects the historical development of engineering and the education system in Britain, where trade and industry never had social cachet.

During the periods of industrialization in other European countries, marriages between people from the older land-owning classes and the newer capitalist class tended to elevate the status of industrial production, lending it social respectability. This did not happen in Britain, where the aim of those with new industrial wealth was generally to forget as soon as possible how their money had been acquired and to emulate the lifestyle of the land-owning aristocracy.[2] Formal engineering education has been considered a very narrow pursuit in Britain; here the object of education has historically tended to be the production of 'gentlemen', with a rounded background in the classics and arts, and possibly also some pure science. As a result there was, and to a considerable extent still is, an emphasis on the *generalist* as the ideal industrial manager.[3] To this day, engineering is considered a second-best career choice for any highly educated young person, male or female. The professions, the media, education and research are more respectable options. Pupils studying science subjects are, therefore, more likely to be channelled into pure science subjects than into engineering.

Given that women are typically concentrated in low-status jobs, we might expect the proportion of women engineers to be higher in Britain than elsewhere. However, Britain has the lowest proportion of women professional engineers in the industrialized world: one in 300, compared with one in 40 in the USA, one in 33 in France, and one in 10 in Sweden. In the Soviet Union (and in China) some 30 per cent of all engineers are women, but there, as in Britain, the status of engineering compared with science is also relatively low.[4]

The reasons for this apparent contradiction are not clear, but it seems likely that the startlingly low representation of women in the British engineering industry is a product both of its historically low standing and of differences in sex-role socialization between countries. Bright, educated girls tend to be encouraged into occupations deemed feminine, and these in the West at least, generally involve the study of languages and the arts. At the same time, the ranks of industrial engineers in Britain are thick with middle-aged men who have worked their way up from apprenticeships. These men are likely to feel deeply threatened by any graduate entrant and especially by a woman, for their contact with women in any professional capacity is likely to be minimal. The small number of graduate entrants into industrial engineering in Britain both results from and adds to its low status, and this may compound the barriers to women's entry.

The present situation

The engineering industry employs a far lower proportion of women than are employed in the economy as a whole. In 1982, women held 43 per cent of all jobs in the industrial and services sector but just under 20 per cent of all jobs in the engineering industry.[5] Table 3.1 indicates the number of women employed in the British engineering industry from 1971 to 1982. In those years, women's employment in the industry fell slightly faster than total engineering employment.

Table 3.1 Women's employment and total employment in the British engineering industry, 1971–82

	Female employees (000s)	Total employees (000s)	Females as percentage of total
1971	753	3,322	22.7
1972	696	3,106	22.4
1973	709	3,127	22.7
1974	753	3,173	23.7
1975	704	3,072	22.9
1976	634	2,890	21.9
1977	643	2,933	21.9
1978	640	2,939	21.8
1979	633	2,915	21.7
1980	608	2,823	21.5
1981	502	2,463	20.4
1982	445	2,230	19.9

Source: EITB *Annual reports*
Notes: 1 Figures for 1982 may be subject to small revisions.
2 Employment figures have been rounded to nearest 1000. Percentages were calculated on unrounded figures.

In order to understand this, we need to look at the types of jobs women do in the engineering industry. Table 3.2 breaks down the employment of women in engineering by occupational category. It shows that over 90 per cent of women employed in the industry work either in office jobs or in semi-skilled jobs (such as assembly) and unskilled support jobs. The overall decline in engineering employment in Britain involves structural changes in the pattern of employment, with the greatest decline being in the clerical and operator categories – precisely those occupations with the highest concentrations of women.

Table 3.3 compares women's employment as a proportion of total employment in each occupational category for 1971–72, 1977

Table 3.2 Occupations of women employed in the British engineering industry, April 1982

Occupational category		Women	Percentage of all women	Women as a percentage of all employees
1	Managerial staff	4,100	0.9	3.2
2	Scientists and technologists	2,500	0.6	3.5
3	Technicians including draughtsmen	4,500	1.0	2.4
4a	Administrative and professional staff	19,000	4.4	13.7
4b	Clerks, office machine operators, secretaries and typists	175,600	39.7	72.3
5	Supervisors including foremen	8,000	1.8	7.1
6	Craftsmen	1,500	0.3	0.3
7	Operators	197,200	44.5	26.7
8	Other employees, excluding canteen staff and seafarers	30,300	6.9	17.3
Total		**442,800**	**100.0**	**19.9**

Source: EITB Annual Report 1982/83
Note: Women employment figures are rounded to the nearest 100; percentages have been calculated on unrounded figures. Any discrepancies are due to rounding errors.

and 1982. Here we can see that the number of women operators declined even as a proportion of the total number of employees in this category. In fact, women's representation increased in all the other occupations, the largest proportionate increases being in the clerical and other office jobs. In the skilled engineering jobs the improvement was greater among scientists and technologists (professional engineers) than amongst technicians (from 1.6 to 3.5 and 2.4 per cent respectively); the proportion of women craft workers crept up from 0.1 per cent to its derisory 1982 level of 0.3 per cent.

The employment of women in the engineering industry varies considerably from sector to sector, ranging from 9 per cent in industrial plant and steelwork to 36 per cent in electronics. In general, women are concentrated in instrument engineering, metal

Table 3.3 Women's employment as a percentage of total employment in engineering occupations, 1971–82

Occupational category	1971–72	1977 (Oct)	1982
Managerial	1.3	1.7	3.2
Scientists/technologists	1.6	2.1	3.5
Technicians/draughtspeople	1.6	2.0	2.4
Admin and professional	10.1	11.6	13.8
Clerical and office staff	63.8	68.0	72.8
Foremen/supervisors	5.8	6.6	7.1
Craftspeople	0.1	0.2	0.3
Operators	33.6	29.9	26.7
Other employees	17.3	16.3	17.3

Source: EITB

goods manufacture, and electrical and electronic equipment and engineering (including office and data-processing equipment).

In part, this concentration reflects the occupational structure of the sectors themselves. The sectors with the highest concentration of women tend to be those with a strong dependence on semi-skilled operators rather than more skilled craft workers, technicians or scientists and technologists.[6] There is a slightly larger female share of some highly skilled jobs in the more technologically advanced sectors, which are younger than the traditional parts of engineering and which suffer from shortages of highly qualified workers – both factors tending to promote women's job opportunities. In electronics, women comprise just under 4 per cent of the technicians and 2 per cent of the skilled craft workers. The highest representation is to be found in office and data-processing equipment, where the proportion of female scientists and technologists is considerably higher than in any other sector, at 7 per cent, and where the proportion of female craft workers is 3.5 per cent. Engineering companies in sectors making products which are primarily used by women tend to employ a greater than average proportion of women at higher levels. (Forty-two per cent of the administrative and professional staff in domestic appliance companies, for example, are women.)[7]

Are things changing?

Training, leading to recognition of skilled status, is a major determinant of occupation in the engineering industry. Women constitute only a tiny percentage of the total number of trainees in the industry for jobs as professional engineers (6.3 per cent in 1981), technicians (4 per cent) and craft workers (a mere 0.28 per cent).[8]

The proportion of women trainees in each of these categories has, in fact, been increasing for some time. Between 1967 and 1982 the proportion of first-year British students studying for engineering and technology degrees who were women increased from 1.5 per cent (141 women) to 9.4 per cent (1,095 women).[9] A similar improvement for women technical trainees is reflected in Table 3.4. There was also a slight increase in the number of women taking up craft apprenticeships, although the proportion of female craft apprentices was, in 1982, less than the proportion of women craft workers. (Management is the only other category for which this remains true.) In theory this trend should be reflected in greater numbers of women working as technologists, technicians and craft workers in future years.

Among the policies introduced by the Engineering Industrial Training Board to facilitate this process was a programme called 'Insight', which offers girls a week's course at a university to enable them to get to know more about engineering as a career. This has been backed up by scholarships for school leavers entering technician training and engineering degree courses. Launched in 1976, the Girl Technician Scholarship Scheme was intended to illustrate – to girls, their parents, teachers and careers advisers – the suitability of engineering as a career choice; to encourage schools to give girls the education necessary to prepare them for such careers; to show engineering firms that girls can be effective technicians, and to encourage them to recruit more. The trainees spent time in their first year in an engineering training centre and a local technical college, and in their second year in two or three different companies for specific training. At the end of the

Table 3.4 Employment of women technician trainees compared with total technician trainees in the British engineering industry, 1973/4–81/2

	Total technician trainees	Total women technician trainees	Women trainees as a percentage of all trainees	Women trainees as a percentage of all women technicians
1973/74	30,000	300	1.0	8.0
1974/75	28,000	300	1.2	8.4
1975/76	25,000	300	1.2	7.5
1976/77	26,000	300	1.3	8.4
1977/78	28,000	500	1.8	11.7
1978/79	30,000	700	2.2	13.8
1979/80	30,000	900	2.9	17.1
1980/81	28,000	1,000	3.6	21.1
1981/82	25,000	1,000	4.0	21.8

Source: EITB Annual Reports
Note: Figures for women trainees have been rounded to nearest 100.
   Figures for total trainees have been rounded to nearest 1000.
   Percentages were calculated on unrounded figures.

scheme they were helped to find suitable jobs. The EITB concluded that the scheme had 'enabled the Board to demonstrate beyond doubt the ability of girls to be trained as engineering technicians and to meet companies' recruitment standards for the job'.[10]

Although the girls often lacked both the traditional scientific and mathematical background and the spare-time activities which develop engineering aptitude, they did as well as the boys in their examinations. The pilot scheme was then replaced by another scheme which encouraged companies to recruit school leavers directly by making a cash grant to firms which offer training places to girls. The objective was the recruitment of 750 girls nationwide by 1982. This target was not reached, partly because of the effects of the recession and cuts in government expenditure, and partly because it proved difficult to get enough girls to come forward and fill even the limited number of places available.

Evidently the importance of a 'nice' job for girls and a 'good' job for boys remains an underlying theme of career choice. Teaching, nursing and other 'caring' roles are considered by parents, teachers and employers as more appropriate careers for women than engineering, and arts subjects as more appropriate for study.[11] With the intention of finding ways of encouraging women into traditionally male areas of work, the Manpower Services Commission produced a report in 1979 entitled *Special Programmes, Special Needs.* The report listed problems facing girls and women, including educational disadvantages, traditional expectations and assumptions on the part of parents, teachers and employers about their aspirations, aptitudes and potential lack of confidence, difficulties with self-expression and self-presentation and a failure to appreciate their need to plan for a long-term working future.[12]

Girls' views of themselves and of what they would like to do with their lives are clearly influenced by all manner of media images, opinions and prejudices. Hinds points out that although a majority of readers of women's magazines work outside the home, only 3 per cent of the magazine covers in 1976 depicted a woman as a paid worker of any kind – never mind an engineer. Sixty-four per cent of the covers illustrated domesticity in some form or other.[13]

Advertising has a very powerful effect, not only in persuading people to buy, but also in reinforcing stereotyped images. Even the advertising of children's toys has a powerful effect. Playing with construction toys such as Meccano is widely recognized as helping the development of both confidence and interest in technical pursuits. Indeed, members of the Institute of Mechanical Engineers recently warned Meccano Ltd. that their closure represented a future threat to British industry by reducing the number of children from whom future engineers would be drawn. Meccano advertised exclusively to boys (and their fathers), and the large majority of Meccano sets were bought for boys. The company was aware that they were aiming at only half of their potential market, but said 'it's not our job to change society'.[14]

Gender stereotyping is very effective. A small survey of school leavers in 1970 revealed that even girls' fantasy occupations were only slightly more glamorous versions of the jobs they actually hoped to do: most imagined becoming an air hostess, pop singer, model or top secretary, for example. By contrast, the boys in the survey produced a list of around 100 different jobs they would like to do, including spaceman, millionaire, vet, footballer, artist and politician. The most 'active' dream occupation of the girls was to enter the women's air force. The top favourites among the jobs they actually hoped to do were nursery nursing and kennel maiding. None of them wanted to work in a factory – in any role – and none were interested in apprenticeships, except for hairdressing. The boys, on the other hand, were nearly all keen to get apprenticeships.[15]

In this context it is hardly surprising that recent policy moves have had only minimal impact. Apart from the low status given to engineering in Britain, there are the additional problems which girls have to overcome if they are to break out of stereotypical career paths. The absence of positive images of women as engineers, plus pervasive social prejudice, are probably much more influential than outright discrimination, particularly at the age at which girls are required to make the important subject choices (see chapter 2). This, of course, is no reason for the engineering industry to be complacent; it has also played its part in creating this situation in the first place.

Engineering doublethink
If you ask why there are not more women doing skilled work in the engineering industry you are very likely to be told that women would not like the work because it is too dirty, too heavy, and so on. Such statements contain a great deal of doublethink. On the one hand they are unlikely to apply to graduate professional engineering (in which very few women are involved anyway), and on the other, they do not discourage engineering firms from employing women in unskilled and semi-skilled jobs which are more likely to be mucky and physically strenuous; they merely discourage them from training and promoting women into more interesting and better-paid work. Ironically these prejudices are most widespread amongst working-class women, those most likely to have heavy, dirty, unskilled and low-paid jobs in the engineering industry. This was revealed in a recent National Opinion Poll survey, in which one of the questions posed was: 'How would you

rate professional engineering as a career for a young person?' Answers were differentiated by sex. Throughout, the respondents rated professional engineering more highly as a man's career. Sixty per cent considered it to be a very good career for a man, and only 25 per cent considered it to be a very good career for a woman. These views were almost identical amongst both female and male respondents. Another 25 per cent of the respondents considered professional engineering to be a very poor career choice for women. Over half of this 25 per cent justified this view with such comments as 'engineering is a man's career' and 'women would not be suited', and over a quarter said that 'women would not be strong enough'.[16]

In practice, of course, professional engineering *is* a man's career, and women predominantly do the menial jobs – whether or not they are 'suited' for them. The only time at which this engineering doublethink has been shelved was during the last two world wars, when women were drafted into all levels of the engineering labour force. Media images suddenly and forcefully endorsed the entry of women into paid work, where previously this had tended to be ignored. For example, the cover of one 1943 edition of *Woman's Own* pictures four women manual workers, two of whom are clearly working in engineering.[17] Needless to say, such women were soon frozen out when the boys returned for 'their' jobs. Official interest in women and in challenging old prejudices is more a function of economic pressure than of a desire to widen women's choice of jobs. Even the relatively progressive stance of the Finniston Committee was prompted by what was seen as a crisis in the engineering industry. Thus, economic necessity also underlies current attempts to attract more women into skilled engineering work.

A recent study in the plastics processing industry indicated that the main reason firms have difficulty in recruiting apprentices and in holding skilled workers, even in the present economic climate, is the low level of wages paid at the end of a long period of training.[18] Skilled workers were constantly leaving to earn higher wages in unskilled work of many kinds, or they were emigrating to earn more money using their skills in other countries, notably Canada and Germany. (The car industry, long reputed to offer high wages, had just as much difficulty finding skilled toolmakers, for the same reason.) Most of the firms visited for the plastics study were not prepared to consider increasing wages significantly, but several of them suggested that a solution to the shortage would be to recruit women. Some managers expressed the opinion that women were more reliable, more skilful and more careful in their work than men. No doubt they expected that women would be more likely to accept the low wages too.

When pressed, even those firms with a positive attitude to recruiting women apprentices did not believe that young women were interested in the work. None had made any particular effort among school leavers to promote the idea of women doing skilled engineering work. The majority of firms argued that women craft workers would, in any case, only leave work to have families once they had been trained. Considering their problem in keeping trained men from becoming baggage handlers, milkmen and so on, the industry's taste for doublethink is clear.

Women would not have to give up paid work when having children if suitable child-care arrangements existed. In 1971 a survey of women with one or more children under school age indicated that over 40 per cent would have returned to work if childcare facilities had been available.[19] The demand clearly exists. There are now more married women in the workforce than ever before (3.8 per cent of the labour force in 1921 and 25.9 per cent in 1979). In 1978, 52 per cent of mothers (aged 16 to 59) and 27 per cent of mothers with children under five were in paid employment.[20]

The attitude of engineering firms to training women workers contrasts strongly with their attitude to unskilled women workers in assembly and packing. Several of the firms visited during the plastics study had attempted to make assembly jobs appeal to women. Shift systems that would fit in with school hours or the return of husbands from work (10 a.m. to 3 p.m. and 6 p.m. to 10 p.m.) had already been introduced. Some firms even said that they were investigating the feasibility of providing creches for young children. Many had made an effort to improve the physical environment, believing this to be more important to women workers than to men. The net result was that none of the firms visited suffered from a shortage of unskilled workers, but rather had a captive supply of potential packers, assembly workers and machine operators in the local housing estates and could get away with paying these women low wages.[21]

On the job

The grosser prejudices which state that women's place is in the home or, if allowed out, in the low-paid, low-status and low-skill occupations clearly abound in the British engineering industry. Few would today argue that women are incapable of doing skilled engineering work but, (as we saw in chapter 2), in practice women who attempt to do so are rarely taken seriously.

The working party set up in 1969 by the Institution of Civil Engineers on the role of women in engineering reported that 'whilst women have certainly established their competence throughout the professional engineering field, there is clearly a built-in or unconscious prejudice against them.' The same report also commented that 'women are welcome so long as they confine their activities to the more "theoretical" departments'. The relative concentration of female graduate engineers into specialties happens, according to the working party, 'not so much because women are particularly good at them but because they are less likely to lead to the women being put in authority over men'.[22]

These conclusions are confirmed in a survey conducted by the Women's Engineering Society. Seventy per cent of the respondents 'experienced prejudice or discrimination in one or more areas of working life'. Further, the highest proportion were working in research and development (R&D) – 32 per cent, compared with only 2 per cent of professional engineers overall. As suggested earlier, there are fewer management opportunities in R&D than in other professional engineering activities. Given that most professional engineers enter management at some point in their careers, the concentration of women in R&D specialties reduces their opportunities for following a normal professional engineering career. Those who do succeed in becoming managers are likely to face even greater problems.[23]

As was shown in chapter 1, the strong historical association between professional engineering and managerial functions related to the organization and supervision of work dates back to the nineteenth-century tradition of inventor-entrepreneurs. It is almost exclusively men who are associated with the management of paid work in capitalist societies. However, the supposed 'problem' of women being placed in positions of authority over men also mitigates against their promotion opportunities in other engineering occupations. Coote warns young women contemplating careers as craft engineers:

> There are few girls at this level of engineering and very few in factories. You may encounter prejudice from prospective employers and workmates. It will probably be more difficult for you to get promotion to the post of chargehand or supervisor than for a man with the same qualifications.[24]

The fear of women supervising men applies, of course, in industries other than engineering, but is perhaps likely to be most critical where the imbalance of the sexes is most pronounced. (And perhaps, too, where the skills involved have traditionally been most jealously guarded by men.) This unusually frank excerpt from *Engineering Today* illustrates the problem:

> Engineering is male dominated, and has a reputation for being conservative. Its views are not necessarily based on the belief that women are biologically unsuitable for engineering. It merely shares the traditional prejudices of British Industry as a whole that women don't make good managers, engineers, or whatever. Why? Well because there aren't any to prove this wrong![25]

Engineering is not an atypical industrial environment; it merely provides an extreme case. Of course, recent equal opportunities legislation has removed legal barriers to women's entry into engineering, but these are of little consequence when compared with the unofficial barriers of prejudice. In practice these appear to operate even more strongly in engineering than in science, perhaps because of the managerial and craft-skilled aspects of the work involved.

The low prestige of engineering and especially production engineering in Britain compared with other countries explains in part the unwillingness of both women and men to enter the engineering industry. But women are also handicapped by lack of information, lack of appropriate qualifications and the yawning gulf between the image of engineering and that of a stereotypical feminine job. All this means that any girl who is interested in engineering and who maintains this interest to the extent of seeking and getting skilled work in the industry has to be fairly remarkable. She can expect little support from school or home. On the job itself her progress, in terms of pay and status, is likely to be consistently curtailed.

These barriers must be confronted if the scattered initiatives so far undertaken are to succeed on more than an individual level. In the United States, affirmative action campaigns have had some success. US colleges and the American Society of Women Engineers have sent out publications to high-school girls, attempting to dispel myths and prejudices about engineering. Affirmative action programmes, backed by US Federal law, ensure that a quota of women is employed in each company. Many companies have themselves responded by campaigning amongst girls and boys in high schools. (The education system in the US, as in many other countries, involves less specialization by subjects during the school career than in the UK, making changes in career direction easier.) Positive action can cover anything from policies to enable working mothers to work hours which suit them to special training schemes to help women obtain jobs for which they lack formal qualifications.[26]

In Britain, the idea of positive action has won remarkably little support, yet the need for concerted policies and campaigns is self-evident. The impact of Women Into Science and Engineering Year is yet to be assessed. It is to be hoped that it will both change attitudes – in the homes and schools, as well as in industry – and prompt the kind of major changes required in educational and employment policies. Only when this happens can we expect a recognition on the part of young women that they have a right not only to a job but also to a skilled job, with all the training and encouragement that implies.

4. Medical technology and the right to heal[1]

Wendy Faulkner

Nowadays healing is increasingly coming under medical control: when we feel unwell we generally consult a member of the medical profession, in a clinic or hospital. Until very recently all medical doctors were men, and even now men remain the vast majority. It is perhaps surprising, then, to discover that in the past women were traditionally the healers, tending their families and each other in sickness as in health. They formed, and in many places still form, a strong solidarity network – passing on their experience and knowledge of both complaints and remedies from one village to another and from one generation to another. Yet the major role played by these 'wise women' has been largely hidden from view, as has been the bitter contest over healing which resulted in the ascendancy of the medical profession.

This contest was marked by the emergence of what is now a very powerful body of technological knowledge concerning disease and illness, and it is this aspect of the story which provides the focus for this chapter. The growth of the medical profession took place against the backcloth of the transition from feudal to capitalist social relations and the development of industrialization, notably in Western Europe and later North America, where these changes first occurred. The story told here is therefore historically and geographically specific. But the battle over healing is spreading to other parts of the world; medical technology has become inter-national. What has happened over the last few centuries in the industrialized world has relevance for women everywhere.

The first medical doctors did not enter the healing scene with their technology already formed: they had to create it. Initially, the newly organized doctors used the influence of other male insti-tutions to muscle in on healing. As their number expanded, the medical men developed a whole series of new techniques for the analysis and treatment of disease, and these became the hallmark of their practice. They also called on the prestige of modern science to legitimate their new role and this, ultimately, placed the doctors in a singularly powerful position over both those they healed and other healers. Healing itself was progressively institutionalized, with the result that when women were eventually reabsorbed into the new, formal system of health care, they came under the managerial control of the medical profession. With the demise of the wise women and their skills, women also lost any autonomous control over our health. Today the battle over healing takes a somewhat different form: medical technology, and the control of it, is part of the equation.

Deskilling the wise women

'Women did not learn to look to an external "science" for guidance until their old skills had been ripped away, and the "wise women" who preserved them had been silenced, or killed.'[2] The conflict referred to here took place in two historically distinct periods each of which carry the hallmarks of the two institutions from which the medical doctors derived their authority – the church and then modern science.

The first medical doctors, called physicians, were trained in the universities which were sanctioned by the Catholic church and excluded women. For the most part the early physicians confined themselves to academic study, but during the thirteenth century they began to put their studies into practice – starting with the treatment of the monarchs and nobility of the European courts. This was an unlikely development because according to contemporary Church dogma, sickness and disease resulted from divine intervention, as penance for sinning. Suffering, it was said, would be rewarded in the next world: any relief brought about in this world thus countered God's will. Yet the Church was prepared to waive dogma and sanction healing – at least for the benefit of the wealthier classes – so long as the practitioners were firmly under its control. (Physicians wishing to treat a patient were obliged to do so in the presence of a priest: he was supposed to safeguard the soul while the doctor attended the body.) Licensing laws were duly established by the fourteenth century to bar all but the university-trained doctors from practice.

Initially attention was focused on barring the better-off and more literate women healers who competed with the physicians for the same urban clientele. In one celebrated case in 1322, one Jacoba Felicie was brought to trial by the University of Paris Faculty of Medicine for 'illegal practice': six people testified that she had succeeded where university-trained physicians had failed, and this ensured her conviction! By the end of the fourteenth century most of the urban women healers had been squeezed out, by similar means.[3] There remained, however, the great mass of peasant women healers, and it was in the silencing of these women that the church stepped in, with full misogynist force.

From the fourteenth to the seventeenth centuries a 'craze' of witchcraft appeared to seize Europe, sweeping from Germany through Italy and, eventually, the British Isles. Suspects brought to trial and found guilty of being witches were usually sentenced to live burning at the stake. The total number of deaths was colossal: estimates put the figure in the millions, and of these some 85 per cent were women, of all ages. With the benefit of historical hindsight, we can see that these events were not so much a craze as a well-orchestrated campaign of terror – organized by the church, and with some assistance from both the state and the emergent medical profession. The *Malleus Maleficarum* or *Hammer of Witches*, written in 1484 by the German monks Kramer and Sprenger, became the legal touchstone of all witch-hunters, Protestant and Catholic alike.

Barbara Ehrenreich and Deirdre English, in their study of this work and contemporary official records, detect three accusations which recurred throughout the witch trials: the committing of sexual crimes against men; being organized, and having 'magical powers' affecting health. Central to these accusations was an ideology which held that women were essentially evil and thus responsible for the sins of men. Female witches, said to have copulated with the devil, were accused of infecting men with 'inordinate passion' or even of making their penises drop off! Witches who worked together were deemed members of the 'Devil's Party' and considered especially fearful. The charge of being organized reflects the intense social upheaval in Europe, during the four centuries spanned by the witch trials, with mass peasant uprisings challenging the established feudal order and

marking both the beginnings of capitalism and the rise of Protestantism. There is evidence that accused women did meet – in
small local groups which came together in crowds of hundreds and
thousands on festival days. It is possible that these women were
celebrating pagan forms of religion, and that they used such
gatherings as an occasion for exchanging information and ideas
about healing. But they were almost certainly also connected with,
if not central to, the peasant rebellions which so threatened church
and state alike.[4]

The church believed that the devil's powers on earth were
expressed through the practice of magic, and it was this belief
which provided them with grounds for the persecution of peasant
healers. It didn't matter whether the treatment provided was
beneficial: this, indeed, was seen as particularly threatening, for it
made people less dependent on God and church. Any cure
resulting from the ministrations of a wise woman was thus deemed
to be the work of the devil. By contrast, medical practitioners were
considered instruments of God: any cures they produced were the
work of the Lord. The partnership between church and medical
profession was therefore never stronger than during the witch
trials. The *Malleus Maleficarum* ruled: 'If a woman dare to cure
without having studied she is a witch and must die.' It was also
decreed that doctors should be brought in to adjudicate as to
whether a person's state of health (good or bad) was the result of
natural causes or of sorcery. Ehrenreich and English comment:

> The trial in a stroke established the male physician on a
> moral and intellectual plane vastly above the woman healer he
> was called on to judge. It placed him on the side of God and
> Law, a professional on a par with lawyers and theologians,
> while it placed her on the side of darkness, evil and magic.[5]

This was to be one of the more insidious effects of the witch
'craze' but there is an irony here, too. One of the objections of the
church (or at least the Catholic church) to the wise women was that
their methods were inquiring and empirical. Yet it was precisely
this approach that the medical men, whose status the church had
so elevated, were to pursue in later years. Fortunately for the
doctors, the ending of their early partnership was not a painful
affair, for the scientific revolution of the seventeenth century

heralded something of a decline in the former authority of the church over many aspects of social life (see chapter one).

During the seventeenth century, also, the mercantile classes of Europe's towns and cities were growing rapidly. Old trades expanded and new ones emerged. Amongst these trades was that of the apothecaries, who blended and sold spices introduced from far-flung regions initially by the Crusaders and later by merchant seafarers. As the range of possible ingredients grew so the skills required to manufacture drugs became more specialized. Thus, in 1617 the London apothecaries split away from the grocers' guild to found the Society of Apothecaries.[6] The apothecaries are important, because during the subsequent two centuries many of them began to practise medicine. (This, incidentally, left a vacuum which was eventually filled by retailing chemists and the modern pharmaceutical industry.) Another of the mercantile guilds which eventually joined the ranks of the medical profession was that of the barber surgeons. From the outset, these new practitioners had a more capitalist approach to health than either the gentleman physicians or their female counterparts. Healing was their trade, entered through apprenticeship rather than academic study; it was a commodity, a service to be sold for cash rather than exchanged for other services. Although the physicians often disdained the apothecaries and barber surgeons, considering both the concoction of drugs and the practice of surgery to be unworthy of their professional status, the commercialization of health spurred by these two groups allowed the physicians to break loose from the potentially restrictive protection of the church. It also brought more *men* into their ranks at a time when the market for healing was growing fast.

It is not clear whether the original apothecary and barber surgeon guilds were open to women and men alike. If they were, they soon (like so many others) became exclusively male preserves. As industrialization proceeded, people were drawn into the urban centres in search of jobs, and the established social networks which had previously linked women healers with those they healed broke down. Many women continued to heal, in the privacy of their homes and communities, but those who sought to earn a living by their healing skills lacked either the protection of the guild system or the social standing of a university training.

Slowly but surely the medical men diversified, their interests giving rise to a number of specialist fields. One of these was obstetrics, whose 'market' – the entire childbearing population – was potentially limitless. During the witch hunts, the practice of midwifery had been singled out for attack. According to the authors of the *Malleus Maleficarum*, 'the greatest injuries to the faith as regards the heresy of witches are done by the midwives'.[7] Yet it was three centuries before the emergent medical profession fully succeeded in muscling into this female stronghold.

By the end of the seventeenth century, doctors from all three branches of medicine were beginning to attend their richer female customers during childbirth. In general they were confined to sitting on the sidelines while the midwives got on with the job in hand; their role, as they saw it, being to intervene if complications arose. Herein lay a problem, for these man-midwives needed to prove – both to their 'patients' and to the more conservative élite of the medical profession – that they were capable of doing something when called on to intervene! They needed to gain experience of childbirth; to observe and record the processes involved, and to develop techniques for intervening. Needless to say, their upper-class female 'customers' were often reluctant to have their bodies used as 'experimental material'. What the man-midwives really needed was the clientele of the wise women. As the nineteenth-century doctor Charles E. Zeigler noted in the *Journal of the American Medical Association*:

> It is at present impossible to secure cases sufficient for the proper training in obstetrics, since 75 per cent of the material [sic] otherwise available for clinical purposes is utilised in providing a livelihood for midwives.[8]

In the end, it was with the bodies and babies of the very poor women who populated the urban centres that the medical men gained their experience of childbirth and trained new generations of obstetricians in their techniques. This was achieved from the mid-eighteenth century onwards in Europe, and later in North America, by the establishment of lying-in hospitals. Lying in probably provided considerable relief for the pregnant women who entered these institutions – it meant, at least, two months food and shelter. In some cases the women were even paid a fee. But the 'co-operation' which was required in return meant their complete submission to the control of the doctors.[9]

By moving childbirth into the hospitals, the man-midwives were able to extend the interventionist role they had established with their richer clients through the development of a series of devices designed both to observe and influence the course of events. The most notorious of these were undoubtedly the obstetric forceps, made public as early as 1733 and popularized by the Scottish apothecary William Smellie. It is commonly assumed that it was the introduction of the forceps which, more than any other factor, gave the man-midwives the edge over their female counterparts. This may be overstating the case, although women were effectively barred from using any instrument deemed surgical. What is clear is that this particular innovation was often used without proper cause. Smellie himself argued that the use of the forceps, a valuable aid during obstructed deliveries, should be necessary only in 10 out of every 10,000 births. Writing only a few years later, one of the more successful obstetric doctors claimed that 'there is little occasion for the present *frequent use of instruments*'.[10] Many midwives, recognizing the threat posed to their livelihood by the male obstetricians, took up the complaint. In 1760, London midwife Mrs Elizabeth Nihill, for example, expressed her 'insuppressible indignation at the errors and pernicious innovations introduced into [midwifery] and every day gaining ground'. She continued her case by describing what she called 'that multitude of disciples of Dr Smellie':

> See the whole pack open in full cry: to arms, to arms is the word: and what are those arms by which they maintain themselves, but those instruments, those weapons of death.[11]

There were, of course, other objections to the male obstetricians: that they had commercialized childbirth, and that the very presence of men was unnatural, if not immoral. But it is significant that the public controversy precipitated by the entry of men into midwifery pivoted around the use of instruments such as obstetric forceps: the doctors' practice of midwifery was becoming distinguishable by its very technical aspect. In this context, the dangerous misuse of forceps may be seen as a product of the fact that most midwives were infinitely more experienced than the attendant doctors and that the doctors lacked any other skills or techniques which might have improved the outcome of childbirth for mother and child. As the number of lying-in hospitals grew, so doctors increasingly emphasized the potentially dangerous aspects of childbirth and, thus, the 'importance' of medical intervention.

The man-midwives duly gained the professional recognition they had sought. In the process they also achieved a reversal in their relationship with the midwife: increasingly it was she who sat on the sidelines while the obstetrician 'managed' the deliveries. Like the pregnant women themselves, those women who continued to practise midwifery were increasingly obliged to accept the doctors' authority. Many organized to protect their skills by seeking legal recognition for their training, but again the threat to the specifically male and technological practice of midwifery was recognized. As one late nineteenth century American doctor commented, training and licensing of midwives would 'decrease the number of cases in which the stethoscope, pelvimeter, and other newly developed techniques could be used to increase obstetrical knowledge'.[12] In fact the 'meddlesome' midwives never became a registered profession in the United States, although their counterparts in Europe were more successful. However, the eventual form of the required legislation was often something of a mixed blessing. By 1902, when the first Midwives Act was passed in Britain, for example, the medical men were strong enough to ensure a controlling position for their profession on the bodies responsible for training and registering midwives.[13]

The story of the doctors' victory over the midwives is particularly poignant because it represents an intrusion into what is a singularly female event. Indeed the virtual taboo which traditionally surrounded *any* male presence at childbirth probably explains why it is such a visible episode of medical history. The battle over healing is less well documented. However it shares important similarities with that over midwifery. Here, the doctors' victory has been even more complete: in most modern health-care systems the midwife is the *only* remaining vestige of the wise women's practice.

The predicament of the man-midwives was also faced by the medical profession as a whole: if they were to increase their 'trade' as healers, they had to increase their knowledge of human disorders. The information they were able to gain from their early clients was extremely limited, for these patients were usually their social superiors who could exercise considerable control over their relationship with the doctors. Like the man-midwives, the general practitioners needed the large hospitals spawned by rapid industrialization to provide them with patients of a lower social class – patients 'compliant' enough to allow them to dictate the course of events. New diagnostic techniques proliferated in the hospital setting. The stethoscope and thermometer, for example, enabled the doctors to monitor ailments without even talking to their patients. These in turn encouraged the development of specialized techniques for treatment. Surgery, which previously had a very low status, became increasingly popular after the introduction of chloroform and ether as anaesthetics in the 1840s. In addition, a whole number of 'patent' medicines found their way into the black bags of the medical men. Increasingly they had something to 'sell'.[14]

The development of new medical techniques did not in itself win the doctor the exclusive right to heal. If they were to succeed in the battle to establish *their* practice as *the* practice, they had to prove first that their methods were the best available and, second, that they alone were capable of using them. In the United States this involved a particularly bitter contest marked, during the first few decades of the nineteenth century, by the rise of a popular health movement.[15] This movement included a multitude of medical 'sects', all of which – unlike the medical men – recognized the value of women's traditional healing skills and had many female healers in their ranks. In 1848, the self-styled 'regular' doctors founded (somewhat pretentiously) *the* American Medical Association with the express aim of persuading the state legislative bodies to deny licences to the assorted 'irregular' lay healers. The mere existence of a professional body was not enough, however. What eventually provided the medical men with the justification they needed was their claim to being more scientific than their competition.

By the end of the century, 'making something scientific had become synonymous with reform'.[16] Pasteur's germ theory of disease gave the doctors a rationale for taking medicine into the laboratories. Legislation progressively upgraded the standards required for registration, with the result that it was increasingly those medical schools with enough money to provide a lengthy tuition in laboratory science which survived and those students with the financial means to sustain such stringent training who entered them. In the United States, where there had been no tradition of university education for doctors, the shift happened a little later and was somewhat more dramatic than in Europe. But in both places the effect was the same: the medical men gained a moral and legal monopoly over healing. In the process, the profession regained the gentlemanly image and status of the earlier physicians, without the restraining influence of the church.

It was, then, the conscious move by the medical men to make their profession 'scientific' which put the final nail in the coffin of the wise women. Although in later years the wise women may have shared the doctors' financial interest in healing, they generally lacked the doctors' means of securing the right to heal. They lacked the allies in the legislative and educational bodies of the day, and the technology – in the double sense of technical gadgetry and scientific authority – which made it possible for men to claim the 'health market' as their own. The medical men had deskilled women not so much by appropriating their skills as by appropriating their role as healers. Their claim to scientific authority rendered the particular knowledge and skills of the wise women 'redundant'. By the same stroke it also excluded women from the new skills and knowledge created by the doctors, and so marginalized women's influence over the emergent *medical* systems of health care. We will return to this theme later, but first we must consider exactly what it was about medical science which ultimately enabled the doctors to claim authority over healing.

Healing and the authority of medical sciences

Most standard histories assume that the demise of the wise women and their replacement by the medical men was a good thing: crudely put, that 'science triumphed over superstition' and that everyone was better off for it. But, as Ehrenreich and English have so exhaustively documented, 'the real story was not so simple, and the outcome not so clearly "progressive".'[17] Many of the skills women lost in the course of the battle were those which today constitute medical technology. A large number of those burnt on the witch hunters' stake, for example, were charged with performing obstetric surgery such as abortions and caesarians. Herbal and other 'natural' remedies were widely used by the wise women. The *Liber Simplicis Medicinae*, compiled by Hildegarde of Bingen in the twelfth century, listed the healing properties of over 200 plants and 55 trees, as well as numerous mineral and animal derivatives. Many of these remedies have substantial pharmaceutical powers – ergot to ease labour pain, belladonna to inhibit contractions of the womb, digitalis for heart problems, to name but a few now incorporated into modern drugs.[18] Contemporary medical men had none of these techniques. In practice they were often far more 'superstitious' than the women healers they sought to displace.

The early physicians understood little about human anatomy and physiology. The church forbade any form of experimentation, and students rarely saw a patient. Their education was largely confined to philosophy and theology. Even when the doctors began to derive their authority from science rather than the church, the training they received continued in this mould and had little technical content. For centuries medical science consisted primarily in classifying diseases according to the symptoms presented by patients. It was widely believed that disease resulted from 'disturbances' in the balance of the body's organs. Treatment involved 'major systemic changes': blistering and bleeding (by incision and the application of leeches) were common practice, as was the use of an increasing number of preparations intended to 'purge' the system.[19]

Needless to say, the effects of the doctors' remedies often proved more dangerous than those of the original ailment. (Poisonous preparations such as arsenic tonics and calomel, for example, were popular all-purpose remedies.) Yet by the late eighteenth century many doctors appear to have persuaded their patients that this form of therapy was desirable:

> The point was to produce the strongest possible effect on the patient, of any kind, as if the physicians were competing with the disease to see which – the disease or the physician – could produce the most outrageous symptoms.[20]

Dubbed 'heroic' medicine – nominally in reference to the efforts required of the doctors! – this practice reflected the wider dilemma of the medical men. If payment was to be extracted from the potential patient, healing had to be made tangible and quantifiable: the greater the effect produced, the greater the fee. The most extreme results of this logic were probably to be found in the United States where, in any case, the conflict between competing groups of healers was most intense. Here the patent medicines and 'book larnin' of the regular doctors were widely distrusted. But the ferocity of the doctors' methods – throughout Europe and North America – also highlights the void, both empirical and theoretical, which existed in medical science right up until the turn of the twentieth century.

We need to be careful here about what we mean by medical science. It may be argued that the practice of the wise women was, like all such pre-industrial activity, a craft and not a scientific practice, meaning that the knowledge so developed was not codified and had no significant theoretical foundation. Unfortunately we do not know exactly how much theory the wise women did develop: little was passed on in written form. What we do know is that their remedies were tried and tested over centuries and that the medical men singularly failed to utilize any of their considerable experience or skills. To give just one example: for many years doctors believed water, air and light to be injurious, and so they closeted the feverish patients, unwashed, in darkened and ill-ventilated rooms. Yet women healers had long understood the value of fresh air, sunlight and frequent washes. The point is that the doctors did not win the battle over healing on the basis of the *cognitive* powers of medical science; their diagnostic and therapeutic abilities were frequently outclassed. Rather it was the *institutional* powers of medical science which, after the simple coercion of the witch hunts, won them their eventual authority.

There were, as we saw in the previous section, two critical events in the institutionalization of scientific medicine: first, the establishment of hospital-based health care, and second the rise of laboratory-based training as a requirement for medical registration. Each of these moves, of course, contributed to the more recent advances in medical practice. The general move into hospitals did enable doctors to increase their knowledge of human anatomy and physiology, and the systematic examination of micro-organisms in laboratories has greatly illuminated the cellular basis of disease. But the most immediate effect of these changes was the exclusion of women and other lay healers from any role in the further development of medical science. In the short term at least, the benefits of the doctors' experimentation – in the hospitals and in the labs – were minimal.

Going into hospital was often a hazardous business in the eighteenth and nineteenth centuries. The institutionalization of childbirth, for example, was rationalized in terms of the need to reduce the startlingly high infant and maternal mortality rates, which the man-midwives were quick to blame on their female counterparts. Given the generally poor state of public health in the industrial centres, however, little could be done to improve the chances of survival for either mother or child. In the event, mortality rates owing to puerperal fever and the like reached epidemic proportions in the lying-in hospitals – because the obstetricians did not adopt the precautions against contagion which many midwives practised.[21] Generally, the development of new diagnostic techniques was not reflected in any parallel improvement in the doctors' therapeutic abilities. By the second half of the nineteenth century, pain relievers such as opium, quinine, cocaine and alcohol were the major drugs used. The only cure the medical men could offer the diseased patient was surgery and without the antiseptics developed later on, this was frequently fatal. In practice the doctors' technical remedies were often just as 'heroic' as the older 'preparations'. Although their germ theory of disease was a substantial improvement on earlier ideas, it was not until well into the twentieth century that the doctors could *apply* the knowledge produced in medical laboratories.

From the outset, medical practice was marked by an overriding emphasis on instrumental intervention. In this respect, the doctors assumed much of the character of modern science even before they adopted its methods. Just as the 'new scientists' saw the natural world as a series of mechanisms to be understood and exploited by technical means, so the scientist doctors viewed the human body as a series of organs, cells and (ultimately) chemicals which, like parts in a machine, could be kept in working order by the use of appropriate techniques. Within this mechanistic framework, which still characterizes medical practice, the biological causes of ill health are stressed whilst the social or environmental causes tend to be discounted. Medical science is thus seen as providing the 'only viable means of mediating between people and disease', and this justifies the use of more and more sophisticated techniques in the name of treatment – which is commonly held to be the best and only way to ensure a healthy population.[22]

This 'scientific' approach to healing represented a radical departure. From what we do know about the wise women, their approach appears to have been based on a much more holistic and positive view of human health, taking account of the well-being of an individual as a whole, and in context. We may assume that the wise woman listened patiently to her clients and interpreted what they had to say about their complaints, and her remedies, on the basis of her own personal knowledge of them: they were, after all, usually friends, neighbours or family, on whose trust she depended. This dependence was undermined not only by the economic changes which resulted in commercialization of health, but also by the scientific imperative to see patients as a series of 'cases', differing only in chemical composition. The assumption that biology alone determines health implies that only the scientist doctor can be objective about the existence of disease. In contrast, the patient's own perception of her or his state of health is devalued: it is subjective, lacking in authority. Although in practice it is not possible for doctors to remain wholly detached from the human suffering which constitutes their 'material', this stance underpins their peculiar power over the patient. It is also, in our society, a specifically masculine stance.

Arguably, the advances we have seen in medical technology during the twentieth century provide considerable justification for the scientific view of health. Now that the functions and disorders of the human body have been subjected to the rigours of systematic experimentation and theory building, there has been a prodigious leap in the healing abilities of doctors. Doubtless this explains in part why we today entrust our bodies to the medical profession. But modern medical practice has also created an enormous inequality between healer and healed, and in this way the rise of scientific medicine has transformed the healing process. The institutionalization of health care resulted in hierarchies both between doctors and patients and between doctors and other health-care workers. Women were not excluded from healing as such, but were effectively denied access to those aspects of the new approach to healing which were to become so central and so powerful – notably the development of scientific and technological knowledge, and of the techniques which emanate from it. To this day women constitute the majority of health workers, paid and unpaid. For the most part, those who work in the 'formal' system of health care do so on terms laid down by the medical profession.

Medical management of women health workers

The women most likely to have succeeded in entering, and so influencing, the masculine bastions of medical science were of course those with access to both money and social status. In western countries, however, upper-class women were generally the first to lose touch with the knowledge and skills of the wise women. They were also excluded from the economic sphere long before other, poorer women. Nevertheless, these leisured ladies were often adamantly opposed to the treatment of women by men, for any complaint. As the prestige of the medical profession grew, so they began to prefer the idea of being treated by a *woman doctor* rather than either male doctors or their more lowly healing sisters. Instead of creating their own forms of health care, they concentrated on gaining entrance to the medical boys' clubs – the schools, hospitals and professional bodies.[23] In so doing they implicitly put their faith in the progressiveness of science for, in order to prove their intellectual equality with men, they had to challenge its assumed masculinity.

This was anathema to the medical men. Female practitioners, pronounced Dr Robert Christison of Edinburgh University, when Sophia Jex Blake first applied to study there in 1869, 'would be injurious to medicine *as a scientific profession*'.[24] Women's role as healers was decidedly not scientific, as was made clear in this parliamentary speech made in 1875 against the granting of medical degrees to women:

> God sent women to be ministering angels, to smooth the pillow, minister the palliative, whisper words of comfort to the tossing patient ill with fever. Let that continue to be women's work! Leave the physician's function, the scientific lore, the iron wrist and iron will to men![25]

In appropriating the healing role, the doctors had in fact split it into two functions: *curing*, which they deemed scientific and thus man's work, and *caring*, which they variously glorified and demeaned, but 'conceded' to women. The result was the most profound sexual division of labour – that between doctor and nurse.

Despite the assumed femininity of nursing, its establishment as a profession represented a clean break with the autonomous tradition of the wise women. The first nurses were generally lower-class women employed in the wealthier homes and in the hospitals. Their healing activities were restricted to a mixture of simple caring tasks and heavy housework. It is not difficult to see why the medical men increasingly welcomed reformers like Florence Nightingale and Dorothea Dix. From the start the professional nurses saw their role as essentially supportive, rather than competitive, in relation to that of the doctors. Initially they set to cleaning up the hospitals – a much-needed reform. Later, as the number of hospitals and medical students grew, the professional nurses were allowed to take over the doctors' more mundane responsibilities – from administering treatment to overseeing the day-to-day running of the hospitals – thereby freeing doctors for the 'more important business' of medical science. Still the quintessential role of nursing did not change. The nurse remained subservient to the doctor's commands, often a kind of office wife in the wards and clinics and a buffer between her boss, the doctor, and his clients, the patients. What did change was the image of nursing for, with the establishment of the nursing schools, the older servant role was glossed with a specifically upper-class version of femininity. The new image persisted, even as more middle- and working-class women were allowed to enter the profession, and the numbers of new nursing students rapidly outstripped the number of women going into medicine.[26]

The association of doctors with the curative aspects of healing served to strengthen their claim to managerial control over the emergent health-care system. When the National Health Service was set up in Great Britain, for example, the British Medical Association was able to ensure that the hospitals – and in particular the teaching hospitals – received the largest slice of public expenditure on health. This is significant because it reinforced the tendency to see progress in terms of 'bigger and better' techniques – whether for purpose of analysis, diagnosis or treatment. Although health service administrators generally have the final say over whether a new technique is purchased, the important decisions about priorities and choice rest with the senior doctors. The commitment to high-technology medicine is now underpinned by the interests of the medical suppliers – especially the manufacturers of precision equipment and the drug companies – who have largely taken over the doctors' earlier role of inventor. They benefit immensely from the influence of the medical profession. Witness the enormous sum of money (currently nearly £1,000 per doctor in Britain per year) spent by the pharmaceutical industry on promoting drugs for prescription.[27]

It is interesting that the doctors with the most influence tend to be those with the greatest stake in continued and rapid technological innovation:

> Power and prestige in medicine are allocated to a very considerable extent on the basis of scientific and technological innovation, and on the extent to which particular specialists are able to exercise their instrumental skills.[28]

In this situation it is difficult for those women who do enter medicine to compete. Around one fifth of all doctors in Britain are women, and in the United States the figure is a startlingly low 7 per cent. In both countries, however, the proportion of medical students is considerably higher. Many women leave medical practice mid-career, nominally as a result of family commitments. As in other occupations, sexism operates covertly as well as overtly. The medical world is extremely competitive, and it is particularly difficult to re-enter after a period of absence. The personal sacrifice required to 'make it', especially in the highly specialized fields, is so great that many women are effectively excluded from (or opt out of) the prestigious areas. As a result, female practitioners are disproportionately concentrated in the lower rungs of the medical hierarchy, and in the lower-status specialties.[29] It is difficult to know which is the more important source of status – being technological or being male. In the west the two seem to be inextricably linked, but in the Soviet Union, where the majority of doctors are women, medicine in general attracts far less social status.[30]

Women health workers have never really had much room for manoeuvre within the doctors' medical system. Some changes have occurred: the Nightingale character-building type of instruction has been replaced by lengthy and highly technical training requirements; some women have become eminent doctors, and there are now a number of 'paramedical' professions, many of which are female dominated and involve work with specialist techniques. All of the women in these areas possess considerable knowledge and skills. Furthermore, women workers outnumber men in formalized health care – by three to one in the British National Health Service. (Doctors account for only 7 per cent of the total labour force, nurses and paramedicals 39 per cent; the remainder are semi- and unskilled ancillary workers.) None of these developments, however, has reduced the power enjoyed by the doctors. Nor have they effectively challenged the doctors' control over medical technology. In the words of Lesley Doyal, 'the highly visible "miracles" wrought by predominantly male doctors continue to rest on a pyramid of invisible and predominantly female labour'.[31]

At a very basic level, the fact that doctors alone are empowered to diagnose and prescribe means that nurses are largely confined to administering the techniques selected. Whilst they usually spend hours tending and encouraging the suffering patients back to health, and often know more about patients' needs precisely because they are more directly involved in bedside care, it is most commonly the doctor – the apparent source of the technology – who receives the credit for the eventual cure. And like the general nurses, midwives also follow very strict guidelines as to what they can and cannot do. A large part of the midwife's job is devoted to observation, and yet the minute anything untoward occurs she is obliged to call on the doctor. Most of the paramedical professions endure a similar relationship with the doctors. This is as true for the occupations concerned with diagnosis as it is for those concerned with therapy. In the pathology labs, for example, women tend to be concentrated in the technician posts where they run tests and report findings for the consultant pathologist (usually male) to interpret and act upon. In a parallel way, X-ray pictures are more frequently taken by a female radiographer for a male consultant radiologist.

The sexual division of labour which characterizes contemporary medically based health-care systems is inherently unequal, and this inequality is founded in no small measure on the fact that women and men health workers have different *kinds* of relationships to medical technology. Thus women health workers have little or no say over whether a particular technique is introduced, or indeed how it should be used, despite the fact that they are increasingly expected to operate or administer these sophisticated techniques. More fundamentally, women are also largely absent from the design of new medical techniques – whether in industry or in hospitals. What is dished out in the name of treatment or analysis depends, ultimately, on what is happening at the frontiers of medical science (where women are largely absent), and on what is considered profitable by way of innovation. Like all companies, those which supply the health services are extremely hierarchical and generally male dominated. Like many, they do not deal directly with the ultimate consumers of their products but instead have a proxy – the medical profession – which, in their case, appears to be an extremely intimate bed partner.

The medical profession remains something of a privileged brotherhood, protected by the very technical armoury it has spawned. From this position it has effectively ensured that the decision-making procedures through which the priorities and practice of modern health care are established bypass its 'producers' almost as much as its 'consumers'.

Our health in the balance
The battle over healing is no longer confined to Western Europe and North America. Where the commercialization of health remains unchecked, the course of industrialization and urbanization continues to erode women's traditional role. Added to this, western forms of health care are increasingly being adopted by, or imposed upon, the rest of the world. Nevertheless, in many Third World countries traditional models of health care co-exist with medical ones, and women's healing skills are still evident. (Predictably, midwifery remains a powerful female role.) In some cases, as in China with its 'barefoot doctor' system, this is the result of conscious policies. In many others, however, simple economics intervene: supporting a medical establishment can be

very expensive. Even in the wealthier countries where the medical profession originated the doctors' influence is not complete. In Britain, for example, it is estimated that for every four general practitioners there is at least one non-medical practitioner (herbalists, acupuncturists and the like),[32] and these figures probably exclude the nameless wise women who still practise in remote or ghettoized communities.

If anything, interest in 'alternative' medicine is going through something of a resurgence, particularly in the west. For many women this has opened up the exciting possibility of finding out about the skills of our foremothers and sisters around the world. These developments are interesting because modern medicine is commonly upheld as the most valuable product of contemporary science and technology. Few would elect totally to reject the powerful body of knowledge which now underpins medical practice, but for many there is a real ambivalence. Part of the problem is that the medical profession remains deeply reluctant to adopt other healing skills and insights, or to listen to what the patient has to say. In addition, our encounters with medical technology have sometimes been extremely hazardous – whatever its benefits or promise.

Women are more likely than men to be on the receiving end of medical technology for the simple reason that we constitute the majority of medical patients. The greater dependence of women on the expertise and technology of doctors may be explained partly by the medicalization of all matters relating to our ability to bear children. The hazards women face here, whether it be through the promotion of modern birth-control methods or through obstetric intervention, are by now well known (see chapters 5 and 6). But medical control over women is not confined to gynaecology and obstetrics. Historically, doctors have also defined us as more sick – or, more specifically, more 'neurotic' and 'psychotic' – than men. In so doing, they have called on the prevalent scientific views of women which themselves merely reinforce the wider pressures to devalue women and all things female. Thus today general practitioners tend to take the complaints of their male patients more seriously, dismissing those of their female patients as either psychosomatic symptoms or signs of mental illness. In Britain one in six women enters a psychiatric hospital compared with one in nine men. We are also twice as likely to be described tranquillisers and other psychotropic (brain-affecting) drugs. In short, the doctors' right to determine whether we are ill, and how we should be treated, has become a very potent source of patriarchal control over women.[33]

At the very least, the care we have received from the medical profession has not always been appropriate to our health needs. This is perhaps most starkly evident in the Third World where sex differences in morbidity (illness) and mortality rates are most pronounced. Here the high incidence of miscarriages and still births reflects the prevalence of *general* poor health amongst women, and yet formalized women's health care is geared almost exclusively to reproduction, and commonly only to birth control.[34] Such failings are not simply a question of resources; medical practice is also inappropriate in a more substantial sense. In a world racked by inequality, any form of health care which ignores the social and environmental causes of ill health, and which relies exclusively on biology by way of treatment, is bound to miss the mark. It will tend to benefit the least powerful least, and this is as true for the woman battling with poverty as it is for her wealthier sister confronted daily by a violent husband.

Health, defined in its broadest sense, involves the emotional and physical well-being which is the foundation of all human achievement and fulfilment; ill health limits the realization of this potential. Women often are more prone to ill health than are men. In part this is due to real sex differences: childbearing can be a dangerous episode. But women's biological functions are frequently made unnecessarily hazardous by social factors, such as the allocation of food within the family or the expectation that women should have children. In practice our health is endangered daily by a network of traditions and institutions which protect male interests. And so, for women everywhere, the extent to which we can exert control over our fates is especially dependent on the state of our health.

In this context the fact that we have, in the wealthier countries at least, largely lost the healing powers of our foremothers is doubly lamentable. With the rise of the medical profession our right to define our own health needs was taken out of our hands. Where women previously depended on one another for the means to good health (all were to some extent healers), scientific medicine makes us individually dependent on doctors. At root the battle over healing is also a battle for control over the health of women. if we are to escape ill health and realize *our* potential to gain power as women we need to build a more 'wise' practice of healing – one in which caring and curing are reunited and knowledge is based on sharing rather than exclusivity.

Without a medical training, it is very difficult for most of us to identify how much the power of the doctors' technology is real and how much is contrived: our access to medical knowledge is tightly controlled. But this is no reason to turn our backs on it. 'Going back to our roots' will not be enough. There is plenty of value to be learnt from the medical establishment, and in particular from those women who work within it. If we fail to take on their struggles to democratize the formal system of health care, we can never hope to transform medical technology into something more progressive for women. Ultimately we will want to be selective: to take that which is good and useful from both medical practice *and* traditional healing. In the meantime, however, one central task is to erode the fundamental inequality between healer and healed. Already women are engaging in that task by building up knowledge about our bodies, by confronting the medical profession and by challenging the wider values which define us as sick and thus vulnerable. Only when we have succeeded will the question of who heals whom cease to matter.

5. Managers and labourers: women's attitudes to reproductive technology

Frances Evans

A number of trends over the last 50 years or so have significantly altered the experience of childbirth for many women. Outstanding among these are the statistically greatly increased safety for mother and child; the actual and potential increase in the use of technology in pregnancy and birth; the change in the usual place of delivery from home to hospital, and the passage of power from the hands of female midwives into those of a medical profession which is controlled and dominated by men. Reproduction is a central issue in women's lives, and it is important that such major changes in its management are subject to informed and critical scrutiny. This chapter addresses some of the issues raised by the use of technology during pregnancy and birth. The first section presents data collected during interviews with women who had hospital deliveries in Britain in 1979 and 1980; the second suggests a theoretical framework for understanding their experiences, and the third assesses political strategies for action around the use of technology in childbirth.

The survey: expectations and findings

In 1981, I interviewed 200 women about their experiences of pregnancy and giving birth. This was part of a research project set up to consider why the number of still births and baby deaths in the first week of life (perinatal deaths) was higher than expected in one particular health district.[1] The survey investigated every perinatal death in the district during 1979 and 1980. Interviews were carried out both with the mothers of babies who had died (Group A) and with women whose babies lived (Group B). Where possible, the latter were the same age as the mothers in Group A, with an equal number of previous pregnancies. Interviews took place in the women's homes: women were asked about their social backgrounds, contacts with medical services and evaluations of maternity care. I was particularly interested in how women perceived their role as 'consumers' of a service.[2]

At the outset I expected that the use of technology as a routine part of maternity care would emerge as an issue of major importance to the women I met. I felt most would be concerned about its excessive and perhaps unnecessary use, for with the advent of the Women's Liberation Movement feminists have generally assumed that most women do not want technological intervention, and that more natural childbirth techniques should be promoted. A number of pressure groups have formed a campaign for greater parental involvement in the organization of pregnancy and childbirth, and as a result there is now a lively public debate about the safety and appropriateness of certain medical techniques.

My expectation was further encouraged by national statistics relating to technical involvement in reproduction. One of the most dramatic changes in maternity care has been the shift in place of delivery from home to hospital clearly evident in Table 5.1.

This change has facilitated medical intervention and control throughout labour and birth. For example, the number of inductions performed nationally increased from 14 per cent in 1963 to 41 per cent in 1974 (as a proportion of total deliveries).[3] Induction rates at the three delivery units in the surveyed health district for 1980 were 67 per cent, 21 per cent and 38 per cent

Table 5.1 Percentage of all births taking place in hospital[4]

Year	
1927	15
1937	25
1946	54
1963	68
1969	81
1973	92
1978	98

respectively. Fifty-four per cent of Group A and 66 per cent of Group B had accelerated labour. In addition, ultra-sound foetal monitoring is now widely used nationally, with many units achieving over 90 per cent surveillance. In this survey, 51 per cent of Group A and 25 per cent of Group B had ultra-sound scans. The use of technology is evidenced not only by the direct use of machines on mothers, as in ultra-sound scanning, but also extends into indirect fields, such as the taking of blood and urine samples for later technical analysis, now routine at most ante-natal clinics.

These trends have been encouraged by central government. Its most recent investigation into this area was the 1980 Social Services Committee Report into Perinatal and Neonatal Mortality, which recommended that:

> an increasing number of mothers be delivered in large units; that selection of patients be improved for smaller consultant units and isolated GP units; and that home delivery be phased out further, and that continuous recording of the fetal heart rate should increasingly become part of the surveillance of all babies during labour.[5]

I felt sure that the research would show that women did not welcome such changes and that there was widespread dissatisfaction with the technology encountered in pregnancy and childbirth. In fact, the mothers in the survey did not fit my preconceived model. They were not particularly concerned about an excessive use of technology. Indeed, many women would have liked it used more often, seeing it as a *basic right* of the pregnant and labouring woman. Just as men with heart attacks are not left to die a 'natural' death, the women felt their pregnancies should not be left completely to 'nature'. There were two main arguments for putting forward this view. The first was that technology should be used as an interventionist measure to relieve difficult pregnancies and labours:

> I wasn't offered drugs at all, except one dose of pethidine. I would have liked something really, they didn't even give me gas and air.

> The baby was two weeks late. I do feel they should induce you when you go that far over.

The second was that technology should be available as a routine service to detect fetal abnormality:

> I think everybody should have a scan. I'm not enthusiastic about it all, I had no fetal heart monitor, only the trumpet. The care was adequate but no more.

> I think I would have liked a scan just to check the baby was all right, but I didn't have one.

Many mothers whose babies had died felt that a scan would have shown up fetal abnormality and that a termination could have been offered, which would have been preferable to the subsequent experience of a still birth or early baby death. Women whose babies lived felt that scanning would have made them considerably less worried during pregnancy.

When asked to sum up their feelings about the ante-natal clinics, many women complained, rather puzzlingly, that staff had done their job but no more than that. Questioned further, 'doing their job' was defined as administering tests. Tests involving the use of technology were seen as particularly useful. Indeed, many women felt that a visit to the hospital was a waste of time if specialist technology was not used:

> It was terrible, I waited two or three hours every time, sometimes longer. It just isn't worth the wait, it's a waste of time – they didn't do anything my GP didn't do.

> All they did was prod your stomach and it wasn't really worth going up there at all. I only went for the baby's sake, I wouldn't have bothered for myself . . . I never had a scan, and I feel I should have had one, especially because of the dates, but also I think you need to be reassured.

It was striking that mothers who had been referred to a London teaching hospital because of complications were very impressed with the advanced machinery they saw there, saying admiringly that it was like something from *Tomorrow's World*. This had made them confident that the best possible care would be given to them, and many commented that it was unfair that this level of technology was not available at every hospital in the UK.

Complaints about too little technology, and demands for its

greater use, should not be taken in isolation. Their context is the total lack of control which women felt over their pregnancy and birth. Indeed, the absence of explanation about, or control over, the pregnancy was the most common complaint. Women felt humiliated and indignant about the way they were ordered around and refused any opportunity to ask questions or to be involved in the decisions about their care. There was also anger about the way the staff had completely ignored the women's own views or worries about the pregnancy:

> The staff didn't really speak to you at all. The doctors didn't even say "good morning" or "how are you?" I was really upset by my internals, and if only someone had explained what they were going to do it would have been better.

> I wasn't really satisfied – I think you should have the same doctor each time . . . when I had the scan . . . the doctor couldn't really be bothered and was very busy and didn't explain.

> I was very disappointed at the attitude of the ante-natal clinic; I always have small babies and knew she was due at the end of March . . . even towards the end the head was well down, and they said she wasn't due. Then I was there the Monday before she was born on the Friday – they gave me an internal and they said it wouldn't be born for another month because she was so small. I knew that was wrong. They just wouldn't listen to me and I *have* had five babies.

> Each time I went I asked them about the bleeding – I was bleeding a lot – and at 36 weeks they gave me an internal and said it was a cervical erosion. It was a long time really to find out what it was. I asked about my breech once and they said it would be OK – they didn't tell me about pushing at all. I was having to ask the questions.

In the language of sociology, women were more disturbed and affected by the social relations within which technology is organized than they were by its use *per se*.

The only complaints made about the overuse of technology concerned excessive drug use. Even in the small number of cases where this was mentioned, the emphasis was on the lack of explanation about or control over drug use, rather than on its possibly harmful effects:

> I panicked in labour and didn't know at all what was going on, they weren't explaining what was happening. I was horrified at all the drugs they used on me. It seems awful. In labour they were sticking needles in me and I didn't know what they were. I was very upset. If they'd have explained what was going to happen, I would have been a lot better. I just panicked.

> I was so heavily drugged that I don't know what was happening. I was moved from one delivery suite to another but I don't remember. No one explained to me what would happen at all. I feel I missed out on the whole of my labour and delivery . . . I wasn't even sure if I'd had a baby. I just don't know what happened.

Generally, women did not mention the public controversy about the appropriateness of some of the techniques used on them. Only a very small number suggested that the use of technology might actually carry risk. It is interesting that so little of the debate inside and outside the medical profession has filtered through to pregnant women themselves.

Finally, women in the survey displayed a great trust in doctors, despite strong dissatisfaction with the service in the clinics they attended, which are often compared to a meat market. Women complained bitterly about both the way they were treated and the physical discomfort of their visits. Long waiting times were recorded, with the most common being between one and a half and two hours. Sixty-four per cent of all mothers felt they were treated as numbers rather than as individuals:

> It's all chaos and confusion. I thought why should we go if they haven't got time to talk to you, it's like them and us . . . I don't like seeing different people all the time . . . I didn't like it – like a conveyor belt really, you felt as though if you did have a problem you couldn't raise it because of other people waiting.

There were other features of the clinics which were clearly intimidating, apart from the rush. For example, 56 per cent of all mothers saw a different doctor each time they went; 25 per cent of all mothers said the doctors had not said anything to them, and 12 per cent of all mothers had not been able to understand 'foreign' doctors. Apart from this, women said that they were made to feel the doctors were very busy and that any questions they might ask would be a waste of the doctor's important time. Yet women did still attend the clinics. They held a firm belief in the capabilities of the medical profession and so felt that not to go would put the baby at risk.

The interviews, then, reveal that women felt they had minimal control over the care they received and were dissatisfied with the way this care was administered. This finding is not new; other publications have made the point well, and a number of pressure groups have formed to press for greater involvement in the way maternity care is arranged. However, a few studies have reported that many women want increased use of technology, as a precautionary as well as an interventionist measure, and that faith in the powers of doctors is often strong. These attitudes have not been adequately taken into account by the Women's Liberation Movement or by many of the parental lobby groups. The interviews reveal contradictory elements – such as a wish for more parental control over pregnancy as well as for more use of technology. This ambivalence presents problems for feminist polemic and strategy which cannot be ignored, and the next section attempts to make sense of some of these apparent contradictions.

The politics of childbirth

The starting point of any feminist analysis must be that women's experiences have political meaning: the personal is political. Women's experiences of pregnancy and childbirth are political in the traditional sense, in that they are moulded by the type of care available, and this itself is the result of political processes negotiated by such bodies as the Department of Health and Social Security and the British Medical Association. In addition, the expectations and experiences of motherhood are affected by political decisions in other areas of the welfare state, those affecting such aspects as maternity rights legislation, nursery school provision or age of entry to full-time education. These decisions in turn reflect a wider politics of womanhood. Thus, in order to understand the specific experiences of pregnancy and childbirth better, it is useful to see maternity as a *managed* event, the actual form of which is influenced by these political processes. In Britain today, most of the important decisions concerning the management of childbirth are made by doctors working in the maternity service. We need therefore to be clearer about how this predominantly male group came to be the 'managers' of childbirth.

Studies of the development of maternity care generally emphasize one of two themes. The first concerns infant and maternal mortality and morbidity. The subject entered public awareness during the Boer War, when the low physical standards of recruits focussed attention on the need to improve the health of the next generation. High infant mortality became associated with 'maternal ignorance' and the remedy was seen to lie with educating mothers through greater contact with professionals. At the same time, it was assumed that concentrating maternity care in hospitals would improve mortality rates. Between the First and Second World Wars, infant death rates did improve. Attention then turned to maternal mortality, which was particularly alarming because it appeared, unlike infant mortality, to be equally prevalent in all social classes. Clinical causes of maternal death became the subject of intense medical interest. Childbirth was viewed primarily as a potentially fatal situation for which medical intervention of any sort could be justified. Success was judged solely in terms of improved mortality rates, which were attributed to the trend towards hospitalized and highly monitored births.[6]

The second theme in the history of maternity care stresses the historical development of medicine as a male science: the gradual exclusion of women from the fields of discovery, knowledge and control, and their containment in the fields of caring, servicing and obedience (see chapter 5).[7] It points out that as the capabilities and extent of scientific knowledge increased, so the battle to prevent women from becoming doctors increased in intensity. Women were stereotyped as unscientific and fragile, and were excluded from the educational establishments which gave professional status to men. The battle was fought not only for monetary and status rewards, but also because of a male wish to appropriate and control women's unique reproductive capacity:

The obstetrician, as distinct from the midwife who is traditionally far less interventionist, seeks to take control of childbirth. It is then almost as if he, and not the woman, gives birth to the baby. The intricate technology has defused the bomb, childbirth has been de-sexed. The previously mysterious power has been analysed, and he has harnessed it to a masculine purpose and according to a masculine design.[8]

Medical knowledge about and control over reproduction would be such a powerful liberating force for women that men have had to dilute that potential by exercising their control through exclusion and domination strategies.

I would argue that modern maternity care has been shaped *both* by the search for increased health and safety in and around birth and by the institutionalization of male control over women. Whilst improved mortality and morbidity statistics have clearly provided a strong justification for the medical management of childbirth, they do not explain why medical control has not been relaxed as standards have risen. The explanation for this has to do with the male takeover of healing. But what are the implications of these observations for the actual management of pregnancy and childbirth, and how do they help us understand the experiences of individual women who find themselves at the receiving end?

Clearly the maternity service is not arranged in a vacuum distinct from all other social arrangements. Its precise form is influenced directly by the wider social structure and in particular by the systematic relegation of women to a position of inferiority compared with men. This can be instanced by considering the commonly expressed dissatisfaction with hospital ante-natal clinics. One reason for the crowded waiting rooms and rushed consultations is the national shortage of midwifery staff, and this in turn is due partly to the fact that, as a 'woman's vocation', midwifery attracts little more than 'pin-money' wages. Another reason for the overcrowding and rush reported in the survey is that the maternity services, and especially ante-natal clinics, are low on priority lists of health-care spending. This state of affairs is commonly justified by the general assumption that maternity patients are physically better able to cope than are patients who attend other out-patient clinics. There may well be some truth in this assumption, but it is of particular interest here because it highlights the extremely contradictory ideology surrounding pregnancy. It is seen as, on the one hand, a pathological condition requiring medical attention, and on the other, as a natural enough event, not warranting any 'fuss' on the part of a perfectly well mother-to-be. Women asking too many questions are easily silenced by a doctor's reminding them that giving birth is an everyday event, and not one to give the mother any reason for worry. The women might well want to retort that, if this were true, there would be no reason to see a doctor!

There seems to be no obvious resolution to this contradiction whose central feature is that although motherhood is often presented as an entirely natural and instinctive goal, providing women with our ultimate fulfilment, it is also so problematic that a welfare state and lengthy socialization are needed to ensure that each generation of women 'chooses' motherhood, and performs it 'efficiently' and 'normally'. This underlying ambivalence about whether a pregnant woman is really ill invites low funding priority, with consequent limitations to care, and is of great importance in affecting women's attitudes to pregnancy and childbirth. In so much as pregnancy is regarded as a pathological condition – and this is after all the popularly accepted and official reason for going into hospital to give birth – it is wholly logical for women to be deeply anxious about the outcome. It is also logical that pregnant women should place their trust in doctors since ignorance about medical knowledge and procedures makes such dependence a necessity if women are to retain some peace of mind during pregnancy. On the other hand, the assumption that maternity patients are better able to cope than are other patients makes it even less likely that women will seek information and reassurance, thereby increasing the potential anxiety.

As it is, women seeing male doctors are at the bottom of two hierarchies: one of gender and one of professional qualification. The professional hierarchy means that doctors are regarded as experts and so worthy of trust. The relationship between experts and lay people is classically unequal – especially when those experts possess knowledge upon which the lay group depends for its own safety, and especially when that knowledge is highly technical in nature. Added to this, the doctor/patient relationship is often a class one, with a confrontation between the middle-class, highly educated professional and the lower-class, less well-educated patient. This has resulted in working-class patients receiving differential and inferior treatment in the National Health Service, a phenomenon which has been documented elsewhere.[9] However, in the case of maternity care at least, the gender hierarchy is of more relevance. My own research revealed no differences in reported care according to social class.[10]

Studies of the clinical relationship have shown the doctor's tendency both to trivialize and discount the viewpoint of the woman patient and cursorily to dismiss any attempts by her to assert her own opinions and wishes. Male doctors have been found to see themselves as in alliance with the female patient's father or husband – against rather than for her. Transcripts of consultations illustrate how male doctors can use sexist banter as a form of social control to which female patients are particularly vulnerable.[11] This is not to say that male doctors are some uniquely cruel breed, but rather that men are the stronger partners in a power relationship with women, and so as doctors can easily intimidate women patients in a society which sees women as less important, less intelligent and less assertive than men.

Women's continued belief in the abilities of doctors, despite deep resentment about their actual behaviour, begins to make sense. It seems now to be a product both of the history of struggle over childbirth in which men assumed the role of managers, and of the confused and confusing picture of pregnancy and motherhood which accompanied that change. It is also consistent with the socialized respect for professionals, and for men, in an area of the health service where 'consumers' are exclusively female.

In this context, the ambivalence women felt about the use of technology appears less surprising. The use of techniques designed to detect abnormalities, for example, can be seen as a palliative for the confused mother-to-be who feels neglected by the doctors in whom she is expected to place so much trust. However, a distinction should be drawn here between monitoring techniques such as scanning, and the wider use of interventionist technology, whose issues are more complex.

It has been argued elsewhere that otherwise unnecessary medical intervention may take place to speed up labour and delivery times and so relieve pressure on over-used beds, or to coincide optimum staff numbers with a maximum number of deliveries.[12] Others argue that the high incidence of induction has less to do with safety, or even financial restraints, than it has to do with the tendency to value technical intervention in *any* medical society.[13] Certainly within western medicine it is the high-technology activities which attract money and professional acclaim, and this explains the *Tomorrow's World* units in the London teaching hospitals. The problem is that access to medical knowledge and expertise is now so restricted that it is impossible for most consumers of, or commentators on, the maternity services competently to evaluate the need for technology in maternity care.

Many women seemed to express a contradictory wish for more control over their pregnancies, as well as a wish for more use of technology, which implies a loss of control to the technicians. It now seems that this is not so much a contradiction as two sides of the same coin: that of women's uncertainty and ignorance, fostered by the male monopoly of medical knowledge and decision making. The technology which was asked for can be seen to be wanted not so much as an end in itself, but rather as a means of achieving a feeling of confidence about the pregnancy and its outcome in the absence of sufficient information or reassurance from doctors.

Strategies for action
Knowing that contradictions exist, and being able to make sense of them by putting them in a political context informed by feminism, is not enough. As feminists we must also consider how our analysis of the effect of power relations can best be translated into effective actions for change. A number of political strategies have developed around the issue of the use of technology during pregnancy and childbirth. In a short chapter it is obviously not possible to do justice to all of these, but here four different programmes for action are briefly sketched out and assessed.

The 'natural childbirth' movement One response to the dissatisfaction many women feel with modern maternity care has been the promotion of more 'natural' methods of childbirth which implicitly challenge the medical approach of seeing pregnancy as a pathological condition warranting the routine use of technology. In Britain this cause has been championed by an organization called the National Childbirth Trust (NCT). It is perhaps the most vocal and best-known opponent of unnecessary obstetric intervention. It has produced a number of books, several of them written by Sheila Kitzinger who has attracted considerable media attention. Some of these contain an almost mystical presentation of childbirth:

> In achieving the depersonalisation of childbirth and at the same time solving the problem of pain, our society may have lost more than it has gained. We are left with the physical husk; the transcending significance has been drained away. In doing so, we have reached the goal which is perhaps implicit in all highly developed technological cultures, mechanised control of the human body and the complete obliteration of all disturbing sensation.[14]

Medical technology is thus characterized as an unnatural invasion which has so dehumanized the experience of giving birth that the only solution, according to some proponents at least, is its wholesale rejection.

The strategy of the NCT is a little more tempered. Its primary purpose is to help women as individuals regain control over their own pregnancies on a practical level. Founded in 1959, 'to improve women's knowledge about childbirth and to promote the teaching of relaxation and breathing for labour', its specific aims are now:

> To set and maintain high standards of ante-natal education; to assess the needs of expectant mothers and new parents and to help to get those needs met; to press for informed choice for expectant parents; and to emphasise the need for good emotional support for women in labour.[15]

The NCT is well organized, with local classes, groups and a newsletter, and it plays a valuable role in filling some of the gaps left by orthodox maternity care. It helps demystify the whole experience for pregnant women, and gives them confidence in their ability to cope with the birth. Its effects over the longer term may well be greater than that of giving individuals support and guidance. Quite apart from the effect of any lobbying activities, doctors may, if consistently confronted by women who have knowledge about their bodies and pregnancies, be forced to reassess the way they generally dispense care.

There are, however, major limitations to the service the NCT can provide. It has limited resources and this brings practical restrictions. For example, many women may live in areas which do not have a local branch and they may not themselves have enough expertise, energy or time to start one. Moreover, the NCT has become popularly identified as a white middle-class organization and so is of limited relevance for many women.

Perhaps most important is the fact that although it provides a useful and supportive short-term action programme for some pregnant women, the NCT lacks any notable strategy for more politically conscious work aimed at permanent reform. It has not analyzed the political process surrounding childbirth and makes no attempt to link women's experience of the maternity service to their general loss of control to the medical profession and their subordination in a patriarchal society. A symptom of this failure may well be that the NCT simply never reaches those women who consider technology as something to which they have a right during pregnancy and childbirth.

A radical feminist view Whereas the supporters of the NCT movement tend to be opposed to technological control over pregnancy and childbirth, Shulamith Firestone is one feminist who generally welcomes this. She argues that women's general oppression in society is rooted in and legitimized by our childbearing capacity, and that the only way to challenge patriarchy is to remove the need for such biological functions. She therefore demands 'the freeing of women from the tyranny of reproduction by every means possible.'[16] Specifically she suggests that women should organize for more research into and implementation of the methods of artificial reproduction so that this may become normal practice and pregnancy and childbirth be avoided altogether. The use of technology in this way is thus seen as a means to revolution and women's liberation.

Putting aside the technical barriers to this objective, the

argument has a certain theoretical cohesion. It does, however, lack any account of the issue of who controls the technology.[17] Firestone urges that the fear of a possible abuse of scientific power should not inhibit discussion about its possible liberating uses. Possibly not, but to ignore the fact that scientific knowledge and power are currently in the hands of men is to ignore the extreme likelihood that any potentially revolutionary capabilities of artificial reproduction will be harnessed and dwarfed by the dominant patriarchial norms. Witness, for example, the eruption of public and media outrage when stories of lesbians giving birth under the AID (artificial insemination by donor) scheme were published.

Firestone avoids the problem of control of and access to technology, as does the NCT. Although the goal of artificial reproduction may in theory have an element of Utopian charm, it has failed to receive any notable support. As a political strategy it promises to increase, rather than decrease, the power of male technologists over reproduction.

Self-help The self-help women's health movement has been gaining strength for some time, and in numerous countries. It is politically conscious, with an ideological home in women's liberation:

> Self-help is women relating to ourselves in order to demystify health care, the professionals, and our own bodies . . . self-help is a political act. It is deeply challenging to the existing health care system. Through sharing our knowledge collectively we have developed skills – we, not only the 'professionals' will know what is done to us medically and why it is done.[18]

It has the dual aim of providing individual women with information and support and of shifting the balance of power in doctor/patient encounters as women become more knowledgeable and confident.

Like the NCT, then, the self-help movement is both practical and campaigning in orientation. But the analysis and strategy it offers seems more politically potent. In attempting to decide why the technology of reproduction is administered in a way which is unsatisfactory for many women, it has not shied away from considering the whole social pattern of patriarchy. The strategy of the self-help movement for maternity care is founded on a clear recognition of the power relationship which operates between pregnant women and their doctors, and on this basis it seems more likely to grasp, and so act upon, women's apparent ambivalence towards the technology used during pregnancy and childbirth.

To date, the self-help movement has made slow progress. Women's health groups are poorly advertised and are usually accessible only through local networks of the Women's Liberation Movement, and so only a minority of women know about them. The Women's Liberation Movement generally has a white middle-class bias and identity, and this may also act to exclude large numbers of women. Similar problems are of course faced by the NCT but, in so far as the women's health movement is more politically radical, greater levels of political awareness and commitment are necessary if women are to become involved in its self-help groups. Most women have particular problems in becoming politically active because of their domestic commitments and taught lack of confidence. Nevertheless the self-help movement is steadily becoming better known, and the publication of women's health manuals such as *Our Bodies Ourselves* by the Boston Women's Health Collective has advanced many of its fundamental principles.

At present, its political impact may be restricted by a certain insularity, but the women's health movement seems to offer the most relevant strategy for women wishing to organize around the right to control our own childbirth. Given the enormity of that task, it is perhaps inevitable that progress will be slow; still, it seems to be in a useful direction. The opening of well-woman clinics by some general practitioners and the spread of 'domino' deliveries are good examples of how the principles of self-help can be accommodated within a flexible National Health Service.[19] These successes also illustrate the value of working politically *within* the maternity services as well as organizing outside of its structures. In this context, it is worth considering the prospects for legislative change.

Legislation The 1980 Department of Health and Social Security Report on Perinatal and Neonatal Mortality had as its starting point official concern over statistics that showed the United Kingdom to be dropping behind the rest of Europe in terms of its perinatal health. It makes a causal link between improvements in mortality and morbidity figures and the increased provision of technology and hospital management.

> Inevitably, the intensive care approach has led to some dissatisfaction – mothers who have not been adequately prepared may feel that the process of delivery is being dehumanised by technology and midwives may regret that they are displaced by doctors in the supervision of labour. Nevertheless, much of the new technology is of accepted benefit to the mother and baby and we regard it as an integral part of modern maternity care.[20]

The report also called for a humanization both of the way in which technology is administered and of the whole hospital environment. It recognizes what it calls 'cattle-market conditions' at the clinics, and makes a number of suggestions aimed at improving the quality of maternity services. These include improving the physical surroundings of the clinics, more careful staff selection and increasing the number of consultants, midwives and health visitors.

Although the reforming spirit of this report is welcome and long overdue, there are major criticisms to be made. The main point is that it fails to question the validity of the assumed link between increased use of technology and decreased infant mortality and morbidity. Indeed, in Britain the possible risks associated with certain techniques, such as induction, have never been properly evaluated by government-appointed bodies. The report also fails to address the problems of why the funding of maternity services has been allowed to drop so low or why the service has become dehumanized. It calls for change without making suggestions about how to challenge the conditions which created the need for change, and so falls into an obvious trap of superficiality. In that its general tone suggests that good mortality statistics are the primary concern, irrespective of women's feelings about the quality of their care, it offers little hope of progress in the feminist struggle to gain control over our ability to have children.

This is not to say that change by legislation can never be useful.

There are a number of ways in which legal reform could significantly improve the maternity services. For example, legislation
could be introduced to provide funds for major research into the
risks associated with childbirth technology so that parents could
make more informed choices. Staff numbers could also be substantially increased by legislation, and even more thorough
selection procedures could ensure that high-risk women receive
the benefits of the most advanced technology while minimizing
unnecessary obstetric intervention. Similarly, changes in legislation could significantly improve the economic status of mothers,
which in turn would affect their experiences of childbearing.

However, there have been few signs of government commitment
to policies of this sort. For the most part, the onus for change is on
the individual woman, and this highlights again the vital role to be
played by movements such as the women's health movement in
identifying and campaigning for policies which *would* alter the
balance of power in the maternity service in favour of pregnant
women.

This chapter has highlighted some of the complexities in the
debate about the use of technology in pregnancy and childbirth. It
has argued that it is misleading to see the central problem as
whether or not the technology is used, and that instead control
over medical knowledge and practice is the crucial issue. There is a
danger of forgetting technology's benefits – whether real or
perceived – because of the patriarchal social relations within which
it is created and administered; that is,'rejecting the technology
itself because we cannot stomach the ideological wrapping'.[21] The
political priority now seems to be the necessarily long and slow
work of changing that wrapping, and this is most likely to be
achieved by a process of consciousness-raising and self-help as
well as by the more traditional tactic of lobbying. This is not to say
that short-term, small-scale change does not provide immediate
help to pregnant women. In the longer term, however, we should
not lose sight of the revolutionary potential of changes in the
organization and management of childbirth:

> The repossession by women of our bodies will bring far more
> essential change to human society than the seizing of the

means of production by workers. The female body has been both territory and machine, virgin wilderness to be explored and assembly-line turning out life. We need to imagine a world in which every woman is the presiding genius of her own body.[22]

6. Who controls birth control?

Elkie Newman

The number of children a woman has in her lifetime is rarely, if ever, under her control or left to chance. Economic necessity, class, social and cultural norms, legal statutes, religious precepts, the availability of health care and the demands of individual men all serve to control a woman's childbearing. Today, medical technology makes it possible for women to prevent birth if they want to. Yet women are no closer to determining how many children they actually have.

Contraception is not a simple matter of choosing from a range of available techniques. Like the decisions about whether or when to have children, decisions about which particular method of birth control to use are mediated by powerful social institutions and expectations. This chapter is concerned with one particular aspect of the forces which today shape the provision and uptake of birth control techniques: the ideology of population control, which itself helped to create an international industry in methods of birth prevention. It starts by outlining that ideology, and then considers why the network of services it has spawned does not necessarily meet women's needs.

Industrialization and the populationist ideology

At different periods in the history of every culture, women have sought to control the number of their children by whatever means were available. Individual preferences and circumstances of course vary, but it is broadly the case that the interest of a community in practising birth control is related to its standard of living.[1] The relationship, such as it is, hinges on the social and economic importance attached to having children. Thus, in poor agrarian communities, where the work which children perform is often essential to the continued survival of the family, birth control is largely irrelevant. Indeed, it may be necessary to have a lot of children, simply in order to ensure that a few survive. Many agrarian societies, having achieved a certain level of prosperity, have managed to keep their populations relatively stable for centuries.

All this changed with the advent of the revolutions in agriculture and, subsequently, industry in the now industrial nations of the world. Initially populations grew prodigiously: more children survived to adulthood and there was (in principle) plenty of work to be had. As industrialization proceeded, however, the economic role of children gradually declined and birth control began to assume a greater importance. Childcare became a burden for women who no longer worked in or around the home, because the traditional support system for looking after children broke down as families scattered to find paid work. In addition, restrictions on child labour and expectations of a higher standard of living meant that children became a drain on wealth rather than a resource. Women in the industrialized countries have fought for birth control almost since industrialization began, and these countries – both in the east and west – now have a very low birth rate – so low that in many countries population growth is at or below zero (that is, the population is stable or shrinking).

Needless to say, economic reasons for limiting childbirth are not in themselves enough to change social attitudes and practice let alone guarantee fertility control for women. The birth-control movement which took hold towards the end of the last century in Western Europe and North America struggled for decades before the increasingly widespread *private* practice of birth control was reflected in public policy. There was no lack of appropriate methods: by 1880 in Britain a whole range of appliance methods – barrier products, spermicides and intra-uterine devices – had been patented and brought onto the (albeit clandestine and semi-legal) market, and many of these techniques had long been in use. In fact the contraceptive Pill, first marketed in 1960, was the only new form of birth prevention to be launched after that time. Although by 1938 the technological prerequisites for the development of an oral hormonal contraceptive existed, prevailing concerns about popular morality and, in some countries, pro-natalist policies delayed this development until the late 1950s. In the event, the change in public attitudes which legitimized work on the Pill, and at the same time made birth control a respectable issue for public debate, was the sudden and popular fear (originating in the US) of a world population explosion.[2] Ironically, this fear focused not on the industrialized nations, where both the pressure for reform and the (initial) market for new contraceptive products was greatest, but on the largely agricultural nations of the Third World.

Much of the wealth of the industrialized countries is produced in the Third World, but the historical links between the industrialized and Third World countries have in effect blocked the economic development of the latter, and resulted in its now familiar poverty trap. Third World struggles for political and economic autonomy thus implicitly threaten to shift the balance of power and wealth in the international economic order away from the industrialized countries. Even the now substantial programmes of economic aid, although couched in philanthropic terms, often serve to reinforce their control over the Third World in the long run (see chapter 9). When fears of a world population explosion caught on in the 1950s and 1960s, the provision of family planning services rapidly became a major part of aid packages to the Third World, tied first to food aid and more recently to basic health-care provision. The idea was that one of the main causes of Third World poverty is the rate of population growth, which is higher here than in the industrialized countries. If the industrialized world could 'help' the Third World to control its population growth, this would also help to combat world starvation and squalor. This reasoning had an obvious appeal to the well intentioned, but it also made political sense to western leaders. Lyndon B. Johnson, for example, proclaimed that investment in population control was better value for money than investment in economic growth.[3] Family planning programmes thus became a panacea: at best, a substitute for the genuine development of the Third World and, at worst, a means of controlling potentially rebellious peoples.

These two aspects of the 'populationist ideology' had in fact already been rehearsed in the industrialized countries during the latter part of the nineteenth century and the first half of this century. Many of the early birth-control campaigners were motivated primarily by the desire to give women the choice of when or whether to have children, but there were other more sinister elements in the movement. In Britain, the most notable of these was the Eugenics Society. The aim of this group was to promote the use of birth control as a means of preventing classes and races deemed 'inferior' from breeding too rapidly – a programme which found its most horrific expression under fascism in Germany. The eugenics movement never became particularly large in Britain, but it reflected a common fear, throughout the middle and upper classes, of the potential threat posed by the growing industrial working class – one which is paralleled today, and with more obviously racial overtones, in the relationship between the rich and poor nations.

The Malthusian League, founded in 1877, was the major force in the birth-control movement of Britain. Its namesake, Malthus, believed that the poverty of the burgeoning industrial centres was largely the result of overpopulation. The League maintained that this poverty could be stemmed by state provision of contraceptive measures to the urban poor, and on occasions this was posited as an alternative to social welfare programmes. Like the Malthusian position, the populationist ideology is essentially founded on a myth: that overpopulation is the main cause of poverty and that the poor are thus responsible for their own poverty. In this way, attention is deflected from the underlying causes of both poverty and population growth.

The ideology nevertheless caught on quickly; it was the catalyst for the investment of big money in research on birth-prevention methods and their eventual production by the drug companies, starting with hormonal contraceptives. Since the 1950s birth prevention has become a major international project, drawing in the drug companies, research scientists and the medical establishment. The provision of services and their administration at a local, national and international level has created a vast number of jobs and professional careers. The study of population trends and population planning is now firmly established in university and government departments and is being incorporated in school curricula in many countries, from primary level on. The resultant growth in birth-prevention services has given some women more control over their fertility. However, the structures which have brought immense potential for progress for women at one level are also a highly developed means of oppression at another – in both the industrialized nations and the Third World.

The Third World response

The professionals involved in promoting birth prevention since the 1950s tended to view the attitudes of western women – who generally want few, if any, children – as a norm for women everywhere. They assumed that if methods of birth control were distributed widely enough and women taught to use them, they would see the benefits and immediately proceed to limit the number of their children, thereby reducing their countries' birthrates. In the event, however, the Third World has not 'responded' as planned. In the few countries where industrialization is occurring rapidly, as in Thailand or South Korea, there has indeed been a reduction in population growth rates. But in most Third World countries the existence of family planning services has not noticeably affected the birth rate, or at least not in isolation from other factors.

The reasons for this are straightforward. In an unmechanized agricultural economy, for example, children represent the only possible source of labour power and family income. Without them poverty is certain. Women's ability to bear children is therefore one of their most valued qualities, and is often central to their role in society. Both women and men rightly reject birth prevention: it is not in their interests. Children are not an economic burden, but a necessity.[4]

Another reason for the rejection of family planning lies in its potentially eugenic applications. South Africa's programme, for example, has been used as a weapon against a whole people. Launched in 1974, the express aim of this programme has been to lower the *black* birth rate. Between 1973 and 1977, the number of family planning clinics – including mobile units – in black areas increased from 2,045 to 7,716; the budget for family planning increased by 266 per cent. This spending must be put into context. The government has forced black South Africans to live on only 13 per cent of the land of their own country and has then tried to persuade them that they are overpopulated.

Yet in the homelands every second child dies before the age of five, and the bulk of these deaths are a direct result of poverty-related diseases and lack of resistance to even minor illnesses. Black South Africans have understandably rejected birth control as yet another form of genocide.[5] But now, because they are resisting government 'help', the black population is being threatened with forced sterilization and forced abortion.

Such policies are an extreme case, but they highlight the implicit racism of an ideology which upholds the reduction of certain *sections* of the world's population. They also remind us that family planning programmes are specifically geared to limiting or reducing the number of children born rather than enabling women themselves to choose whether and when to have children (regarded as a right by the women's movement internationally). The rejection of family planning services is not based on irrational obstinacy, backwardness or prejudice, but on the well-founded belief that family planning is being used oppressively, as a means of control.

It took over a decade for the professionals to admit that family planning services alone did not do the trick,[6] even when these were as drastic as the mass sterilization programme instituted by Mrs Gandhi in India in the early 1970s. National governments are now being taught that they can affect the birth rate by using a combination of economic, social and health policies, and they are increasingly doing so.[7] Thus the introduction of industrial production techniques and mechanization of agriculture, the drafting of women into paid work, the introduction of benefits such as better housing for couples with only one or two children, and combinations of such policies are bringing about a drop in the birth rate of some countries. (This is not to say, of course, that population control is the *only* objective of such policies.) However, where women's general health is eroded by lack of food, poor housing and sanitation and this is ignored – and where health problems specifically related to women's ability to reproduce (for example, infertility and pelvic infection) are widespread and not treated[8] – the sole provision of family planning is a gross insult.

The types of technology imposed on Third World countries in the name of development are not always appropriate to their needs. This is no less true for health programmes in general than it is for the various economic programmes where, in many cases, the introduction of new techniques creates new forms of suffering and exploitation.[9] It is in this context that we must understand why women's needs are not being met. For if we go one step further and look at the specific techniques which have become available since the 1950s, the influence of populationist thinking becomes even clearer.

Birth-control research

Until recent fears of overpopulation took hold, there was little advance in the development of contraception, abortion or steriliz-ation techniques. A vast and often highly imaginative array of 'traditional' methods existed for centuries throughout the world, many of them highly effective. These included herbal teas to bring on a miscarriage; abdominal massage for the same purpose; mixtures of natural substances inserted into the vagina as a spermicide; animal skins used in the manner of condoms; stones and other objects inserted in the uterus; infanticide and taboos on sexual intercourse during proscribed periods. Many of these techniques are still being used today. However, as the medical profession began to claim responsibility for the provision of birth-prevention services, traditional methods have been uniformly rejected as primitive, cruel, dangerous or simply nonsense. What has replaced them?

Every traditional method in fact has its counterpart among the so-called modern range of techniques, because there are only a limited number of ways in which birth can be prevented:

- by preventing the sperm and egg from meeting – through female and male sterilization, the condom, cap or spermicide;
- by preventing the egg or sperm from maturing – through contraceptive pills and other hormonal methods such as injections;
- by dislodging the fertilized egg or foetus – through intra-uterine devices (IUDs), abortion, or 'morning-after' pills;
- by avoiding conception altogether – through abstinence from sexual intercourse altogether or during 'unsafe' times in a woman's menstrual cycle.

Two major discoveries have led to the additional techniques

available today. The first, which transformed all surgical techniques was the discovery that surgery was safe only if carried out under aseptic conditions. Without the use of sterile techniques, safe abortion and sterilization on a wide scale would never have been possible. The second was the accidental discovery that oestrogen and progesterone have an effect on fertility. It was this discovery which laid the basis for the development of numerous types of Pill, injectables, and other methods, like implants, still being tested.

Considering how much time, money and energy is now spent on birth-control research, we might expect to be able to choose from among, say, 10 different kinds of barrier method or perhaps a range of 'morning-after' methods. Instead, our options are confined to essentially 2 barrier methods, the various hormonal methods, a few IUDs and abortion techniques, and a small but increasing number of sterilization techniques. The emphasis on hormonal contraceptives is justified on the grounds that they are nearly 100 per cent effective, cheap to produce, and easy to market and dispense. Most notably, the use of hormonal methods does not require many visits to a clinic, and neither needs to be explained at great length to the woman nor requires her to make constant decisions about continuing to use them. Of course the injectables (which are generally administered every three months) require even less 'responsibility' than taking a daily pill – as do the IUDs. Now that operative techniques for sterilization are improving, the number of sterilizations has risen dramatically. This is the only method which needs be used only once in a lifetime and so is strongly favoured by the populationists. By contrast, barrier methods have been heavily neglected. They continue to be classed as old-fashioned, and their failure rate is stressed above any advantages they might have. They are, in fact, 'underdeveloped' in every sense of the word.

Major flaws have now appeared in all of the 'developed' birth-control techniques, and this has necessarily, alerted women to the actions of those responsible for developing and introducing new methods.

Testing and sales
When the modern contraceptive techniques were first introduced, no

one expected them to have serious (i.e. unwanted) side effects. We now know that the hormonal methods, IUDs and female sterilization can all produce quite nasty effects (ranging from thrombosis and increased risk of heart attack to painful periods and pelvic infection) – as well as the desired one – but these have shown up only after long-term use by masses of women. There have been repeated attempts by pharmaceutical companies to deny these effects and, when these have failed to convince, the effects have been played down. Now that the companies and professional groups which provide these new methods have had sufficient experience of them to be able to assess the risks involved, we might expect these same people to exercise much more caution when advising women about what to use. As it is, ideology conflicts with caution, and women's health hangs in the balance. The majority of women who turn up at family planning clinics are still not told adequately of risks they are taking – an abuse which is most glaring in the Third World, but which is widespread everywhere.

Of course many women do not suffer any deleterious effects and continue to use these methods because of the obvious advantages. But the drop-out rate is high – up to 50 per cent of women in the first year, in some studies of women using the injectable Depo-Provera.[10] With sterilization, unfortunately, you cannot drop out. A presently unpublished study of 'regret rates' following sterilization internationally highlights the conflict between the aims of the population controllers and the needs of women. We must give credit both to those research scientists who are doing their best to refine hormonal methods so that the unwanted effects are reduced along with the dosage, and to those who are trying to make sterilization a reversible and safer operation. Needless to say, the World Health Organization, which funds research centres in a number of countries, has only limited amounts of money to support this kind of work: it is not an international priority, whereas population control is.

The drug companies have shown little compunction in testing and selling dangerous drugs and devices in the Third World, particularly in rural areas. Before the Pill was marketed, it was not initially tested on western women but taken to countries like Puerto Rico for experiments. At that time the dosage was much higher than is allowed today, but as the priority was to establish the contraceptive effectiveness of the preparation, other effects were not assessed. The racism which made Third World women more 'suitable' than white women was exacerbated by the fact that legal restrictions on trials of untested drugs were far less stringent in the Third World than they are in the richer industrialized countries.[11]

This discrepancy still operates today, with the result that when a particular brand or dosage or method is determined to be unsafe and is partially or wholly withdrawn from the market in western countries, it turns up in clinics in the Third World. Called 'drug dumping', this practice is an exercise in not losing profits on already-produced drugs and devices.[12] No international policy exists to stop it – yet.[13]

The disasters which have resulted from these abuses are not a thing of the past. Nor are they confined to the Third World. The case of the Dalkon Shield, an IUD which was barely tested before being marketed, is by now well known. The device was inserted in millions of women, causing 17 known deaths and an unknown number of cases of pelvic infection and infertility. It is estimated that 10,000 women in Britain alone may still be walking around with a Dalkon Shield inside them. As yet the British Government has steadfastly refused to impose a total recall on the device.[14]

National and international protest in the face of such abuses has already had some effect. Wishing to avoid accusations of discrimination, the World Health Organization now has a policy to the effect that newly developed methods should be tested equally in 'developed' and Third World countries. Trials of current methods, however, are still being run by the WHO, mainly in the Third World.[15] Campaigning against drug dumping has been vociferous in recent years and has checked its practice somewhat. But the fightback by the drug companies to protect their interests is just beginning. Despite the overwhelming evidence of drug sales abuse gathered by the pressure group Health Action International, the World Health Organization failed to agree a code on drug distribution in the Third World at its annual meeting in 1982.

What is really needed is an international policy which covers all stages in the development and promotion of birth-control techniques – from exploratory research and testing to marketing, distribution and follow-up studies. In practice, the service at this end of this process, where women 'choose' from the techniques available, is no more neutral with respect to women's interests than are the earlier stages.

Birth control services

The distribution of birth-control methods and devices is carried out mainly by national family planning associations (or their international umbrella, the International Planned Parenthood Federation), by aid agencies or, directly, by the drug companies. In the industrialized world, clinics are either funded by government or are private and usually profit-making. In countries with mainly private medicine and a strong feminist movement (such as Australia and the United States), many feminist controlled clinics now exist, but as yet these do not have the means of providing services for the majority of women. Most services are controlled almost exclusively by the medical profession; women (or men) wishing to practise birth control are treated as 'patients', the underlying assumption being that 'doctor knows best'.

In theory, every contraceptive method on the market is available to consumers in the western world. Medical bias, however, restricts choice even here. In particular, attitudes about race, class and age influence what (if any) methods are recommended most strongly to individual women. Poorer women and women from ethnic minorities are often assumed to be the least 'responsible' when it comes to birth control and so they are often recommended those methods, such as Depo-Provera or even sterilization, which require the lowest level of decision-making for continued use. Despite all the publicity about birth control, countless women still spend years thinking the Pill is the only form of contraception. It appears to be the number one choice of many doctors, if only because it is simple to prescribe. It is interesting that in Japan neither the Pill nor the IUD are available, owing to government policy for the 'protection' of women's health. This policy does not prevent mass production of the pill in Japan for export to other Asian countries – though it does protect the profits of gynaecologists doing abortions.[16]

Choice in the Third World is, predictably, much more restricted.

Governments generally have little money to spend on the sophisticated services so taken for granted in western countries. Although family planning programmes receive international aid funds, the provision of services is often severely restricted by cash limits – affecting not only the number of clinics but also the training of staff, the provision of sufficient doctors and equipment and the range of methods provided. Clinics may be half a day's journey away; women cannot visit regularly or easily and, because staff numbers are low, little time can be spent with any one woman. These conditions explain why some methods are favoured over others, irrespective of their suitability, and why women may not be fully informed about the technique they are using.

Limited funding is also a contributory factor in the dramatic recent increase in the use of sterilization. In Colombia, for example, a high proportion of the money available for birth control is channelled into sterilization clinics. 'La Operation' (words used in the same way we use 'the Pill' to mean contraception) is inexpensive and much more easily obtainable than either contraception, which can be costly, or abortion, which is illegal.[17] Populationists are quick to say that such sterilizations are voluntary. Certainly if we compare this practice with the physical coercion and blackmail which occurred in India in the 1970s, we cannot call it forced sterilization. We can, however, call it sterilization abuse – a more sophisticated form of coercion if you like. And when we are told that women in Thailand are choosing Depo-Provera in large numbers, along with the Pill and the IUD, we must ask what other choices they are given.

Dissatisfied women have forced the professionals to become more sophisticated in their methods of control but, like the drug companies, the family planners now have a vested interest in maintaining their markets and are unlikely to hand over power without a struggle. In the face of growing anger in the Third World that Depo-Provera is considered safe enough for them but not for western women, advocates of the injectable are lobbying fiercely for restrictions to be listed in the United States and Britain. Population controllers are offering funds to feminist groups in the Third World to set up services. They are increasingly co-opting our language – saying, for example, that it is 'a woman's right to choose' Depo-Provera. And they are using women's liberation demands as a means of population reduction – for example, if women had equal opportunities at work they would have fewer children. They have not, however, come any closer to accepting the politics of choice.

The most gaping hole when it comes to lack of choice is in the area of abortion, not mentioned often in this chapter because it has not yet achieved the same status or level of acceptance as other forms of birth control. Contraception, despite limits on availability, is rarely illegal and its practice is widely accepted. Legal restrictions on sterilization are also rapidly disappearing, as the populationists succeed in selling it as 'permanent birth control'. Yet when used at an early stage of pregnancy, abortion involves only a minor operation, with few risks. It is estimated that at least half of the 30 to 55 million abortions which take place worldwide every year are illegal and not done under safe, medical conditions. In Turkey and Venezuela septic abortion cases take up about 60 per cent of beds in the urban maternity hospitals and use between 40 and 50 per cent of those hospitals' blood supplies.[18] Antiquated laws, dating from European colonialism, remain on the statute books of many a Third World country, and anti-abortion movements intimidate many a government. They even intimidate the population controllers, who have shown a tremendous reluctance to take on the Catholic church, Islam or other religious ideologies opposed to abortion. It is ironic that in Mexico the women's movement has campaigned for legal abortion for years to no avail but that as soon as the National Council of Population (the government office which studies population policy) recommended legalization the government promised to consider it – before 1988, when elections are due. In the meantime, complications from dangerous abortions are the second or third largest cause of maternal deaths in many countries – an unacknowledged and particularly gruesome form of population control.

Sexism and birth control

Any analysis of how women's fertility is controlled must start and finish with the reality of male oppression. In a world divided by class and imperialism, some women inevitably suffer more than others. But we are all affected to some extent; our bodies are pawns in the playing out of power relations between different groups of men. Neither the process nor the outcome is neutral – for any woman. If the state provides the services and women reject them as a means of control they are accused of backwardness and ignorance.

On an individual level, men who want children often want also to know that those children 'belong' to them and so they attempt to control when 'their' woman should get pregnant – either by deciding if and when she uses contraception, or by themselves using male contraception (condoms). In Yugoslavia if a man fails to do anything to prevent pregnancy, the women rely almost exclusively on abortion.[19] In Japan, where sexuality is not openly discussed, women also have to rely on men for contraceptive information and decision-making. Condoms are consequently the most widely used contraceptive, but in the end abortion is a widespread backup method.[20] When men refuse to practise birth control, women may have little choice but to accept this. Going against a man's decision on this issue can be dangerous. In Britain and New Zealand individual men have tried (unsuccessfully so far) to take out court injunctions to stop their wives from having abortions. Worse still, men have been known to pull out IUDs and to destroy pills, caps and other visible techniques. (This is one reason why a method like Depo-Provera is sometimes preferred: it is almost invisible – unless the woman's menstrual cycle changes and gives her away.)

Men hold the top positions in most international companies and agencies, as well as most national governments. Thus, decisions about the distribution of birth-prevention methods and the provision of services are generally made (and changed) by men, as are laws concerning contraception, abortion and sterilization. Similarly, most of the research into birth control is done by men. Women, of course, are the guinea pigs for new methods since most are intended for use by them. Some male techniques have been developed, but here the dangerous effects tend to be played down far less than is the case with female techniques. Disadvantages considered 'tolerable' for women are deemed an unacceptable burden for men. In fact men have been very reluctant to volunteer for experiments with male methods of any kind, just as they have been generally reluctant to be sterilized. The World Health Organization recently decided not to put much money into research on male methods in the future – they simply cannot persuade enough men to try them![21] (In any case, women are understandably reluctant to rely on male birth control methods especially when these are 'invisible': men don't get pregnant!)

Regardless of what we might want in an ideal world, or of what is technically feasible, many women continue to have children they do not want and many are unable to have children when they want them. In a very real sense we are denied control over the whole of our lives when control over the capacity to give birth is not in our own hands. Women are often penalized for taking that control – whether to increase or to decrease our fertility. Women are in some places, as in China, made to feel criminal for wanting children, or, in others, criminal for not wanting children, as in Eastern Europe and the Soviet Union. If women want services from the state, and the state refuses to provide them, women can find themselves in prison for helping each other, as in Spain, where abortion is illegal.

A woman's right to choose

It is wrong to assume that women in every culture and in every country have the same needs or interests with respect to children. It is also wrong to assume that they are always individually motivated to do what is economically or socially required of them. As is true of all oppressed peoples, women are not passive victims of the extremely complex controls on their fertility. Traditionally women used and controlled their own techniques for birth control, just as they did for childbirth and pregnancy. And women are beginning to take that control back again – all over the world and in a wide variety of ways.

We are making demands on men individually and collectively. We are rejecting birth-control techniques we don't like and demanding access to techniques which are denied us. We are setting up our own clinics and health services and influencing the type of services provided by the state. We are experimenting with traditional methods and beginning to influence the research being conducted internationally. We are campaigning for laws that reflect the needs of women and, slowly, we are getting them.

Most important of all, women are meeting and working together, nationally and internationally to reject the ideologies of control imposed on us, to articulate what we want and to build alternatives which will provide it.[22] It is simply not enough to talk about women's choices on an individual level: we need to talk about the right to make choices, and the right to determine what those choices are.

7. Housework and the appliance of science

Erik Arnold and Lesley Burr

Housework, in the sense of work done in the home by a housewife, is a relatively modern invention. It is a uniquely industrial phenomenon because it resulted from the reallocation among family members of work done in the home which was prompted by industrialization. It is also uniquely patriarchal, because it is done by a particular gendered person: the house*wife*.

During the Industrial Revolution in Britain the application of technology and science to the world of paid work brought enormous social and economic upheavals, but the pattern of relations between genders inside individual families provided an important source of continuity. In the money economy a new ruling class emerged in the form of the owners of capital. In the home the rulers remained the same: male dominance continued largely unchallenged. As men, single women and children increasingly undertook paid work outside the home, so married women tended to be left to cope with the mess left behind – in other words, to do the housework.

This new sphere of housework was, however, not fixed and unchanging. Crudely, we can regard it as having passed through three phases since the Industrial Revolution. In the first phase, lasting perhaps until the 1870s in Britain and the USA, more and more of the goods formerly produced in the home began to be made in factories. Combined with other technical changes (such as improved water supplies and newer types of house design), this reduced the amount of housework necessary to maintain previous standards, and tended to create what Barbara Ehrenreich and Deirdre English have called the 'domestic void'[1].

The second phase, lasting through the last quarter of the nineteenth century and into the twentieth until roughly the First World War, saw efforts to fill this void and sustain the feminine role of the housewife in the home. These efforts involved the domestic science movement and the introduction of domestic science education. They fostered rising standards for housework and therefore higher expectations about the quantity and quality of the goods and services consumed in homes. The introduction of science and of quasi-scientific ideas brought with it the idea of 'progress' in standards: specifically, the idea of progress without effective limit.

The third phase involved the increasing use of technology to pursue these ever-rising standards. An important aspect of this has been the acquisition of consumer durables to help supply the increasing demand for services in the home. In this latest phase, new technologies – especially domestic appliances – have been brought in to enable family members to produce certain goods and services in the home instead of buying them from outside. This latest period may be thought of as the self-service phase in the development of housework.

This chapter concentrates on the first two phases, looking at social and technical influences on housework in the first phase and domestic science in the second. It deals first with the construction of housework as a feminine activity during the Industrial Revolution in Britain, and some of the processes by which it was deskilled and devalued during the nineteenth century. Next, it describes changes in ideology which both enabled and justified the creation of housewifery as a separate feminine sphere. Finally, it describes the application of quasi-science to housework by the domestic science and home economics movements. These movements paved the way for the 'appliance revolution' of the twentieth century.

In thinking about social and technological changes, it is important to recall that people's behaviour and ways of life are subject to a good deal of variation at any point in history. Just as people's lifestyles vary today, so they did in the past. However, in any period people have an idea of what constitutes 'normal' (or stereotypical) family life. Whether this stereotype actually represents the 'average' does not really matter in so far as the *idea* of the norm influences people's aspirations and behaviour. Tension between ideology and material reality has been a constant feature of family life and housework in the capitalist period of history.

The invention of housework

Before the Agricultural and Industrial Revolutions, the family was generally the major unit of production, making goods both for immediate consumption and for exchange on the market. There was little distinction between the home and 'work', as the home was the place where most types of work were performed.

In both the cities and the country, people often lived in extended families. Farmers would have single male labourers living as part of their households, while urban craftsmen ruled over households which included their apprentices. Domestic servants would also live in. They were generally young single women whose wages were of more use to their parents than their work in their own households. Women played a vital role in production together with men. The conception of women's proper work embraced a much wider range of activities than today, including brewing, dairy work, the care of poultry and pigs, the production of vegetables and fruit, spinning, nursing and doctoring.[2] The division of labour in the family was based on age, gender and ability. Unskilled work was the province of unmarried girls and boys who worked alongside other family members. Marriage did not relieve a woman of the necessity to work and to provide for her children. Single and married men generally received the same wages; neither expected fully to support other family members out of these wages.

Urbanization has been a corollary of industrialization in the developed countries. In England, as elsewhere, the pattern of economic development was very uneven, and this unevenness was mirrored in the development of housing. The early industries of the Industrial Revolution were dependent on water for their primary source of energy and this limited their choice of factory location. Entrepreneurs like Strutt and Arkwright were therefore obliged to build not only factories but also whole hamlets to house workers and their families in the 1780s. The transition to steam power, however, allowed factories to cluster together in towns, promoting the development of local labour markets and loosening the ties between employers and employees. Employers setting up in the towns did not have to attract and house labour but could rely on it to be available locally. In the early nineteenth century, building houses for the labouring masses became an industry in its own right, with so-called jerry-builders erecting cheap housing in great quantities for rent at high prices.[3]

Despite the unattractiveness of many aspects of factory work and life, the availability of industrial work represented an important avenue of escape from traditional patriarchal households, in which women's subordination was considerable. 'The new girl of 1832 caused many a headshake. She was dangerously independent because she had her own money. Even a wife began to adopt airs unbefitting her position.'[4]

For many country girls, the route to the factory and independence – or to marriage to a socially mobile urban worker – lay through domestic service. In many cases, domestic service provided an apparently safe occupation for single girls and women not needed in their parents' homes. The role of the employers *in loco parentis* was especially important for girls, and while the work was onerous it provided training in housework skills and thus increased servant girls' prospects of marriage. Domestic service also spread middle-class values and notions of propriety into working-class families. The Reverend J.S. Brewer urged on his middle-class listeners the importance of:

> The female servants in your household, whom you have instructed in their respective duties – whose manners you have softened – who have learnt from you how to manage a household – who have caught up from you, insensibly, lessons of vast utility, lessons of order, lessons of economy, lessons of cleanliness, lessons of the management of children, of household comfort and tidiness; these women eventually become the wives of small tradesmen and respectable operatives. They carry into a lower and a very extended circle the influence of your teaching and your training. Visit a hamlet or a village where the cottager's wife has been a servant in the squire's mansion, and you shall see the result immediately, in the air of comfort, order, and neatness which reigns around – in the gentle and respectful manner of the woman – in the tidyness and respectability of her children. Even her husband, though rude and habituated to rough toil, has caught something of the gentle manners of his wife.[5]

This role of domestic service as, in sociological terms, a

'bridging occupation'[6] helps to explain the recurrence of the 'servant problem' as a middle-class concern throughout the nineteenth and well into the twentieth century. According to Carol Dyhouse, one in three women in Victorian England spent part of her life in domestic service, most usually at some time between the ages of 15 and 25 years.[7] Experienced servants content to stay in service were hard to find precisely because service was so often a means to acquire geographical and social mobility through training in the domestic arts.

People moving from the country to the towns in search of work tended to leave their extended families behind and live in smaller family units. In the overcrowded slums, generations of women and men grew up working in factories from early childhood, never learning the most basic domestic skills. Cooking was elementary; washing was hired out; domestic crafts such as needlework were largely absent.[8] The contrast with the domestic life of people two or three generations earlier was complete; so too was their deskilling with respect to the domestic arts. The servant problem and the low level of housework skills possessed by working-class girls were to be important motivations for middle-class philanthropy and efforts to promote domestic science education.

While the form of modern housework and the gender of the housewife were established during the first century of the Industrial Revolution, the content of housework has changed continually. Changes in technology have played important roles, and in the nineteenth century new techniques facilitated many changes in the boundary between housework and paid work. Fay Pierce, writing in the USA during the 1870s, complained about the takeover of housewives' (that is, largely married women's) work by single women under the management of capitalist men:

Hitherto, men have allowed us at least to make up . . . the fabrics they sell us. But this last corner of our once royal feminine domain they are determined now to wrest from us. They have invented the sewing-machine, and already it takes from us not far from five hundred million dollars' worth of sewing annually. Our husbands are clothed entirely from the shops and in all the large dry-goods firms they have marshalled the pale armies of sewing girls to ply the wheel from morning to night.[9]

Product after product formerly made in the home began to be made in factories, either by men or by (largely) single women under male management. Beer, butter, buttons, starch, medicines and bread went this way, as had textiles bleaching in the past. Washing was an important task which tended to move out of housework throughout the nineteenth century (though it was to move back during the twentieth, partly because of the spread of domestic washing machines). In England until the late 1840s, when piped water became common, washing was done very infrequently indeed by modern standards, and even after that time it was undertaken reluctantly. Washing involved carrying and heating great quantities of water as well as the laborious work of hand-washing itself. Crude, hand-cranked washing machines which agitated clothes in soapy water were developed in the 1810s, but they did little to relieve the sweat and boredom of the task and were not widely used. Nonetheless, through the nineteenth and well into the twentieth century, many married women took in laundry or hired themselves out as washerwomen because this could easily be combined with childcare.

From the 1860s, partly mechanized laundries were established, again staffed largely by single women. These undermined the activities of married washerwomen, while also providing a welcome escape from the drudgery of washing for many. Ironically, the impetus the commercial laundries gave to washing-machine development eventually rebounded on them in the form of domestic washing machines, which in turn undermined the market for laundry services.

Urbanization encouraged the process whereby new business enterprises and new techniques successively stripped off aspects of unpaid housework and moved them into the capitalist money economy. When, in 1889, the editor of the *Ladies' Home Journal* advised women to stay out of politics and stick to their own sphere, the suffrage paper *Woman's Journal* commented that if the sexes were to keep to their respective spheres;

the baker, the laundry-man, the manufacturer of underwear and ready-made garments, the caterer, the tailor, the man-milliner, and many more would have to go, for if woman is not to encroach on man's especial domain, then he must keep his own side of the fence and not intrude on hers.[10]

Throughout the nineteenth century, the removal of individual tasks from housework into the money economy represented a genuine deskilling of housework: a housewife needed knowledge of fewer traditional skills (such as soap-making) at the end of the century than in its early years. And as housework was deskilled, so its status – which had never been high – declined further.[11]

The takeover by men and single women of the paid and unpaid work which housewives could do was undoubtedly one reason why the proportion of married women engaged in paid work fell through the second half of the nineteenth century. In 1851, about 25 per cent of married women were economically active, but this proportion fell to about 13 per cent in 1901 and went as low as 9 per cent in 1921, before increasing through the rest of the twentieth century to its current level of about 50 per cent (Table 7.1). In contrast, the proportion of *all* adult women economically active in Great Britain remained remarkably constant for a century from 1851, rising substantially above a third only in the early 1950s

Table 7.1 Proportion of married women 'economically active', Great Britain, 1901–74

1901	13.2%*
1911	9.6%
1921	8.7%
1931	10.0%
1951	21.7%
1961	29.7%
1966	38.1%
1971	42.0%
1974	49.0%

*England and Wales

Source: Census, except 1971 and 1974 *Social Trends*, London: HMSO.

(Table 7.2). This apparent stability of women's involvement in paid work nevertheless conceals significant shifts in the type and content of both their paid and unpaid work.

It would be wrong to view changes in the position of married women during the nineteenth century solely in terms of their being squeezed out of paid work through competition from their unmarried sisters and from men, important though this was. Capitalist industrialization also brought with it changes in attitudes about the right place of women in society, and these attitudinal changes enabled men to consolidate their supremacy in paid work during the nineteenth century. The creation of housework resulted not only from changes in the technical and economic organization of society but also from shifts in ideology: the social ideas which governed people's expectations about housework and house-wives.

Separate spheres and the ideology of housework

From the end of the eighteenth century, it began to be recognized

Table 7.2 Proportion of all women 'economically active', Great Britain, 1841–1971

1841	25%
1851	35%
1861	36%
1871	35%
1881	34%
1891	34%
1901	32%
1911	32%
1921	32%
1931	34%
1951	35%
1961	39%
1971	43%

Source: Census.

that it was more difficult for people to make their own independent living in the crowded capitalism of the growing cities than it had been in the rural past. Migration meant that urban areas were filled by people with few family ties. In order to avoid the responsibility of having to feed and house too many unemployed migrants, urban parishes needed to place primary responsibility for families on someone else. In the event, the 'natural' choice was the male household head. Following a decision by magistrates at Speenhamland in 1795, the Poor Law was changed so that a wife and children became the financial responsibility of the husband: in the past a woman was able to look to the parish for relief in her own right if she was unable to support herself and her children independently of her husband. This event began to provide justification for paying a higher, 'family' wage to men than to women.

Women's exclusion from paid employment was reinforced by the need of working men to organize against their capitalist employers, monopolizing skills to keep up wages. Exclusion of women from apprenticeships helped keep skills in short supply, and the new idea of married women as their husbands' dependants enabled men to demand a family wage.

It is, perhaps, not surprising that the late eighteenth and early nineteenth centuries were marked by evangelical movements in Britain: religion provides an important source of continuity in times of social upheaval. While the Methodists campaigned outside the established churches, other Evangelical sects worked within the Church of England on a programme of anti-slavery and moral reformation of the family. This reformation was made especially urgent by the terror which the French Revolution inspired in the British property-owning classes, who feared a working-class revolution in Britain.[12] Moral reformation could pre-empt this by transmitting middle-class ideas to the working class.

The Evangelicals saw women as the means to improve the moral qualities of the opposite sex, who were liable to be polluted by their involvement in the world of industry and paid work. Wives had a particular duty to encourage their husbands' religious sensibility so that, as Wilberforce explained, when the husband should return to his family, worn and harassed by worldly cares or professional labours, the wife, habitually preserving a warmer and more unimpaired spirit of devotion, than is perhaps consistent with being immersed in the bustle of life, might revive his languid piety.[13]

The idea that women and men belonged in 'separate spheres' of activity grew up in part because of a conjunction of economic and religious interests. The Evangelicals were as sharply critical of aristocratic moral laxity as they were of working-class immorality; their natural allies were the new bourgeois industrial classes. More than any other group, the Evangelicals set the moral tone of nineteenth-century society which allowed women and children to be 'protected' by successive factory reforms and the sphere of paid work to become dominated by men.

Among the principal factory reforms was an Act in 1832 limiting children's hours of work. This led in many places to the replacement of child labour with women's labour. In 1844 both women and children were restricted to a 12-hour working day. In 1847 this was reduced to 10 hours, but because it was not laid down which 10 hours in the day could be worked, many employers adopted a relay system. In 1850, however women's and children's work was restricted to particular hours of the day.

The reforming legislation did not solely protect women; it also focused attention on children. By the first half of the nineteenth century the image of childhood was being altered quite as much as were notions of women's 'rightful place'. In pre-industrial Britain and during the first century or so of the Industrial Revolution, children were treated as miniature adults in most respects; they were allocated work on the basis of ability from an early age. The reformers effectively succeeded in extending the period for which children were considered as dependent and in need of nurturing. This reinforced pressures on married women to leave paid work in favour of childcare and housework and bolstered arguments for paying men a family wage. In so far as the movement of many aspects of production formerly done in the home into factories left married women at home with less to do, this change in the way childhood was seen helped fill the so-called domestic void.[14]

The separation of the masculine sphere of work from the

feminine sphere of home and children had geographical as well as occupational significance, especially for the middle classes. In the early years of the century, masters still tended to live 'above the shop', or very close to it. *Sub*urbanization began on the basis of horse transport in the first part of the nineteenth century, but it was facilitated from the middle of the century by innovations in transport infrastructure, especially railways. This led the spheres of home and work to become physically separated in the middle classes, as they had also become for working people. The new capitalists attempted to force their wives into the mould of the aristocratic 'lady of leisure', and inevitably this stilted (and, no doubt, infinitely tedious) role came to be the ideal of other people in society who wished to 'better themselves'. As Carol Dyhouse says, in the suburbs dominated by females during the daytime:

> The distinction between the mother's world – the private, comparatively leisurely routine of the home and neighbourhood activities; and the father's world – a public world of regular time-keeping and rather vague but decidedly important activities, was abundantly clear.[15]

Domestic science

One result of middle-class Evangelism's mission to reform the family through women and a revitalized Christianity was the practice of 'visiting'. From the 1830s, various visiting societies fielded thousands of largely unoccupied middle-class women to visit the homes of their working-class sisters, offering charity, education in household economy and evangelical Christianity[16]. Visiting, like domestic service, provided a channel for transferring middle-class values and notions about women's place to working-class families.

A further channel for this transfer was domestic science education, which sought to raise the status of both its proponents and housewives and housework in general. The domestic science movements represented a channel for the energies of intelligent middle-class women who found that the only way to gain admittance to a profession was to create one. In the UK, this professionalization was reflected in the National Training School of Cookery, set up in 1874 at South Kensington, and it was followed by others in Liverpool, Leeds, Edinburgh and Glasgow in 1874–75. These institutions were a source of domestic science teachers to the schools. By 1897, UK domestic science instructors were established as a professional interest group in the form of the Association of Teachers of Domestic Subjects.[17]

The deskilling of aspects of housework, and the lack of domestic skills among many working-class girls which led to the recurring 'servant problem', had brought a need to stress the importance of women's increasingly devalued role in the household. This is a recurring theme in domestic science and instructional writing about the home in the nineteenth century. Isabella Beeton, whose best-selling 1861 book of household management retains its fame in the UK today, urged:

> Such are the onerous duties which enter into the position of the mistress of a house . . . [that] . . . She ought always to remember that she is the first and the last, the alpha and the omega in the government of her establishment; and that it is by her conduct that the whole internal policy is regulated. She is, therefore, a person of more importance in a community than she usually thinks she is.[18]

Childrearing was explicitly included in the programme of the domestic science movements and its importance – and the high status which it should attract – was continually stressed. In 1869, Harriet Beecher Stowe co-published a book with her sister on *The American Woman's Home, or Principles of Domestic Science*, which aimed 'to elevate the honor and remuneration of domestic employment'.[19] The following year, she proclaimed to mothers that:

> You are training young minds whose plastic texture will receive and retain every impression you make, who will transmit what they receive from you to their children, to pass again to the next generation, and then to the next, until a *whole nation* may possibly receive its character and destiny from your hands! No imperial queen ever stood in a more sublime and responsible position.[20]

The scientific aspects of domestic instruction proved a valuable means of enhancing the status of housework. Among the important virtues taught was cleanliness. The germ theory of disease, which became popular from the 1890s, provided a rationale for continuous cleaning of the home, in contrast with the pre-industrial practice of 'spring cleaning'. It justified the frequent washing of clothes – a far cry from the old habit of washing them at monthly or even greater intervals – and this was reinforced by the middle-class ideal of presenting oneself and one's family 'well turned out' to the world, an ideal promoted by the domestic scientists. The increasing importance of children in family life in turn made absolute cleanliness in all things more urgent, since they were continually threatened by dirt-borne germs and disease.

Domestic science education was not solely a means to create new high-status roles for women. It also involved the philanthropic aims of bettering the condition of the urban poor through teaching the efficient use of meagre domestic resources and, in the USA, of assisting the socialization of immigrants into American society. Like other domestic science enthusiasts, the middle-class women who congregated annually at Lake Placid from 1899 and who were to form the core of the American Home Economics Association had their own peculiarly middle-class vision of 'right living', and their attempts to apply scientific principles in the homes of the poor were strongly coloured by this vision. In particular, it involved casting out the last vestiges of economic production (such as keeping poultry) from the home, making the housewife's sphere exclusively one of consumption.

Model 'settlement houses' were set up in the slums where the poor – and specially the daughters of the poor – were taught useful domestic virtues such as middle-class American cooking, decorating, table setting, manners and the giving of tea parties. One domestic scientist explained the incongruity of teaching middle-class consumption patterns to poor children in terms of shaping their aspirations:

> While it may be impossible for them at present, owing to poverty-stricken conditions, to make practical use of all they learn, we are teaching for the future and the world, and when the opportunity does present itself they will be able to embrace it intelligently.[21]

The enthusiasm with which domestic scientists taught middle-class techniques to working-class girls had a similar effect to the teaching of higher cleanliness standards. It introduced the idea that progress in the standards of domestic life was both possible and – at least partly – attainable through improved organization and technology in housework. This idea of progress in standards was to play an important role in counteracting the labour-saving impact of domestic appliances in the twentieth century, leaving the actual time wives spent doing housework substantially unaffected by technological changes.

From the 1870s in the USA, domestic science or home economics movements promoted the idea of formal training for girls and women in the domestic arts. Harriet Beecher Stowe herself set up 'female seminaries' in Hartford and Cincinnati. In the UK, attention focused more on the role of the school system in providing this type of instruction, although individual middle-class philanthropists such as the Birmingham women who organized evening classes in needlework during the 1850s were also in evidence.[22]

The stress on education was important because British Victorians held the poor personally responsible for their poverty. Education therefore gave the poor the means to alleviate their condition in the proper manner – through self-help. However, some types of education also had useful side effects for the middle classes. Notably, most charity schools set up during the nineteenth century had the training and provision of domestic servants as their major objective.[23] Needlework had been among the domestic skills taught since the 1820s, and in country districts this often meant making and mending for the gentry patrons of the schools. There was recurrent conflict over the extent to which needlework taught should be plain or fancy (that is, useful to working-class girls in their own right or in their potential roles as servants) – a debate which was to be repeated over the type of cookery taught later in the century. In 1862, the revised code covering practice in state-supported schools made plain needlework a compulsory subject for girls.

The Education Act of 1870 replaced the previously patchy provision of schooling in the UK with a universal right to primary education. The National Association for the Promotion of House-wifery, organized by Lady Brabazon, campaigned during the

1870s and 1880s for the inclusion of domestic science in board schools' curricula, both to fit girls for adult lives as wives and to ensure the supply of servants. While the Education Department would not countenance the use of elementary schools as servant-training establishments, domestic science textbooks of the 1880s and 1890s promoted service as a 'nice' job and as providing an important training for life.[24] Partly as a result of lobbying by the National Association for the Promotion of Housewifery and other organizations, the Education Department did, however, put pressure on schools to teach domestic skills, offering grants for the teaching of cookery from 1882 and for laundry from 1890.

The independent schools of the Girls' Public Day School Company set up in the last quarter of the century tended to resist the encroachment of domestic subjects on the curriculum. These schools had been founded expressly to match the type of academic and intellectual education available to boys. Their opposition to domestic subjects was atypical at the start of the twentieth century, when women not prepared to dedicate their lives to housewifery were seen by many as shirking, selfish or as failing to discharge their national duty. Following revelations about the poor state of health of male volunteers for the Boer War from the large cities, a UK government inter-departmental committee in 1904 squarely laid the blame on city-dwelling women for their ignorance and neglect of wifely duties.[25] It was a preposterous charge, especially at a time when married women's labour participation rate was close to its lowest recorded point, and it was one on which contemporary feminists heaped scorn.

Feminist fury was no smaller in 1908 when the King's College for Women began to offer a three-year course in Home Science and Economics, a course eventually awarded degree status by the University of London in 1920. The role of such professionalization in imparting status to housework was stressed by Hilda Oakley, the college warden, who described the aim of the course as 'the using of the educational forces at our disposal to combat the depreciation of the activities related to household work due to both social and industrial courses'.[26]

Domestic science appears to have contributed little to our understanding of the world – not even in areas such as cleaning methods, which supposedly lie among its central concerns. Instead it has provided a means for applying the 'wisdom' of other, more male-dominated sciences to the home, thus elevating the sphere of women through contact with the fruits of male intellectual labours.

As well as specifying what the housewife should do, the domestic science movement was also keen to specify how. This involved imitating industrial practice as far as possible through maximizing the 'efficiency' of housework. Enthusiasts like Lillian Gilbreth tried to apply F.W. Taylor's ideas about industrial management and efficiency to housework but rapidly encountered major difficulties. Taylor stressed that 'conception' and 'execution' of work should be done respectively by management and by workers. The housewife was indivisible in this way and therefore had to do both these things herself; unlike the worker in a factory she had both to set and to meet her own quality standards. Equally, it was not clear what the point of increased efficiency was, especially when it saved time. Perhaps an appropriate use for any time saved through the application of the principles of domestic science was the study of domestic science!

Few members of the domestic movement thought that this time saved should be used to allow women to enter paid employment. Dissenters from this point of view, notably Charlotte Perkins Gilman, who advocated the industrialization of the tasks remaining to the housewife as a means of liberating women into capitalist society, had precious little influence on the thinking of the movement as a whole. In the event, the housewife of the twenteith century was to be neither the freed industrial citizen envisaged by Gilman nor the smiling and efficient domestic manager envisaged by the domestic science movement. Rather, as single and married women's economic activity rates rose, her lot was to be the worst of all possible combinations: menial paid worker and housewife combined.

Science, domestic technology and liberation

The relationship between science, technology and housework is complex. The description here is necessarily sketchy – for example, the roles of domestic architecture and urban planning in structuring housework have not been discussed. Nonetheless, it is clear that while some of the character of housework depends on the state of development of technologies inside and outside the home, we have to look to social relations to explain its existence, its content and the quantity undertaken.

If housework was created through an unholy alliance between patriarchy and capitalism, then religion provided the ideological cover-story for ensuring that a woman's right place was seen as the home. Later, the prestige (rather than the content) of science was used to justify keeping her there. One of the heritages of the domestic science movement's uncritical imitation of scientific and industrial methods is a continual search for higher standards in the absence of criteria for knowing when those standards have been reached. The range of domestic technologies devised to ease the increasing burden placed upon the housewife has partly been brought into being by this search for higher standards which the domestic science movement initiated. However, the adoption of the scientific idea of progress involves seeking progress without effective limit: no matter how much the family standard of living rises through increased efficiency and the use of domestic technologies, there is always scope for further improvement. As long as being a wife involves also being a housewife, any spare time and effort created is likely to be devoted only to a further improvement in standards.

The shape and size of household technology developed since the heyday of domestic science in the late nineteenth and early twentieth centuries reinforces the pattern of living in nuclear as opposed to extended families. Alternative shapes and sizes for household technology are not explored, presumably because manufacturers see no market for them. Women are urged to buy all manner of machines which promise to make their lives better and easier. To be sure, no one in her or his right mind would willingly abandon the benefits of vacuum cleaners or any of a good number of other useful domestic innovations. But the ideological clap-trap peddled along with these and other labour-saving techniques for the home is not merely insulting but work creating. Does the fast-food dinner taste good enough for the husband to eat? Are the clothes white enough? Will mother-in-law criticize the inadequate sparkle of the kitchen floor?

We must expect the shape of technologies to be influenced by the social circumstances for which they are designed. As this chapter shows, these circumstances have changed over time, and they continue to do so. Existing designs can constitute a drag on social change. Since the Industrial Revolution our society has built housing, provided infrastructures, manufactured appliances and developed food preservation, transportation and preparation techniques which are primarily appropriate to nuclear families. It would be difficult simply to throw away our housing stock, our appliances and our hard-won knowledge about existing technologies. Equally, it takes a good deal of time to change social attitudes, as the events discussed here themselves make clear. The oppressive social construction of housework continues in many places in our society, from the schools through the advertising media to employment legislation.

Just as housework has been socially constructed, however, so it can also be socially reconstructed. Science and technology can easily be applied in ways which bolster existing power structures, but they can be applied, too, in ways which promote alternative structures. They can be used in this way only as adjuncts to social movements for change. Techniques generally reflect the interests of their designers. Techniques designed by those who dominate in our society are unlikely to reflect the interests of the dominated. Domestic technology, therefore, is unlikely to be liberatory until it is taken up as a weapon by people with an interest in lifestyles other than the nuclear family. It is not only the women's movements which have such an interest: single people, pensioners, gays, working couples, communal households and extended families all work with domestic techniques which are not designed for them and which are often inappropriate. Enlisting science in the redesign of domestic technology is an important challenge which involves contesting one of the most important sites of women's oppression: housework.

8. Kitchen technology and the liberation of women from housework

Philip Bereano, Christine Bose and Erik Arnold

In industrial countries, many household functions have been taken over by the market. People generally assume that much of the work remaining in the home will be eliminated by the application of technology. We have 'fast foods' to save time, 'convenience foods' for ease and 'labour-saving devices' to lighten the workload. Only recently, with the rise of women's, consumer and technology-assessment movements, has research been done to test whether the promises of these technologies have been fulfilled.

The time women spend on housework has not declined very significantly in the last 50 years, despite the increased availability of modern 'conveniences'. Rather, new household technologies have helped maintain the number of hours required for household tasks, causing technological unemployment among women domestics, seamstresses and laundresses.

What we can say here is limited by the patchy nature of the evidence available. We have drawn on information from several fields since no one discipline covers all the issues involved. The stimulus to research provided by the US Bureau of Home Economics and the interest of other US government departments means that we have more detail about technology and housework in the USA than in some other countries. However, there is almost no information on variations across ethnic groups, and few data about different social classes. There has been little examination of single-parent households, people living alone, group houses or gay couples. The focus of technology studies has been the 'ideal' adult man-woman household of the white middle class, usually with children.

The traditional view is that new household technologies add interest to housework and make it more pleasant. Unfortunately, this view does not distinguish between the actual tasks which make up housework and the peculiar, gendered social role of housewife[1]. Housework is decentralized, labour-intensive and occurs on a small scale, so it is inherently inefficient. Housework tasks are basically manual work, and mechanization means only that the worker has to tend machines. Much work in the home is isolated, involves monitoring several activities at once and has many emotional burdens which are not subject to rationalization or mechanization. All this may limit the degree to which technology can ease housework. Modern types of domestic technology tend to reinforce the home system, keeping women economically marginal to the larger society.

Different technologies can affect household work and structures in different ways. How should we, for example, compare plumbing, the vacuum cleaner and the wire whisk? In this chapter, we have categorized household technologies in a way which expands on work by Heidi Hartmann,[2] distinguishing them by their form and capital cost into four major types:

- *utilities* – the infrastructure of the household, such as running water, electricity, gas and sewage;
- *appliances* – machines used in housework;
- *foods* – new forms of packaging, preserving and 'convenience' foods;
- *services* – which can replace household functions, such as fast-food restaurants and nappy (diaper) services.

These provide convenient groupings for use in the following sections, which discuss the spread of domestic technologies during the last century or so, the way in which time spent on housework has changed in that period, the division of labour between household members and, finally, the extent to which it makes sense to see household technologies as liberatory for women.

The spread of domestic technology

Technical change in the home was slow during the nineteenth century. Perhaps the major innovation was the introduction of piped water. Gas ranges appeared in Britain in 1841, but the modern gas cooker was not invented until later in the century. Electricity, which began to be commercially generated and distributed in Britain in 1881, was to have a much greater influence. Initially, electricity was used solely for lighting. The generation and distribution infrastructure was therefore designed for relatively small loads, and this made some early electrical appliances impractical. An electric hot-water geyser built in the 1890s, for example, consumed some 10 kilowatts of power and dimmed the lights for miles around.[3]

The development of small electric motors in the 1890s paved the way for endless quantities of domestic electric machines and gadgets. Electrification, however, took time, and its progress was slowed by fears that the new 'electric fluid' might be a health hazard. The first Hoover patent was taken out in 1908, and marketing of vacuum cleaners followed. Practical electric washing machines were available from 1916. While electric cookers had been available since 1893, domestic refrigerators first appeared in 1913 in Chicago and 1919 in London.

The diffusion of new domestic technologies through society is not instantaneous. The upper and middle classes are usually the first users, with cheaper mass-produced versions trickling down the socio-economic hierarchy later on.[4] Thus, many basic amenities were only partly spread through US society in 1940 (see Table 8.1). Consumer durables spread sooner in the USA than in Europe. In 1951, for example, the USA had some 22.28 refrigerators and

Table 8.1 Trends in labour-saving technology, US homes (per cent)

Facility	1940	1960
Bathtub or shower	61	88
Wood, coal or oil stoves	45	5
Wood or coal for heating	78	16
Electricity	79	99

Source: John P. Robinson and Philip E. Converse, 'Social Change Reflected in Time Use', in Angus Campbell and Philip E. Converse (eds.), *The Human Meaning of Social Change*, New York: Russell Sage Foundation 1972, p. 48.

18.54 washing machines per 100 of population, as against 1.29 refrigerators and 2.18 washing machines in the UK, where levels of ownership were broadly in line with other European countries.[5] Table 8.2 shows the percentage of UK homes owning selected consumer durables between 1965 and 1982, and suggests that only since the late 1960s and 1970s can we assume that many major domestic appliances are in very widespread use in British society. Even then, they are less likely to be owned by working-class and older women. Older working-class women often own older (and therefore less effective) vintages of a particular machine.

The custom of the more affluent buyers of early generations of appliances enabled manufacturers increasingly to mass-manufacture and to reduce prices sufficiently for less-well-off social groups to buy later versions of those machines. However, the continuing presence of servants in affluent homes initially slowed down the adoption of 'labour-saving' machines, since saving servants' labour was rarely a priority of their employers. Besides, the new appliances were very expensive. For example, the first Hoover vacuum cleaners imported into Britain cost £25: the equivalent of a maid's annual wage. The long opening hours of shops and the relative abundance of servants to send shopping made the domestic refrigerator unattractive (though refrigeration was widely used in business), with Frigidaire's 'cheap electric ice box' selling for £60 in 1923.

Table 8.2 UK households owning selected consumer durables (per cent of all UK households)

	1965	1970	1975	1980	1982
Washing machine	56	64	71	77	80
Clothes dryer	19	25	31	38	38
Vacuum cleaner	78	84	90	93	95
Central heating	16	32	49	58	61
Food mixer	8	24	40	47	N/A
Television	87	93	96	97	98

Source: Audits of Great Britain, Home Audit Division, The Research Centre, West Gate, London W5 1UA.

Mass production of refrigerators did not begin until the 1930s. Of all the new electric appliances, the cheap electric iron spread most rapidly, despite the unfortunate fact that a prototype had exploded in 1889, killing its inventor. With the exception of cookers, the more expensive appliances appeared in most homes only during the 1950s and 1960s.

Price competition and the continual search for expanding markets meant that while early models were expensive, appliance manufacturers tended eventually to produce smaller, cheaper devices in the hope of selling one to every household, irrespective of social class. From about 1920, manufacturers and public utilities began to employ women domestic scientists to help in marketing. Christine Frederick, one of the founders of the domestic science movement in the USA, wrote a book in 1929 entitled *Selling Mrs Consumer*, in which she credited the domestic science movement with being the advance guard of the 'appliance revolution'.[6] She was right, in that the combination of home economics with the discovery of germs had provided a rationale both for extending (almost without limit) the amount of housework 'needing' to be done and for finding new methods of tackling this workload. Appliance manufacturers' interest in mass markets coincided exactly with the ideological preoccupations of their domestic science advisors, whose belief that a woman's place is in the home led them to think that appropriate appliances would be designed for the individual woman user, rather than for communal or shared use.

Following the entry of women domestic scientists into the appliance companies, small electric appliances such as mincers and mixers began to appear in the 1920s and 1930s. Manufacturers of large kitchen durables consistently painted them white, leading this category of machines to be known to the trade as 'white goods'. Their whiteness at once promoted the ideas of cleanliness and efficiency and made them difficult to keep visibly clean.

Domestic appliances were promoted not merely as labour-saving devices but as ways to improve standards in the home. The British Electrical Development Association assured the public that electricity made 'Spring Cleanliness Every Day' a possibility,[7] while the Vacuum Cleaner Company stated that:

Your valet or maid can keep all your garments free from dust, and in spotless condition. The dust that blows on them from the street can be removed at once upon your entering the house. Think what this means to you: in greater ease, in more economy, and in better health. Germ infected dust removed from the room forever, and you and your children protected from it. You can imagine how improved your condition will be with your house absolutely clean.[8]

Ideas derived from domestic science combined with the productive possibilities of new appliances were to provide a rationale for rising standards in housework, thus absorbing many of the benefits which women could have gained from new technology if standards had remained more constant.

Housework time

Common sense suggests that the amount of time spent by married women on housework should have declined in the industrial countries, especially since the First World War. During this period, piped water and electricity have reached almost all homes, enabling most social classes to use labour-saving devices in housework. The average number of children per family has fallen, implying that less time strictly needs to be spent in childcare. However, many studies have suggested that housework time has gone up rather than fallen during the first half of the twentieth century (Table 8.3). More recent data from the UK, the USA and Holland show an absolute decline in the average amount of time spent in housework during the 1960s and 1970s.[9] While we need to be rather cautious about relying on individual studies for evidence on time use, the overall impression from these studies is that the average amount of time wives spent in housework rose in the first half of this century and then began to decline slowly.

However, this generalization hides a number of important underlying trends in housework. It involves, for instance, using a contemporary notion of what tasks make up housework and imposing that on data about earlier times. We now tend to think of housework as involving the consumption of goods and the production of services within the home. In earlier times, when more of the population still lived on the land, a good deal of farm

Table 8.3 A comparison of data on housework hours

Study, and country carried out in	Date	Average weekly hours of housework
Rural studies		
Wilson: United States	1929	64
US Bureau of Home Economics: United States	1929	62
Cowles and Dietz: United States	1956	61
Girard and Bastide: France	1959	67
Urban studies		
US Bureau of Home Economics: United States	1929	51
Bryn Mawr: United States		
(i) small city	1945	78
(ii) large city	1945	81
Stoetzel: France	1948	82
Moser: Britain	1950	70
Mass observation: Britain	1951	72
Girard: France	1958	67
Oakley: Britain	1971	77

Source: Ann Oakley, *The Sociology of Housework*, London: Martin Robertson 1974, p. 94.

work involving the production of food for family consumption fell to wives. If we omit this farm work from consideration, we omit significant housework tasks which wives performed.

Joann Vanek[10] analyzed studies of married US women's time use from the 1920s and compared these with research done in the mid-1960s. Many of the 1920s data relate to rural women, while the 1960s data relate to town dwellers, reflecting US urbanization over this period. In 1924, rural women without paid jobs spent about 52 hours per week in housework, while urban women in the 1960s spent 55 hours on the same set of tasks. This stability is, however, apparent only because in defining the same tasks as housework both for the 1920s and the 1960s, some 10 hours of farm work per week were ignored. In 1924, rural households produced about 70 per cent of their own food, while urban households produced on average only about 2 per cent. Urbanization, then, may have reduced the amount of time spent by married women on producing goods but there appears to have been little change in the overall amount of time spent on the tasks we now regard as housework.

On the other hand, the allocation of time between these tasks has changed. For example, the amount of time spent on shopping has increased with urbanization and the subsequent trend towards self-service supermarkets. Supermarkets gain price advantages over small shops partly by transferring the work of collecting goods off shelves from paid shopworkers to unpaid shoppers, and by centralization, which increases shopping journey times. John Robinson and Philip Converse show that housewives' shopping time rose between 1952 and 1967–68 in the USA.[11] There is also evidence that in the UK some of the extra shopping has been done by men.[12]

Many domestic technical innovations represent new and improved versions of pre-existing equipment. Many also involve the ability to provide services inside the household which might formerly have been bought from outside. The classic examples are the washing machine replacing some laundry services and the television replacing certain types of entertainment. In each case, households generally consume more of the final service – clean clothes, entertainment – than before.

The fact that many major domestic appliances diffused into US homes in appreciable numbers only from the 1940s, and into European homes from the 1950s, implies a need to be careful about relating the dates at which they were commercially available to changes in the amount of housework done by wives. Thus, although the refrigerator, for example, was marketed in the late nineteenth and early twentieth centuries, it can have had little impact on total housework time until well after the Second World War. The increases in housework reported in time-use studies took place largely before this time and so appear to relate only indirectly to changes in domestic technology.

There are probably two ways in which this happened. First, the influence of the domestic science movement, domestic science education and other cultural factors such as advertising raised women's standards in housework and probably increased the desire for appliances. Although new appliances may not always have been widespread, they may have had a demonstration effect, leading people to expect higher standards even in homes without the new technology and therefore raising the amount of housework to be done. Second, early versions of new appliances are not necessarily very productive, and they may generate demand for extra services in the home that outweigh any productivity improvements. Competition between manufacturers means that later versions of appliances tend to be more productive, allowing more services to be produced in less time than was originally spent on the old level of provision.[13] This, and the relatively recent widespread ownership of many major appliances, implies that we should expect reductions in housework time only in very recent years – and is consistent with the available time-budget data.

There are, in addition, reasons for the increase in housework time quite unrelated to changes in domestic technology. The loss of servants from middle-class households meant that there was a sizeable group of women whose housework time was rising. Gershuny compared data about housework in the UK from the 1930s with more recent statistics, distinguishing between the amount of time spent in housework by non-employed or part-time employed middle-class and working-class women (Figure 1). The rapidly diminishing importance of domestic service through and after the Second World War implies that middle-class wives' housework load grew between the mid-1930s and about 1960 as they had increasingly to do their own housework. From that time on, time spent in housework tended to decline.

The participation of women, and especially married women, in the paid labour force is probably the factor with the greatest single impact on total housework time. During the first few decades of the century when, according to the time-use studies described above, the amount of time spent doing housework was increasing, married women's employment sank to an all-time low. In the last 50 years, the percentage of women employed in the US has more than doubled. In the UK, the rise has not been as steep for women overall, but married women's work has increased by a factor of more than five. This has led to a reduction in the overall amount of time spent on housework, because employed

Figure 1 Housewives' domestic work hours (non-employed or part-time employed women)

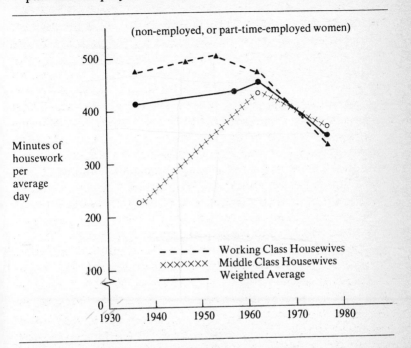

Source: J.I. Gershuny, 'Changing Use of Time in the United Kingdom: 1937–1975, the Self-Service Era', *Studies of Broadcasting*, no. 19, 1983, Nippon Hoso Kyokai, pp. 71–91, p. 81.

women do less housework than non-employed women. Housework time is also strongly influenced by the number of children (especially young children) in the family,[14] although women with young children tend not to have paid employment, especially in countries where the level of childcare provision is particularly low. We will return to these themes later, but first we have to consider the direct effects of specific household technologies and of commonly held assumptions about the benefits brought by the wide spread of domestic technology.

The effects of specific technologies
Utilities probably changed housework more than other technical

improvements because they eliminated several burdensome and time-consuming tasks. Hot and cold running water ended the pumping, carrying and heating of water; electricity and gas eliminated chopping wood, carrying coal and continuous cleaning and stoking of stoves. We have few data for the early part of this century. What we do know is that the transition from rural to urban lifestyles through which industrial societies have passed increased the availability of utility services and therefore the opportunities to use appliances which depend on an electricity, gas or constant water supply. In one study comparing provincial households in Eastern Europe without running water to urban households with not only running water but also other mechanical amenities, there was no significant difference in the total time spent on housework.[15] In 1917, running water saved between one and a half and two hours a day in pumping and heating.[16] Yet another study of the same era suggests that time spent on certain tasks was little different for housewives who had the newer utilities than for those without them.[17]

Although these studies imply that utilities have had no impact on total time spent in housework, we must remember that they were carried out with small samples of farm households. Clearly, utilities did save time and effort on individual tasks which had also been done before their introduction, but the saving on those activities appears to have been passed on to other household activities. Time-budget studies comparing rural and urban time allocations all show an increase in childcare, shopping and management, and a decrease in time spent in meal preparation. The introduction of utilities was a primary force behind this decline in meal-preparation time, but in terms of total time urban women were no closer to liberation from housework than their rural sisters.

The limited data on appliances reveal contradictory effects on housework. Almost the only appliance to have been studied in detail is the dishwasher. Most studies do show a reduction in dishwashing time, although figures vary.[18] A gas stove may save up to half an hour per day over a coal range because there is no need to clean up coal dust or carry it out.[19] In a 1929 study, the combination of modern plumbing, electricity and equipment was found to have saved two hours per day for meal preparation and cleaning up, and 0.7 hours for routine cleaning and care of fires.[20]

(In this context, it is interesting that one study found satisfaction with housework to be unrelated to the number of appliances owned.)[21]

By contrast, there is a small positive correlation between the number of appliances owned and household work time in some middle-class families, suggesting that the proliferation of small appliances has been task-extending rather than task-eliminating.[22] Even the US business magazine *Fortune*[23] has cited the fact that appliances require a great deal of time to take out of storage, assemble, use and clean up. Repair of appliances has become more difficult and mysterious, and many are designed to become obsolescent and so sustain demand.[24]

In examining food technologies – that is, convenience foods – and their effects on easing housework, our assessment must be based primarily on speculation. Most tests of 'starting from scratch' versus convenience foods have not compared shopping, planning and management time, or meal types. On the whole, while convenience foods may save some time, they cost more than home-prepared foods. The US Department of Agriculture found that 64 per cent of the processed foods it studied were priced higher than equivalent amounts of home-made food.[25] In another Department study of 158 convenience foods, only 42 cost less than their fresh or home-prepared counterparts. To the extent that convenience foods require less preparation and fewer ingredients they may save some effort, but they impose different planning, shopping and storage activities, which may require more exertion. The sheer number of choices available at the supermarket, together with the need to serve nutritious, attractive and tasty meals, can make meal planning and cooking time consuming, as is shopping at a centralized shopping centre, transporting the goods home, and storing them.

One could argue that the smaller meals often served today have decreased the time spent in meal preparation. But the larger meals of past eras were made up of similar ingredients, with the same type of food being served (perhaps reheated) at breakfast, dinner and tea. Modern meals involve serving different types of food at different times of day, making three separate periods of meal preparation necessary – and often more if there are children in the family.

Market services allow housework to be done by others outside the home, reaping scale economies which are not available to individual households. Laundry services and home food delivery have declined since the Second World War. But eating out became necessary and acceptable during the war with the mass entry of women into the labour force, and it continues to grow in importance. Supermarkets and the appliance industry, faced with the threat to profits posed by people eating out, have launched massive advertising campaigns, pointing out that it is cheaper to eat at home – if the cook's time is not counted. The existence of male chefs notwithstanding, eating out often shifts food preparation from women in the home to women in paid work: the division of labour in the home may alter, but the sexual division of labour in society remains the same.

A family that eats out spends less time in meal preparation. In the USA, one meal in three is eaten away from home, with some experts predicting that this will rise to one in two in the near future,[26] and fast foods seeing the quickest growth.[27] These trends are mirrored to a lesser extent in other industrialized countries. However, much of the use of market services is related not to their technological convenience but to the increase in women's paid employment and the decrease in average family size.

Rising demands on housewives' time come partly from new standards set by domestic science and partly from new possibilities created by household technologies. Many 'labour-saving' devices really do save labour in housework, but only if used to do the same amount of work as before. In practice, early versions may raise expectations so far as to generate more work than they save. Different types of household technology obviously have varying effects on housework time, but new technologies often bring other factors into play and these must be traded off against any savings in time.

The cost of using newer kitchen technologies is an important factor affecting the amount of time and effort spent in housework. When a housewife does not have paid work it is difficult to ascribe a money value to her time and it makes strictly 'economic' sense for her to work long and hard in order to save small amounts of money, rather than pay more for convenience foods. Households' willingness to spend extra money on time-saving technologies or services partly reflects their valuation of the housewife's own time. As women's participation in the labour force increases, their time becomes scarce and potentially of greater monetary value. Thus time could be counted more heavily in the costs of home food preparation, possibly giving a cost advantage to eating out. However, we must also look at why women take paid work. If women are working as heads of households or to provide a needed second income they may still not be able to afford to eat out.

The household division of labour

The effect of modern domestic technologies on the amount of time spent on housework is negligible compared with the effects of factors such as family size and women's employment rates. Available studies are unanimous in finding that women employed in paid jobs do less housework than women who are not employed. Vanek points out that US employed women spent only 26 hours per week on housework in the 1960s, as against the 55 hours spent by their non-employed sisters.[28] Few US women in either category had servants in the 1960s and, even more importantly, husbands did little to 'help' employed wives with housework other than shopping. Since the gender allocation of housework is little different between households in which the wife is employed and those in which she is not, the finding is not surprising: there are hardly enough hours in the day to do both full-time housework and a paid job. As it is, a women's total number of working hours (in paid labour and unpaid housework) under these conditions is about 60 hours per week in the US.

One conclusion to be drawn from available studies is that housework both expands to fill the time allocated to it and contracts when time is set aside for other things – such as paid work. (Interestingly, television ownership correlates with reduced housework time,[29] and this reinforces this idea.)

Non-employed married women are more likely to have young children, with all the work that they generate, but non-employed women without children still do more housework than their employed sisters, both on weekdays and at weekends. Vanek concludes that the low status of housework relative to the activities (especially paid work) of other family members leads non-employed women to 'make up' by doing more housework and by scheduling some of it at times (such at weekends) when it is visible to other family members. Thus, housework's low status helps explain why men are so reluctant to assume any responsibility for household chores, even when their wives put in the same number of hours as they do outside the home.

Whilst employment clearly reduces the amount of time spent in the home, it is not at all clear that it frees women from housework. Married women do the bulk of household work whether they are also in paid employment or not, so although women's paid employment changes their own use of time it does not alter the household division of labour. (Furthermore, the social division of labour remains largely unchanged: the paid jobs women enter are frequently in the service industries involving tasks akin to housework.) Yet the reasons for women to take paid work are pressingly evident and have little to do with the number of household gadgets they can call on. Even when not driven to work through financial necessity, women prefer paid employment to housework.[30] To be 'just a housewife' is debilitating: fewer working wives suffer from nervousness, insomnia, trembling hands, nightmares, perspiring hands, headaches, dizziness and heart palpitations than non-employed wives.[31] The problem is not confined to middle-class women: this 'housewife syndrome' has also been found among working-class and Native American women.[32]

The ability to purchase household technologies is clearly dependent on the financial means of households. (It is interesting that the primary purchasers of appliances in the US are white households with higher incomes or full-time housewives. Blacks purchase appliances at a slower rate than do whites of the same income level.)[33] Women able to choose whether to try to obtain paid work tend to be in families which can afford to buy more appliances and convenience foods than most. Rather than freeing women for paid work, it may be that domestic technology is most heavily used in households with the most sex-stereotyped division of labour.

Appliances are bought because people believe they save time and because they have symbolic value: if a woman believes that the latest equipment increases the quality of her housework and home life she has a powerful incentive to want a well-equipped home. A man's household domination is reinforced by an ability to provide a comfortable standard of living for his family. Thus the purchase of these appliances is symbolic of patriarchal power.

Husbands in all social classes do little housework. In the USA in the mid-1970s, they spent an average of 1.6 hours a day on all household tasks, irrespective of whether their wives were employed.[34] Household technologies have had little effect on the division of labour between wives and husbands. They have generally been marketed as though designed exclusively for use by the woman of the household, although there have been some changes of emphasis in recent years. Convenience foods, for example, are often claimed to be a 'role equalizer' for the household cook – partly because they save time and partly because they offer a solution to the man who needs or wants to cook but thinks that he cannot. In general, however, the sex-based allocation of household work does not change as a result of technological change, and time and effort saved are seen as becoming available for other family needs.

Some household appliances may in fact be used as substitutes for a more equal allocation of household labour or can mean that women take over tasks previously done by other family members. For example, in families with garbage disposal units, wives are more likely to dispose of garbage than in those without. Lugging a large garbage can around is generally seen as a male task, because men are socially expected to be big and strong and women to be small and weak. Since garbage disposal units allow rubbish to be got rid of piece by piece, much of the heavy carrying work disappears, and with it the social rationale for male involvement. There is a similar pattern with dishwashers, where the loss of much of the traditional form of washing-up involves removing tasks which some households regard as 'male' and replacing them with a new type of 'female' work.[35]

The tendency for men to do slightly more housework in recent years has had little impact on wives' housework time. Where men do housework, they usually do non-routine tasks (such as repairs), while women do the more routine cooking and cleaning. Women spend much more time in these routine housework tasks than men do in the non-routine ones. Jonathan Gershuny[36] has used time-budget survey data about household tasks from a sample of couples to create an index showing the extent to which women or men dominate the use of particular machines. Figure 2 shows his

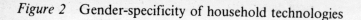

Figure 2   Gender-specificity of household technologies

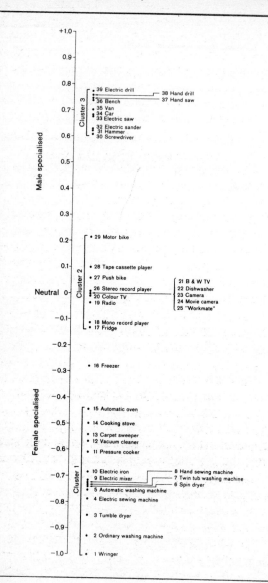

Source: J.I. Gershuny, 'Household Tasks and the Use of Time', in Sandra Wallman and associates, *Living in South London*, London: Gower 1982.

results, with three distinct clusters of technology: one in which men dominate; one in which women dominate, and one relatively neutral cluster. In most cases, the more nominally 'high-tech' a device is, the more male-dominated is its use. So motorbikes are more male-dominated than pedal cycles; stereos more than mono record players; automatic washing machines more than twin-tubs. To the extent that non-routine work is intrinsically more satisfying than routine work, and high-tech machines are more interesting, (though not necessarily more difficult) to use than low-tech ones, then male involvement in housework tends to lead to the appropriation of the more interesting and rewarding tasks.

Historically, services probably had the greatest potential for redefining the household division of labour. By 1900, households in the industrialized countries were becoming smaller, with the extended family, boarding and employment of servants all declining. This meant that there was potential for reducing housework by bringing household functions into paid work outside the home. In practice, the idea that a woman's place is in the home was reinforced by the activities of the domestic science movements, which sought to raise both the status and the standards of housework. As a result, housework stayed largely in the home, with technology brought in to help wives take over tasks previously done by other family members and servants.

Technology and liberation

Conventional wisdom holds that household technologies lead to an increase in women's paid work. Even if it were the case that technology had reduced housework to a nub of undemanding tasks, and even if it were the technology which had caused women to (re) enter the labour force in large numbers, the technology would not itself have removed the assumption that it is women who should do the remaining housework. The reasons for this lie in the realm of social relations, not in the realm of technology. The low status of housework has already been mentioned, but this is only a reflection of the marital power relation which, reinforced by expectations about what is 'normal', keeps a wife tied up with housework and discourages her husband from sharing in these tasks. Men benefit from the assumption that housework is women's work – both materially, in the personal servicing they receive, and psychologically, in the assurance of masculine authority which their very distance from housework grants them.

The form taken by developments in domestic technology in our society fits in well with the nuclear family but is poorly adapted to other lifestyles. For example, convenience-food packet sizes are frequently oriented to small families. Appliances are engineered to a price which can be paid by a single family. Their robustness is limited by the need to manufacture relatively cheap goods for relatively mass markets and the amount of use their designers expect them to have in isolated households. The actual techniques which are produced on the basis of domestic technological knowledge therefore reflect the interests both of husbands in the nuclear family system and of industrialists who need large markets.

The prime gains achieved through the application of technology in the home do not appear to have gone to women. While technologies may have decreased the physical effort of housework, they have not significantly reduced the time or the psychological burden involved, changed the household division of labour or released women to enter the paid labour force. Rather, they have allowed housework standards to rise, providing household members with a higher standard of living in return for an expenditure of the housewife's time which is substantially unchanged. Purchasers may believe that appliances and foods do save time, effort or cost. Often, they are purchased for symbolic reasons as well. But the largest impacts on housework have come from non-technical changes, such as reductions in household size.

Nonetheless, household technology could help widen women's options and improve women's position in the sexual division of labour. Since basic household maintenance need not require full-time work, it is possible for people to live alone or in alternatives to the nuclear family. Housework could be eased through the shared work of collective living with a non-stereotyped division of labour. Reductions in housework could also occur because of smaller family size, lower cleanliness standards or women's adoption of other roles, such as that of paid employee outside the home. Since consumption and childcare are now major housework tasks, community or home-based childcare centres and the decentralization of shops would help alleviate this responsibility. Neighbourhood houses could supervise children after school; work could be restructured through shorter or flexible working hours to allow parental responsibility for all, and housing could be redesigned to facilitate family forms other than the nuclear one.

Some work currently done in the home could be replaced by equivalent services such as domestic help, fast-food services and laundries or communally provided services outside the home, such as the group cooking proposed over 80 years ago by Charlotte Perkins Gilman.[37] Public or market services have the potential to replace home food production and other work, lightening women's burden in the home. However, if women take over the resulting new service-sector jobs, the sexual division of labour in society itself would remain intact.

Social change and political intervention is therefore needed to challenge the 'naturalness' of the nuclear family and the housewife role. We cannot rely on technology to liberate women.

conclusion

9. The Green Revolution and women's work in the Third World[1]

Ann Whitehead

The work done by Third World women is enormously varied. A pauperized Bangladeshi woman who does not want to work in public enters the homesteads of her secluded and slightly more affluent neighbours to husk rice with the dheki – a modified, foot-operated pestle and mortar – in return for meals and clothing. Young Senegalese matrons leave their children with the older kinswomen of their homesteads to travel by truck to the local multinational company factory to pack peppers and strawberries. These are then airlifted to the European market while the women are cooking and serving their husbands' evening meals. Daughters of poor Indonesian peasants leave home well before daybreak to trek many miles to the farms of the richer peasants. There they spray growing paddy with carefully calculated amounts of chemical weedkiller in return for pitifully small incomes which shore up their families' survival. Gambian wives, who weed and cultivate their food farms in the morning, refuse to weed their husbands' irrigated rice farms in the afternoon without pay, preferring instead to earn a direct income by weeding the rice of unrelated and richer farmers in the community. The list of farming and family circumstances, of techniques and tools, of crops and activities and of forms of reward for Third World women is endless.[2]

Despite such bewildering variety, these women workers have many things in common. Their work is undertaken within an organized sexual division of labour, implying economic interdependence between women and men. The division of labour varies in flexibility, but invariably the result is a sexual hierarchy in which men exert power over women. The specific nature of the sexual division of labour in any one case depends on the wider cultural forms of female-male relations and on the way the rural economy is organized. The relative social power of women and men is influenced by the links they have with each other within marriage and the family. In so far as these links are related to work and production or involve ways of sharing out income within the family, what connects the prevailing economic conditions with female-male relations is the organization of household and family life.

In fact, economic conditions in rural societies in the Third World are changing fundamentally as a result of processes euphemistically known as 'development'. Technological change plays a major part in this economic transformation, both at the level of the work involved in production processes and at the level of the products made. This amounts to the transfer or imposition of technologies developed in the First (industrialized) World, and it has begun to change the sexual division of labour in the Third World. Where new forms of work organization have emerged, male power over women is generally maintained and sometimes increased, although it may take new forms.

This transformation and its effects on the work of rural women in the Third World are the subject of this chapter. Although social and economic circumstances do vary, the chapter is organized according to very broad themes, with detailed examples used to illustrate some of the generalizations made. I discuss first the general character of the rural economy in the Third World, the nature of 'development' and the role of technical change in it. The second section considers the example of the Green Revolution: a major group of agricultural techniques introduced into many Third World countries during the last 20 years. This example sheds light on the differential effects of technical change on women and men, and thus on the sexual hierarchy, which are discussed in the remaining three sections. These look at the changing division of labour in the rural household and the impact of the Green Revolution on both the unremunerated work women perform as 'family' labour and the entry of women into paid work.

Technical change and underdevelopment
The rural economies of the Third World are all changing as a consequence of processes which are variously called development, underdevelopment, or distorted or peripheral development. These

processes have gone on side by side with the historical development of industrial capitalism in the economies and societies that we call the First World. Non-industrial economies in the Third World have not been able to escape the influence of the capitalist First World economies. Rather, they have been brought forcibly into contact with them in such a way that wealth is extracted from them and channelled into the more industrialized countries. Although people argue about the most illuminating way to describe the links between international capitalism and Third World countries, and the implications of capitalism for the form of economies in the Third World, the basic character of these links is clear. Whereas pre-capitalist production is primarily undertaken by people who themselves use what they make, capitalist production is primarily for profit via exchange through the medium of money. Non-capitalist production in the rural Third World has come to provide capitalists with an opportunity to transform production for use into production for exchange, thereby opening up the possibility of making profit from the production that takes place. The implication of this for Third World communities is that instead of producing to meet their own needs, they produce objects in such a way that wealth is created and then taken away from those who have laboured to produce it.

The drive to transform the purpose of economic activity in the Third World is masked by the elaborately developed language, with its own codes and symbols that makes up the repertoire of those who speak approvingly of 'development'. Some of the most powerful of these codes and symbols use women and children to convey their messages. The starving elderly woman with her staff and begging bowl; the desperate mother cradling the pot-bellied child; the woman scratching the stony earth with a clumsy hoe – all these images communicate the idea that development rescues the weak and the powerless from rural impoverishment.

For the proponents of development, the key problem of the rural economies is seen as that of raising their low productivity. The need for higher productivity is normally inferred from the fact that the cash economy is poorly developed. The weakness of the cash economy is taken to imply that little is produced and that no surplus is generated for investment. As a result, the subsistence farmer is seen not as producing most of life's necessities within the household, but as someone who has only barely enough for survival. Sometimes the activities of people in the cash economies of the rural Third World are also deemed too unproductive, and their techniques and skills too poorly developed. Whatever the perspective taken, however, technological change has come to be seen as a critical element in raising rural productivity.

Rural development packages always involve an element of technical change in the farming system, if only to increase the amount of raw product which is turned into cash. (Cash, of course, provides the link with the international monetary system.) Thus, in much the same way that the development of advanced capitalism was accompanied by changes in social relations and in techniques, the development of the peripheral capitalism characteristic of 'underdeveloped' countries is also accompanied by technological and social changes. We meet these changes most often under the label of commercialization – that is, as the creation or development of a market for land and labour where none existed before and which occurs as an outgrowth of the simultaneous developing market in agricultural products. Importantly, in addition to affecting the relation of some rural people to their resource base and to each other, technological change also affects women's and men's rural resources and their relation to each other.

In fact, the need for technological changes in Third World countries, in order to raise productivity and cope with the poor and starving, is itself created by the development process; that is, it is created by economic contact with industrial capitalism. The massive poverty and malnutrition of the contemporary Third World is not a product of the intrinsic inefficiency of the pre-capitalist farming economy. Although this economy is not necessarily one of abundance, there is much evidence to suggest that the problem of, for example, inadequate food supply, is a created one.

Pre-capitalist societies often occupied land at levels of population density that could be adequately sustained with existing techniques and levels of trade and exchange. Numerous political, social and economic means were developed to cope with environmental vicissitudes.[3] The use of rural areas by distant capitalists as sources of raw materials or products or of migrant labour, and the resulting dominance of capitalist relations over non-capitalist ones, changed the purpose of rural production. Famine, disaster and impoverishment came with the consequent disruption of the ratio between people and land, and the upset in the previous balances between ecology, techniques and knowledge. The integration of the pre-capitalist rural economy into the world market, therefore, tended to undermine its stability. It was this instability which led to famine on a wide scale. The pre-capitalist economies became incapable of maintaining their levels of productivity and could not retain as much of what they did produce for their own use. The need for technological intervention to raise levels of productivity is thus a consequence of the link with international capital and not of the absence of such a link.

This understanding must be the starting point for our analysis of the character of technological intervention. Far from being a benign handmaiden of the wise physician, as much of the terminology of development would suggest, technological change in Third World societies is more about the health and well-being of the First World. The transfer of technology creates dependency in which the Third World needs constantly to purchase inputs (often in the form of technology embodied in machines or specialized raw materials) which are manufactured in the First World, and in which the Third World comes to rely on First World markets for its agricultural products as a source of cash. As a result not only technology, but also social relations are transferred to the rural Third World when new techniques are imported.[4] These social relations are, as the example of the Green Revolution illustrates, both capitalist and patriarchal in nature.

The Green Revolution

The 1960s was the decade of the Green Revolution to transform Third World agriculture. Many proponents of development, in both the First and the Third Worlds, were enthusiastic about the Green Revolution. It was seen as providing a 'technological fix' for the problems of malnourishment in the greater part of the world. The essence of Green Revolution technology was the introduction of new hybrid strains of rice, wheat and maize, which had been bred for higher yields – so-called high-yielding varieties (HYVs). These 'miracle' seeds were promoted on a massive scale in Asia and Latin America. They were expected if not completely to solve the problems of feeding the rural and urban populations of these continents, then at least to make substantial inroads into them. An important aspect of the HYV packages was that they were considered a scale neutral innovation – that is, they were expected to benefit small and large enterprises equally. Third World countries were encouraged to promote the new seeds because they could be sold in small quantities. The gains to be had from growing the higher-yielding varieties should have been accessible to all those willing to experiment with them. Richer farmers, who have an advantage in larger-scale technological packages such as mechanization which are more costly, should not have benefitted disproportionately. Another selling point of the new seeds was that because they did not require large-scale mechanization they should have created work and employment in rural areas rather than displace labour.

Despite these characteristics, however, the new technology brought very serious (if unintended) consequences. Third World farmers took up the packages, which were largely offered in state-backed schemes, and yields of cereal were increased. But the pattern of adoption was very uneven and the effects on income and consumption were markedly unequal. By and large, cultivators with small acreages failed to innovate successfully, while the large and middle-sized farmers who took up the new technology became increasingly prosperous. Moreover, the success of the new technology for some farmers accelerated the transformation of the agricultural economy into a more commercial form.[5] In the event, the supposedly scale-neutral innovation of HYVs was accompanied by the enriching of some sectors of the rural population and the increasing poverty of others. Using the large surpluses of grain built up through the use of the new technology the larger farmers were able to purchase land from small farmers, especially those in debt. These smaller farmers swelled the ranks of the landless rural labourers.

Investigations have since shown why and how the HYVs were not, in practice, scale neutral.[6] Optimum conditions for the new varieties required inputs additional to the seeds themselves. They needed fertilizer, other chemicals such as weedkillers, and a flexible, controlled and reliable water supply. To purchase these other inputs, individual farmers had to have a source of cash. This could be income from selling farm surplus or through additional cash earnings, but cultivators who were not already producing some surplus or had no other income could not begin to experiment. The problem was further complicated because successful HYV innovation required that certain key areas of infrastructure – especially roads, irrigation schemes and sources of credit – be developed in the countryside. In most places these were provided by the state. The new seed programmes were accompanied by extensive irrigation schemes, the widespread provision of credit facilities, extension programmes to distribute fertilizer and other chemicals and marketing facilities which often included a system of guaranteed prices. However, the farmers who were the clients of these public policies often came from markedly different agrarian classes, and this affected their ability to profit from the new technology in a large number of ways.

The reason for this is that there are considerable economies of scale associated with these various other inputs required in order to benefit from the Green Revolution. In other words, the larger the original farming enterprise, the cheaper – relatively – are the total costs of production. Thus, for example, the unit cost of water supplied by irrigation to small farmers is often higher than it is to large farmers. The cost of credit varies considerably according to its source, with middle and large farmers (who have more collateral) being able to get the cheapest state-aided forms of credit and the poorer rural dwellers having to rely on the local money lender, who invariably charges higher rates. There are also economies of scale in the management of the new inputs. Thus, although both the larger and the smaller farmer have to spend a day in town to arrange the sale of produce, get a loan, to collect fertilizer and so on, the larger farmer will eventually have more produce to sell than the smaller farmer in return for this 'wasted' time spent away from the fields. Smaller farmers tend also to lack the education, bureaucratic skills and social and political contacts which oil the social wheels essential to implementing technical change efficiently.[7] All these factors affect the profitability of innovation.

The introduction of new techniques occurs as a result of the individual investment decisions of farmers. Their decisions are made on the basis of perceived benefits, which revolve around increased profits or surplus. Whether through a system of guaranteed prices or through market mechanisms, the price received for the extra cereal produced tends to reflect the average cost of its production. The fact that these costs tend to be lower for the larger farmers gives them larger unit profits. With higher unit costs, small and marginal cultivators cannot derive the same level of profitability and their attempts to innovate may fail. Thus, having been 'sold' as a package suited to the technology and resource levels of a substantial majority of the peasants of Latin America and Asia, the Green Revolution instead enriched the rural élite.

Although this was partly a result of the nature and scale of the implementation of Green Revolution technology, it also happened because the profit motive set other processes in train. The initial large-scale investments of the rural élite led to profits which were ploughed into land accumulation. Those who were dispossessed were often those who had got into debt in an attempt to use the new techniques on small plots. Higher levels of cereal production were achieved, but the work that could have been provided for the growing army of those squeezed off their land disappeared as mechanized technology for land preparation and other tasks emerged as a further type of profitable investment. Indeed, this was another major unplanned change: the opening up of opportunities for mechanization, which spread wherever the new HYV technology became established.

Technical change and gender
The example of the Green Revolution indicates some of the general problems of rural technological innovation in Third World agriculture. It is also one of the few situations to have been sufficiently well researched for us to generalize about what happens to women in these circumstances. It illustrates the ways in which the institutional basis of technological change, and the processes set in train by innovation, interact with and influence the structure of rural female-male relations in such a way as to continue, yet transform, women's subordination.

It must be said immediately that few women in Green Revolution areas are in a position to be innovative farmers in their own right. A proportion will be heads of households and farm their own land, but all the cards which are stacked against small male farmers are doubly stacked against them. In general, their acreages are small, they themselves are poor and often illiterate, any credit they obtain is expensive, contacts are impossible to make and unconventional behaviour is quickly and often cruelly dealt with by neighbours. By and large, women farm as members of households – as wives, daughters, sisters, mothers, and so on. In those rural households which have profited from the new technology women have generally shared in the gains. However, they are unlikely to have gained as much as the men.[8] Further, access to increased material resources is likely to have been gained at the expense of some personal freedom. Where religious and cultural precepts sanction women's physical seclusion in the home and attach shame to their being seen by men to whom they are not related, purdah or purdah-like restrictions are often used as a critical mark of increased affluence. Even outside these particular belief systems, high status is symbolized by restrictions on behaviour for many Third World (as for many First World) women.

Prior to International Women's Year in 1975 – a year which saw unprecedented worldwide discussion about what was happening to women – there was an almost universal belief that the processes of development were sex blind or gender neutral in effect: that there is nothing inherent in economic and technical change which could alter the balance of advantage and disadvantage between women and men. As part of this prevailing view, rural dwellers were treated by planners as family and household units and not as individuals, female or male. (Women's development issues were confined to questions of infant mortality, maternal health care and the provision of birth control.) Of all the areas of development policy, the one in which the failure to distinguish the gender of farmers or the rural workforce is most marked is that concerned with technological change. The implication is that technological change is emphatically not about social categories and social relations; that since it is defined by the objective and concrete world, technology cannot distinguish whether the wielders of hoe or chemical pump, the drivers of bullock plough or tractor, are female or male. Countless pauperized and overburdened Third World women bear witness to the falsity of this proposition. In order better to understand why innovations like the Green Revolution are not gender neutral we must first look more directly at the agricultural system.

A crop cycle is often an annual affair. It involves many different activities, which may be highly dependent on one another, so that individual crops must fit into a pattern where different crops or forms of husbandry are maintained simultaneously. Superimposed on the technical division of labour is a sexual division which allocates female and male labour to certain tasks within crop cycles (and farming sectors) in a stereotyped fashion. One of the most critical characteristics of technological change is that it does not intervene simultaneously in all parts of the labour process, all parts of the crop cycle or all aspects of the farming system. Typically, technological change alters the technical division of labour, creating new forms of interdependence and changing the pace and volume of work at different points in the annual cycle. As a result, in technological revolutions the sexual division of labour in agricultural work tends to evolve out of previous forms of sexual division rather than being completely changed. Some, but not all, of what is happening to rural women as a consequence of technological innovation derives from the way in which these changes work through the sexual division of labour.

Several researchers have examined both the farming processes by which HYV-increased yields are produced, processed and marketed and the effects these have had on work burdens, employment and income; Palmer is one of the few, however, who has taken into account the sexual division of labour.[9] She finds that increased yields affect all points of the crop cycle and so have a potentially work-augmenting effect on both women's and men's work. Extra efforts are required from men in more careful and frequent land preparation and in the harvesting of a thicker crop, and from women in the great increase in transplanting and weeding work, in applying chemicals, and in the harvesting and processing necessary to get the bigger crop ready for market or for their own use. However, the work-augmenting effects of the bigger yields are somewhat offset by the tendency to mechanize certain parts of the crop cycle. The most frequently mechanized tasks are land preparation (male), harvesting (female and male) and some processing (female). Once mechanized, these tasks become male areas of work whatever the initial gender designation of the task. For example, rice milling employing male labour is replacing the hand pounding done by women on a wide scale in Sri Lanka, Southern India, Bangladesh and Java. Overall, the effects of the

Green Revolution on women's work are contradictory, with both increased work burdens and loss of work occurring side by side.

The ways in which specific women experience these contradictory effects appear to depend on the social relations within which they perform their tasks in the sexual division of labour. Much of the work that both women and men do is as members of household production units. This activity is 'non-productive' in that it is not paid and includes tasks such as house repairs, cooking and childcare. According to conventional wisdom the (male) household head is the farmer, and his wife, children and other dependants work as 'family labour' under his direction. Indeed, the availability of this extra family labour to the male farmer is often assumed in development planning, and in cases where it is not customary it may be actively promoted. It is important to remember, however, that women everywhere bear an especially heavy burden of the domestic and reproductive work which comprises family labour.

In addition to this unpaid household work, tasks within the sexual division of labour may be undertaken for wages. These tasks may differ widely in skill, productivity, rewards and security of employment. Although rural production systems differ markedly in the amount and type of wage labour within them, the casual wage labour that women of the landless classes undertake in the hard and seasonally peaked harvest and post-harvest tasks is a significant, but often largely invisible and neglected, category.

In practice, both types of female work – family labour and casual wage labour – are socially and politically invisible. Both the productive contribution that farming wives make to the farming enterprise and the income contribution that landless women make to the household budget are hardly recognized – by researchers, policy makers, agents of aid and development, and male peasants alike. What is happening generally to women in situations like the Green Revolution is that their work burdens have intensified in the area of family labour, whilst in the area of wage labour, although in some cases employment may have been created and work intensified, there is also an opposing trend. Opportunities for casual income (which, although small, is nevertheless vital to the annual maintenance of the household) are decreasing or disappearing. The social relations obtaining in each of these two areas is discussed in turn.

Women as family labour

The inescapable conclusion is that the major factor affecting women's increasing work burdens within family labour is the ability of the male household head to allocate increased work disproportionately to them. In this he is often helped by the fact that the sexual division of labour is not simply a practical matter of how tasks are divided: it also underpins a gender ideology – or, more specifically, the set of often firmly held beliefs about the kinds of work which should be done by women and men and which, in some fundamental way, are associated with notions of femininity and masculinity. These beliefs can and do change, but their relative inelasticity means that the women's intensity of effort can easily be increased quite a lot without this resulting in a changed allocation of tasks. The fact that women bear more of the burden of increased work on a day-to-day basis illustrates the point that the interests of the household and those of individual family members do not necessarily coincide: marriage itself can be a labour relation which contains the potential for exploitation.

It is perhaps not surprising, in this context, that it is the cultivation work such as sowing and weeding, most often done by unpaid female family labour, which is generally not mechanized. The cost to the farmer of this work is an annual overhead, namely the cost of the 'upkeep' of the female members of his household. This annual cost cannot be saved by mechanization, although if the women's work burdens were reduced this might (in principle) free them for more productive or income-generating work. By contrast, the purchase and use of mechanical substitutes for the tasks already done by casual *hired* labour may well cut the farmer's monetary costs quite markedly. Of course, this does not wholly explain why husking and processing are more often mechanized than sowing and weeding. The range of technical possibilities must also be important, as is the fact that mechanical processing creates a more uniform product which is more acceptable in markets (some of which are western). Mechanized processing is also more amenable to state control than is processing in the homestead.

The capacity of husbands to get more work out of wives who are their family labourers is affected by one of the common characteristics of HYV packages. The way in which the link is made between the farming enterprise (the household) and the outside institutions delivering the inputs for new technology often immeasurably strengthens the dominant position of the male household head. Monetization – relying on money, rather than simple barter – itself implies greater links with the market and with credit agencies in which, as one author argues, 'prominence is given to the male head of household as the selling agent of the domestic unit. The male takes on a stronger patriarchal and entrepreneurial role as the custodian of family labour and cash earnings.'[10]

I have already mentioned the tendency for development projects to be constructed on the assumption that it is the male and husband who runs the farming enterprise, owns the farming resources and controls the disposition of the product. These projects typically treat this male household member as its representative and give titles to land and credit to him, as well as assuming that the crops produced belong to him. Such practices reflect an extremely ethnocentric view of the relations between women and men in marriage – one which is 'lifted' from European norms and imposed upon direct producer households in the Third World. Globally, rural production systems differ considerably in the extent to which wife and husband are seen as a single economic unit sharing productive resources and co-operatively meeting their needs. In many areas of Africa, for example, husbands and wives do not share a common purse, nor do they meet individual and family needs out of a main domestic fund.

Although ethnocentric, the stance of development projects nevertheless captures an important truth about economic relations within marriage and the family. The conventions which govern economic actions within them are not those of the market place; they are ones to which a different ideology attaches. This means that access to the products of the work that household members do is not seen to be a direct reward for the work itself. Instead, families tend to allocate resources (such as food) on the basis of some idea about relative needs. Unfortunately, conventional ideas about needs are linked to sex and age, and inequalities in access to resources within families often stem from the way in which the relative power of different members is filtered through these ideas about needs. So it could be argued that the problem is not that rural women are working harder as a result of technical change but that the benefits of their greater effort do not accrue to them directly because they do not have sufficient purchase on the political and ideological processes which determine distribution within marriage and the family.

Women's work as paid labour

In the farming systems under consideration, female casual paid labour (as opposed to unpaid family labour) tends to be in harvesting and post-harvest processing, and it is here that there has been a tendency to mechanize. A good example is the widespread and growing replacement of a modified traditional technique for husking paddy in Bangladesh using a dheki with a diesel-powered custom huller. The dheki was used by female family labour in middle-income households, and by landless poor women who went to the homesteads of richer women in order to work under conditions of seclusion. The new custom huller employs a male driver, and sometimes another male helper, and is estimated to be some 300 times more productive than the dheki on an hour-by-hour basis. This difference is reflected in the much larger payments that men receive for operating the mechanized technique compared to the incomes that poor women derived from using the dheki. It is possible for the farmer to cut costs markedly by switching from hiring casual female labour to using the mechanized mill. Not surprisingly, therefore, in those regions of Bangladesh in which HYV innovation has been most successful, with consequent increases in rice yields, there has been a massive displacement of female paid labour.[11]

This particular technological story is in fact very complex. Some households process paddy using entirely (unpaid) family labour. For women of these households, the custom huller marks a reduction in the time taken for a back-breaking and lengthy task. They have undoubtedly benefitted as a result, although it should be noted that their workloads have risen in other tasks. In some areas of successful innovation it is reported that men are taking additional wives, who provide the extra labour for the increased agricultural work at other parts of the crop cycle.[12] For landless women, on the other hand, the same technique represents the removal of one of the very few sources of income available, and arguably threatens their very existence. Bangladesh rural areas have witnessed an increase in the number of women paupers who are apparently homeless and kinless and must roam around to find some kind of a living. For some landless households, families are splitting apart, with individuals forced to go their own way. Women who can no longer bring in any income and who do not have a role in childcare are probably being abandoned.[13]

This stark example illustrates a fairly general phenomenon in the relation between gender and wage labour. In Third World rural areas, as in First World cities, wage labour itself is characterized by a sexual division of labour, or what may more properly be termed a sexual hierarchy. Where women's and men's jobs are linked together it is very rare for the chain of command and control to run counter to a sexual hierarchy in which women are subordinate to men.[14] In the Senagalese agribusiness factory referred to earlier, for example, the women packers are supervised by male foremen.[15] In the rural Third World there is a pronounced sexual hierarchy in the whole labour market, rather than simply a sexual division of labour.

One of the interesting aspects of women's employment on a global basis is that one can never predict what work women will be doing. Sometimes they do mainly casual, ill-rewarded and technically backward farming tasks; sometimes they have relatively secure jobs involving the use of modern techniques; sometimes changes in agriculture force them into fragmented areas of the informal (or non-money) economy. Women in the Third World are not universally associated with wage labour of a particular kind, so that we can rarely speak of a sexually segregated (or dual) labour market of the kind that exists in advanced industrial society.[16] However, women are nevertheless located in jobs whose major characteristic is that they rank lower in terms of skill, security, techniques and rewards than the available male employment in the same locality. Indeed, I would argue that a key element in determining which of the sexes fills new jobs created by technical change is the wage rate, or relative return to labour. Where employment is created whose returns to labour are higher than those in existing employment or economic activity, then it is done by men, and where employment is created with relatively low wages it is done by women.

The regularity with which sexual hierarchy is reasserted when technological innovation changes the pattern of paid employment in the Third World suggests that very powerful processes are at work. Few have studied at first hand the ways in which this happens, although one researcher was struck by the rapidity with which the jobs introduced by a multinational company into the Senegalese countryside became seen as women's and men's jobs, although not introduced as such, and how rapidly they then became filled by only one sex or the other.[17]

The maintenance of other areas of hierarchy between women and men seems to be fundamental to these processes, and this is especially true of hierarchy within families, marriages and households. In households where both women and men work for wages both may contribute to the family budget, but the effect of the kind of hierarchy described earlier is to place male household members in a more economically powerful position than female ones. This seriously limits the potential political gains accruing to women who enter paid employment. In households whose subsistence comes entirely from waged work, the wife is not subject to the patriarchal authority of her husband in production work as she is in peasant producer households. Some of her economic activities are outside the domestic sphere, and so an important material element in the unequal relation between wife and husband is removed. This gain is offset where the patriarchal character of these family relationships affects the terms on which wife and husband enter the employment markets of the countryside. Since women tend to be squeezed into the more disadvantaged jobs, a new form of hierarchy serves to bolster up these unequal gender relations.

Examples which on the surface appear to run contrary to these generalizations turn out to have special features. The modern technological industries such as electronics in Asia and Latin America are run almost entirely on the wage labour of young women. This could hardly be termed a backward sector, and one might be tempted to agree with management protestations that the workforce is chosen for its 'nimble fingers'. (The work certainly uses and abuses the good eyesight and co-ordination of these women.) However, recent discussions show that it is the women's position in the family which is being exploited.[18] As daughters they are making a contribution to the family budget, but this does not include the maintenance of dependants, so they are paid poor wages. They are already habituated to obedience and male authority and are reputed to be a docile workforce. In some cases, the paternalistic style of management segregates the girls into work in which their reputations can be protected (and freedom curtailed) in deference to their fathers' wishes.

This chapter began by sketching the enormously varied ways in which the work of rural women in the Third World is being affected by new techniques and new kinds of work relations. The countless changes affecting so many women can be generalized in a few pages only because of the strength of the tendencies indicated. Technology transfer can disrupt the sexual division of labour and existing forms of economic interdependence between women and men. This creates conditions in which women and men often find themselves struggling across divided material interests. This chapter has described how these struggles may concern investment decisions in the choice of new crops or techniques especially with regard to where any increased work burdens fall. They also concern how increased rewards are distributed or impoverishment experienced. In short there is a powerful tendency for sexual hierarchies of male dominance to reassert themselves, albeit often in new forms, when technology changes. This male dominance results from two political processes: the movement of technology and the conflict of interest between women and men within the household.

Nevertheless, it should also be said that although it is important to stress that sexual subordination is not eliminated by technological change, there is more to it than this. Women's political struggle to gain greater freedom is affected by the type of work relations they encounter in marriage as well as in society at large. It is impossible to generalize: specific situations provide specific opportunities for women in their struggle. These situations and opportunities involve not only the family but also capitalism, because technology transfer is primarily a capitalist dynamic. The very different effects that development and technology transfer have on women and men in the rural Third World serve to add to the already existing rifts between peasants. If rural communities are rent by conflict between women and men over the costs and benefits of imported technology, it becomes even more difficult for these communities to unite against the wider social ills of capitalism.

10. Microelectronics and the jobs women do

SPRU Women and Technology Studies*

New microelectronics technology affects women's and men's jobs in very different ways. In this chapter, we discuss how the particular jobs women hold and the status attached to such jobs – in terms of pay, security and bargaining power – combine to make them particularly vulnerable to being degraded or destroyed as a result of the introduction of the new technology. We concentrate on the effects of microelectronics on women's paid work in the UK (which is relatively typical of western industrial societies). But women's paid employment does not exist in isolation: it is inextricably linked to women's unpaid work in the household and the community.

While there is a widespread belief that the nuclear family, comprising an employed husband and a non-employed wife who keeps house and minds children full time, is the normal form of family life, it is statistically abnormal. Nonetheless, assumptions about women's household, childcare and community responsibilities – assumptions based on the stereotype of the nuclear family – continue to determine many aspects of their work, both paid and unpaid. Women are concentrated in occupations which reflect their roles as 'housewives', working predominantly in low-status and poorly paid female ghettoes, often at or near the bottom of male-dominated hierarchies. Microelectronics tends to displace

* Charlotte Huggett, Christine Zmroczek, Flis Henwood and Erik Arnold of the Science Policy Research Unit, and Nuala Swords-Isherwood of the Technical Change Centre. This article is based in part on Nuala Swords-Isherwood, Christine Zmroczek and Flis Henwood, 'Technical change and its effect on employment opportunities for women', a paper to Section X of the British Association for the Advancement of Science, Annual Meeting 22–26 August 1983. That paper developed an early version of this chapter, and was subsequently reprinted in Pauline Marstrand (ed.), *New Technology and the Future of Work and Skills*, London: Frances Pinter 1983.

jobs low down in hierarchies and create new, more technical jobs higher up. Until we find ways to change the social forces which tend to confine women to low-status jobs and exclude them from the new, higher-status technical jobs, one important effect of the adoption of microelectronics will be a reduction in women's job opportunities relative to men's.

Women's jobs

In western countries, the likelihood of a woman being in paid employment varies according to her marital status and the number and ages of her children. Women's hours of work and the types of jobs women do are restricted by domestic responsibilities in a way that men's are not. A woman's domestic responsibilities are thought to be more important to her than her paid work, and many women feel torn between responsibilities to their families and their jobs. Careers are for men, families are for women – or so the story goes.

The 'problem' of combining paid work with family responsibilities is still seen largely as a woman's problem or a women's issue, as if men had nothing to do with it. The care of the young, sick and elderly, the provision of goods, clothing and shelter are vitally important tasks which are essential in all societies. There is no objective reason why these tasks should be deemed to be women's work and given the low status that they presently are.

Shelley Coverman has analysed US employment data to show that 'there are important linkages between the familial and economic spheres, whereby sexual inequality in the family division of labour helps perpetuate sexual inequality in the labour market.'[1] The effects of the unequal division of labour between women and men are so large that they outweigh class differences in explaining women's earnings in paid employment. Employers prize and reward employees who put in long hours and who are expected to remain within the same organization for a long period. Household responsibilities and childrearing often preclude women in both these respects. The expectation that women employees will probably give up work in order to have children or if their husbands change jobs leads them to be viewed as unstable workers.

Both women and men who are seen as unstable tend to be discriminated against in more responsible, predominantly male types of jobs.[2] While only some men are seen as unstable, all women are regarded in this way because they are expected to sacrifice their careers to childrearing. Women's perceptions of themselves reflect this expectation. Many single women see themselves as 'pre-married' rather than as single: that is, they plan their careers as if they were to become wives and mothers.[3] In contrast, older women who have never married, and who can be seen as more committed to avoiding the nuclear family stereotype, tend to follow career patterns more similar to men's. Nonetheless, even these women have drastically lower earning potential than their male contemporaries, irrespective of their educational attainments. Men's earnings tend to rise through most of their careers, while women's – on average – flatten out much sooner.[4]

In Britain, most married women and mothers who have jobs work part time. In the absence of adequate arrangements for childcare and domestic work, 'choosing' part time work is – for most women – not a matter of real choice at all. In 1981, 73 per cent of women had paid work. Only 5 per cent of single women worked part time, as against 32 per cent of married women.[5] There is a similar pattern for women with children. In 1980, 61 per cent of all women with children were in paid work, compared with only 30 per cent of women with children under four years. While 62 per cent of women with children aged five to nine had jobs, 42 per cent worked part time.[6]

Part-time work is both a cause and an effect of women's peculiarly exploited position in society. Women's daily work does not finish at the end of the paid working day. The main reason for taking on part-time work is to enable domestic responsibilities to be fitted in around it. As a result, many women working part time are employed in jobs for which they are overqualified. The National Training Survey showed that one part-timer in 25 who has a teaching qualification works in a low-skilled cleaning or catering job, as does one part-timer in 12 who has a nursing qualification, and one in 6 with a clerical qualification.[7] Employers often obtain skilled workers for unskilled rates of pay. In 1978, three-quarters of women working part time earned hourly rates which would qualify full-time workers for supplementary benefit. Few had any entitlement to sick pay, holiday pay or a pension, and 40 per cent were denied meal and tea breaks during work.[8]

Women's predominance in part-time work highlights several widespread myths about women's work. One is that women work for 'pin money' – marginal income to pay for luxuries. Another is that women do not achieve, or to want to achieve, at work in the way men do. A third is that equal opportunities legislation has corrected injustices in the treatment of women in paid work.

The idea that women work only for 'pin money' is inherently middle class and predominantly male. Throughout history, most women have worked. It was really only with the arrival of the factory system of production and later the 'family wage' that some women could choose whether to take paid work. As is still the case, many families were solely dependent on a woman's income. In 1979, over 700,000 single-parent families were headed by women, as against 100,000 headed by men.[9] Again, the Department of Health and Social Security found in 1971 that the number of two-parent families where the father was in full-time employment and which fell below the supplementary benefit threshold would treble if mothers did not also have a job.[10] Eligibility for supplementary benefit is often taken as a measure of poverty. Middle-class women are not immune to financial need: in a survey of women working in 1965, just over two-thirds of manual workers' wives and a little over half non-manual workers' wives said they worked because they needed the money.[11] It has only ever been a small minority of women who do not undertake paid employment for financial reasons.

However, women – like men – work for reasons other than solely to earn money. In one survey undertaken in 1977, three-quarters of employed women said that they would work even if they did not need the money. While women's reported higher absenteeism than men's is often thought to indicate their lack of commitment to work, it is probably more sensible to regard it as a function of the type of jobs that women do: men in low-grade, low-paid and low-skilled work also have high rates of absenteeism.[12] Equally, in the absence of proper childcare facilities, women's responsibilities as mothers sometimes enforce absenteeism. For example, mothers – not fathers – are generally expected to look after sick children.

The Equal Pay Act of 1975, which was introduced to reduce and then abolish differences in pay based on sex, failed to equalize rates of pay and to bring the equality at work that was supposed to follow. In 1961, women's average earnings were less than half those of men. By the 1975 deadline for implementation of the Act women's average earnings had risen to 58 per cent of men's. However, by 1978 this improvement had gone into reverse. The 1978 New Earnings Survey showed an average rise of 13.4 per cent in male manual workers' gross pay, while female manual workers' pay rose only 12.9 per cent. Male non-manual workers' earnings rose 13.9 per cent, while women's rose by only 12 per cent.[13]

The prevailing view of men as breadwinners is a key factor in maintaining women's subordinate position in labour markets. As long as men can bargain for a family wage, women's wage labour will be organized as supplementary and subordinate to men's, irrespective of individual circumstances and of whether the reality of people's lives and needs corresponds to the ideal type of nuclear family which underpins men's superior earning power.

Women's occupations

One important reason why the British equal pay and opportunities legislation of the mid-1970s has had little impact on equalizing women's and men's earnings is that it was based on the principle of equal pay for equal work. Yet women and men do not in general do the same types of jobs. Women's employment has grown enormously since the last world war, but the new jobs involved have largely been in 'female' occupations rather than occupations comprising mostly men.[14]

Table 10.1 shows how women are concentrated in a few occupations, where they constitute the great majority of workers. Almost two million women work in occupations where more than 90 per cent of workers are female: typists, secretaries, maids, nurses, canteen assistants and sewing machinists. The majority of restaurateurs, cooks, kitchen hands, bar staff, office cleaners, hairdressers, launderers, clothing-makers, waiting staff, house-keepers and knitters are also women. These occupations mirror in the paid sphere the unpaid work of women in the home.

In any occupational group, women tend to be over-represented in the jobs with low skills, status and pay, while men are over-

Table 10.1 Women in occupations with 20,000 or more women employees (Excluding occupations with less than 26 per cent women workers)

| | Percentage of employees who were women | | | |
	26–50	51–75	76–90	91
Clerks, cashiers		1,406		
Typists, secretaries, shorthand writers				715
Shop assistants			686	
Maids and related service workers				391
Charwomen, office cleaners			376	
Nurses				352
Primary and secondary school teachers		285		
Canteen assistants, counter hands				272
Sales managers	210			
Hand and machine sewers				206
Packers, labellers		197		
Office machine operators			135	
Hairdressers, manicurists			113	
Cooks		112		
Kitchen hands			93	
Telephone operators			86	
Waitresses		71		
Barmaids		70		
Launderers, dry cleaners			61	
Electrical assemblers			61	
Service workers n.e.c.*	61			
Teachers n.e.c.*	54			
Food processors n.e.c.*	52			
Inspectors (electrical and metal goods)	52			
Clothing makers n.e.c.*		47		
Production process workers	44			
Laboratory assistants and technicians	44			
Cutters, sewers, lasters		42		
Printing workers n.e.c.*	40			
Restaurateurs	38			
Social welfare workers		38		
Tailors, dressmakers		38		
Pressworkers and stampers	32			
Domestic housekeepers				31
Textile workers		29		
Housekeepers, matrons			28	
Bakers, pastry cooks	28			
Paper products makers		26		
Publicans and inn keepers	25			
Winders and reelers			23	
Craftsmen n.e.c.*	23			
Hotel and boarding house managers and proprietors	23			
Workers in plastic	23			
Hospital orderlies	23			
Professional workers n.e.c.*	22			
Knitters		21		
Total in listed occupations	**794**	**2,382**	**1,662**	**1,967**
Per cent of female labour force	**10%**	**29%**	**20%**	**24%**

*n.e.c. Occupations that could not be classified in the more specialized categories of work within each occupational group.

Source: OPCS and GRO(S). *1971 Census, Great Britain, Economic Activity, Part II (10% Sample)*, Table 15. Figures for England and Wales. See *Department of Employment Gazette*, November 1978.

represented in skilled and managerial jobs (Table 10.2). Thus, in textiles, 85 per cent of winders and reelers are women, as against 6.5 per cent of dyers; in warehouses, 72 per cent of packers and labellers are women, but only 16 per cent of 'warehousemen' and storekeepers are female.

This type of segregation of women into job categories at and near the bottom of employment hierarchies, where they receive relatively low status and pay, is present right across the economy. It makes women's jobs peculiarly vulnerable to technical changes which differentially affect jobs involving low skills.

The development of microelectronics

Electronics is specifically concerned with information – the data which form the basis of knowledge – and is used to control various types of productive activities, often by so-called 'control engineers'. It is as suitable for the control or monitoring of people as it is for machinery. Electronics has been the fastest-growing industry this century. In the first part of the century, electronics involved valve ('tube') technology. Its problems of heat production and poor reliability meant that making sophisticated computers would have been virtually impossible. The introduction of transistors improved both reliability and performance but there were still problems with the numerous interconnections between transistors. Further development led to the possibility of sculpting large numbers of electronic devices onto the surface of a thin silicon wafer. The first chips produced in this way in the late 1950s brought together what would earlier have been several components. This bringing together of several components onto one chip of silicon is known as integration, and the circuits produced are called integrated circuits, microelectronics or 'chips'.

The development of integrated circuits from the start of the 1960s reduced the cost of the individual circuit components and made it feasible to build large, complex and reliable systems. Until the 1970s, computers were still expensive and bulky, and they usually needed a protected environment. Through the long period of economic growth after the Second World War they had relatively little impact on employment. It is only since so-called 'large-scale integration' began in the late 1960s, with large circuits being integrated onto single chips, that this technology has become a threat to the number and quality of jobs available. This type of microelectronics can be used where automation was previously too expensive or difficult, such as in clerical work or in repetitive, monotonous tasks in manufacturing like assembly and packing.

This description of electronics technology is necessarily brief. Fuller accounts can be found in books by Forester[15] and Braun and MacDonald.[16] Our purpose here is to show how and why women's employment is particularly susceptible to the effects of microelectronics. This depends crucially on the type of paid work that women do.

New technology and women's jobs

The flexibility of microelectronics makes it hard to think of many areas of our lives which cannot be affected by it. In many cases, the use of microelectronics involves rationalization (using less labour in production), although microelectronics also forms the basis of new products and services. The overall effect of this new technology on employment depends on the balance achieved between new jobs created because of the possibilities microelectronics offer and jobs lost through its use in rationalizing existing types of production. Many people currently expect that this balance will be negative because in recessionary times industrialists tend to be more interested in rationalization than in investing in new production capacity.[17] Whatever the effects on the total number of people in employment, the fact that (even within rationalizing uses of microelectronics) there are job gains as well as job losses means also that there are winners and losers. A look at sectors of industry where women work suggests that it is generally women who are the losers.

Wherever microelectronics is used to rationalize production, women's jobs are affected, either by direct application to the work that women do, or indirectly, as when microelectric controls are added to a production line, reducing the need for clerical data collection and processing. The spin-off effects are not limited to clerical workers: where microelectronics saves labour in production, fewer women are needed in supporting services such as cleaning and catering.

Table 10.2 Sex splits in occupational groups, 1971 (the two occupations listed after each occupation group are those with the lowest and highest proportion of females respectively within the group)

	Number in each group	Women as a % of all employed
Farmers, foresters, fishermen	640,350	14
Fishermen		0.5
Agricultural workers n.e.c.*		24
Miners and quarrymen	229,250	0.2
Coalmine—workers underground		none
Workers below ground n.e.c.*		none
Coalmine—workers above ground		1.1
Gas, coke and chemical makers	125,580	9.0
Furnacemen, coal gas and coke ovens		0.001
Chemical production process workers n.e.c.*		9.5
Glass and ceramics makers	87,450	32
Furnacemen, kilnmen, glass and ceramic		3.9
Ceramics decorators and finishers		76
Furnace, forge, foundry, rolling mill workers	153,040	5.4
Furnacemen-metal		1.2
Fettlers, metal dressers		12
Electrical and electronic workers	559,190	14
Linesmen, cable jointers		1.4
Assemblers (electrical and electronic)		84
*Engineering and allied trade workers n.e.c.**	2,552,750	11
Steel erectors, riggers		0.1
Pressworkers and stampers		50
Woodworkers	377,800	3.1
Carpenters and joiners		0.3
Woodworkers n.e.c.*		14
Leatherworkers	110,000	50
Shoemakers and shoe repairers		3.6
Cutters, lasters, sewers, footwear and related workers		59
Textile workers	266,040	53
Dyers of textiles		6.5
Winders, reelers		85
Clothing workers	370,100	80
Upholsterers and related workers		26
Hand and machine sewers and embroiderers, textile and light leather products		96
Food, drink and tobacco workers	325,630	30
Butchers and meat cutters		6.9
Food processors n.e.c.*		42
Paper and printing workers	287,520	29
Compositors		2.7
Paper products makers		53

*n.e.c. Occupations that could not be classified in the more specialized categories of work within the occupational group.

	Number in each group	Women as a % of all employed
Makers of other products	295,800	35
Workers in rubber		26
Workers in plastic		37
Construction workers	501,860	0.3
Plasterers, cement finishers, terrazzo workers		0.05
Builders (so described), clerk of works		0.6
Painters and decorators	261,300	3.0
Painters, decorators n.e.c.*		2.2
Aerographers, paint sprayers		8.2
Drivers of stationary engines, cranes etc.	278,160	1.3
Boiler firemen		0.1
Stationary engine, materials handling plant operators n.e.c.*, oilers and greasers		2.3
Labourers n.e.c.	1,087,310	11
Railway lengthmen, labourers and unskilled workers n.e.c.*		none
Textiles (not textile goods)		23
Transport and communications workers	1,281,440	11
Drivers, motormen, second men railway engine		none
Telephone operators		84
Warehousemen, storekeepers, packers and bottlers	729,990	37
Warehousemen, storekeepers, assistants		16
Packers, labellers and related workers		72
Clerical workers	3,275,820	70
Office managers n.e.c.*		14
Typists, shorthand writers, secretaries		99
Sales workers	2,032,770	47
Roundsmen (bread, milk, laundry, etc)		7.1
Shop salesmen and assistants		80
Service, sport and recreation workers	2,661,980	69
Fire brigade officers and men		2.5
Maids, valets and related service workers n.e.c.*		96
Administrators and managers	860,920	8.5
Managers in engineering and allied trades		3.0
Personnel managers		31
Professional, technical workers, artists	2,501,460	38
Civil, structural, municipal engineers		0.2
Nurses		91
Armed forces	231,610	4.9
Inadequately described occupations	591,620	57

Source: OPCS and GRO(S), *1971 Census, Great Britain, Economic Activity, Part II (10% Sample)*, Table 15. Figures for England and Wales. See *Department of Employment Gazette*, November 1978.

Clerical work A substantial proportion of the women employed in every sector of the economy do clerical jobs, essentially handling and processing flows of information. The introduction of microelectronics – for example, word processors – into offices undoubtedly benefits some women clerical workers, bringing a chance to learn new skills and eliminating some boring and repetitive tasks (such as retyping and correcting documents). In principle, time savings could be devoted to more interesting work, but in practice many women have found themselves sitting in front of a word-processor screen for hours on end, with no upgrading in terms of either pay or status. It is difficult to see this as an improvement on traditional typing-pool work. The quality and conditions of work can be affected: machine pacing, performance monitoring, eye strain, headaches, backaches and stress have all been cited in recent studies of office work (see chapter 11).

During the 1960s, computers were used to displace women clerks and created new job opportunities – mostly for men – in the data-processing departments which programmed and operated the machines. This had no visible effect on employment because the volume of clerical work available was growing faster than women could be displaced by computers.[18] More recently, increasingly powerful and cheap computers combined with economic recession have probably led the balance to shift in the opposite direction, causing job loss among women clerks but not necessarily in the newer and more technical types of work. For example, one mail-order firm recently reduced its full-time clerical staff from 1,000 to 550 and its part-timers from 100 to 50; a city council reduced typing staff by half (from 44 to 22) while producing 19 per cent more work.[19] Of course, factors other than new technology can and do cause job losses, but it is significant that new technology can allow organizations to do more work without hiring more people, producing so-called 'jobless growth' in output.

Sales and distribution Approximately 1.5 million women work in sales and distribution, mainly in shops and stores. Major changes in the organization and structure of selling, implemented through microelectronics, are expected, both by outside observers and by senior management of the large supermarket chains,[20] and again it is clear that women's jobs are particularly at risk. The most significant threat is electronic Point of Sale and data capture equipment (POS). POS systems are now being installed in shops in the UK, and they are likely to be widely used in the near future by organizations such as Tesco, which plan to invest £90 million in computerized equipment for their stores by 1990.[21] A POS terminal looks very much like a cash register. It may incorporate a scanner which can 'read' bar codes printed on the products by manufacturers, removing the need for someone to key in information about purchases. With bar-coded products, only the shelves or counters need price-marking, and this eliminates the job of pricing each item. The POS terminal adds up purchases in the same way as a cash register, producing a more detailed receipt; it stores information about sales and can often record information about the checkout operator's performance. There has been some resistance to this – women in Danish stores, for instance, refused to work with POS terminals until the monitoring function had been disabled.[22]

When linked to a computer, POS equipment can use the checkout sales data it has captured for automatic stock control and re-ordering. Even small stores which cannot afford a complete POS computer system can use bar coding for automatic stock control. Shelves can be checked by using a portable data acquisition unit to record which items need replacing. The information captured electronically in this way can be transferred directly to a computer at a central warehouse through the telephone network. The potential job loss is huge in the areas of checkout and till operating, restocking, pricing and customer assistance – which has already been substantially reduced in the last 15 years by the spread of self-service stores. The behind-the-scenes clerical work in inventory, stock control, ordering, invoicing, payrolling and the typing and calculation that accompany it are also threatened. All these jobs are mainly done by women.

POS is likely to reinforce the trend towards centralized, self-service shopping by making it even more difficult for small 'corner' shops to compete with supermarkets. As well as reducing employment in these small shops, this trend has already made life more onerous for women as consumers. Shops no longer deliver groceries, and the costs and time involved in travelling to a central supermarket and finding goods have been transferred from the shops to the shoppers. Some new jobs may be created by the predicted boom in mail-order and video shopping, by which customers will be able to order items through a home computer terminal, although it remains to be seen how successful such schemes will be and whether it will be profitable to apply them to cheaper items as well as to expensive consumer durables like washing machines. Women, who usually have the major responsibility for shopping, may be reluctant to make purchases – especially of items like fresh food – without the opportunity to examine them. Since this kind of shopping would largely be at the expense of traditional shops and stores, jobs created here are unlikely to compensate for those lost overall through the introduction of microelectronics in selling.

Banking, insurance, finance Banking, insurance and other financial institutions employ large numbers of women – over 685,000 in September 1982,[23] and the use of microelectronics in these areas is already quite well advanced. In insurance, computerization has largely affected clerical work. In banking, the growth of self service by means of automated telling machines, and the computerization of internal and inter-bank transactions through electronic funds transfer, point to a radical restructuring of banks and the services they offer. It seems likely that the banks will move the 'back office' work to computer centres handling transactions for several local 'satellite' branch banks. These would be increasingly automated, with staff available for non-routine banking or special services such as loans or investment advice.[24] This kind of restructuring particularly affects the clerical and counter-service banking jobs in which women are clustered.

Some of the new banking jobs require specialized skills which, in the present hierarchy of banking employment, are not being acquired by women in any numbers.[25] Much new job creation is in computing, and employees with technical knowledge are often recruited from outside – especially for the higher-level positions. It is more likely to be men who will have these technical skills.

Manufacturing The labour-intensive, repetitive and monotonous tasks usually done by assembly workers are also increasingly prone to automation with microelectronics technology. This has already substantially reduced women's employment in parts of the engineering industry, the major manufacturing employer of women in the UK. The phasing out of electro-mechanical teleprinters and typewriters, for example, and their replacement by new electronic types, eliminated the need to assemble hundreds of mechanical parts, which were largely replaced in the new versions by a small number of chips. The assembly of electronic components into finished products (for example, computers and consumer electronics) is also affected – first, because one microcircuit replaces many discrete components, so reducing the number of parts to be assembled; and second, because of the introduction of specialized robots (automatic insertion machines) to assemble components onto printed circuit boards and the increasing use of other new assembly technologies such as surface mounting and thick film. In television manufacture, many women assembly workers have lost their jobs since the use of microelectronic components reduced the number of components to be assembled into a typical 22-inch colour television from about 1,400 to 400 in the last 10 years.[26] A new generation of digital television components will probably reduce this latter figure by a factor of about 10 over the next few years.

The food, drink and tobacco industry is the second largest employer (after engineering) of women in manufacturing. Here, women's jobs have mostly been in badly paid, labour-intensive tasks such as cooking, cleaning and packing. Microelectronics can reduce the need for workers in all these areas. Indeed, the potential exists for almost completely automated food production in some cases. In one factory the production of 40,000 pies per hour requires only one worker: a woman who feeds the foil dispenser.[27]

The 'caring professions' Education, health and welfare are also very important areas of employment for women. At present, public spending cuts are probably limiting the speed with which microelectronics is introduced. Another constraint is the personal nature of many of these services. In nursing, for example, personal contact with patients is essential. In teaching, one of the main functions is control of students, a task which cannot be easily transferred to a machine.

Teaching is a very sexually segregated occupation. Women

make up 99.1 per cent of infant-school teachers, 77 per cent of primary-school teachers, 44 per cent of secondary-school teachers and 7 per cent of university teachers.[28] In the UK, government schemes have ensured that microcomputers are most widespread in the schools which deal with the youngest age groups and where teachers are overwhelmingly female. To date, available educational software has largely been limited to helping with the rote-learning and practice involved in young children's acquisition of basic skills. Government may well be encouraged to try to increase the pupil-teacher ratio in early education with the aid of such computers, mostly affecting women teachers. With the spread of new technology an increasing number of teachers of technical subjects will be needed at all levels. Unless there are improvements in women's technical education, men with technical skills will continue to have a considerable advantage in the competition for such teaching jobs. (Equally, the continuing lack of women teachers in these technical subjects is one of the factors discouraging girls from taking them up.)

The use of computers for keeping medical and social records – tasks usually done by women – is increasing. Sales of electronic medical equipment are growing and although it is hard to detect an immediate effect on women's employment, nursing is one area in which new technology could improve services. However, given the cuts in public expenditure on health, and the experience of the use of microelectronics in other areas, this seems unlikely.

New jobs, old problems

Overall, the picture looks gloomy for women's employment in the traditional fields, but what of the new opportunities arising through microelectronics? It is important to differentiate between new jobs and the movement of women into areas formerly the preserve of men. Microelectronics increasingly supplies electronic substitutes for craft skills and physical strength, sometimes allowing women to enter traditionally male areas of work. However this is by no means unproblematic, for when women compete with men for jobs the contest is unequal.

Microelectronics creates a demand for types of skill which are not necessarily held by women. The barriers which prevent most women from acquiring technical knowledge at school, combined with other assumptions about skills and domestic responsibilities, result in women being seen as less technically adept and less suitable than men for jobs or training with the new skills. Sometimes discrimination takes a very subtle (or even unconscious) form, such as recruiting trainees from 'people in the factory who have shown mechanical aptitude'[29] when women are unlikely to be employed in areas where there are opportunities to show such aptitude. At other times discrimination is anything but subtle. Comments such as 'we would not recruit a female technologist because her job would require her to supervise males' were typical of personnel officers' attitudes to women in one survey of recruitment methods.[30]

So, microelectronics creates a polarization in which many of the newly created jobs go to men whilst women continue to work in jobs defined as low skilled. But what is skill? It is often defined in terms of formal qualifications or experience, but other factors such as the 'negotiability' of job classifications are equally important. Whether a job is classed as skilled or unskilled may be the result of negotiation between workers and employers, and depends more on their relative power than on the requirements of the particular job. Women's representation in most trades unions is woefully inadequate and union policies overridingly reflect men's interests. Heidi Hartmann argues that men, through their unions, are able to maintain women's inferiority in the labour market by manipulating skill definitions.[31] The assumption that work done by women is low in skill leads unions to fear that employers can redefine the skill levels of tasks if women are allowed to do them. Instead of uniting with women to struggle against this, men use the power of the unions to retain skill definitions and pay rates by uniting against women.

The newspaper industry is a case in point.[32] The introduction of microelectronics has meant that composing, traditionally done by men and requiring a high degree of skill and physical strength, can now be done by means of a keyboard and visual display unit (VDU). But women with keyboarding skills have not been able to move into these jobs in great numbers. Men in the UK print unions have organized effectively to keep women out of 'their' jobs.

These new keyboarding jobs also highlight one of the problems associated with jobs created by microelectronics: they are often temporary, existing only because they involve tasks which are too complex or too expensive to automate at first, but which become obsolete with further technical development. For example, voice-recognition technology, which is presently under development, may eventually reduce the need for keyboarding.

Women are notably absent from the design and development of technology. As a result, technology is designed to suit male expectations and male bodies rather than being appropriate to all people. For example, the size and weight of the formes containing type which are used in the printing industry mean that they are too heavy to be moved by many women, although men working in the industry have little difficulty with them. Women are effectively excluded from certain well-paid printing jobs by the necessity of carrying these formes about. Health and safety considerations can also be inappropriate. Thus, high miscarriage rates have occurred among VDU operators at Sears and Roebuck in Dallas, and at other workplaces in North America. It seems unlikely that male VDU designers even considered the possible effects of VDU work on the foetuses of pregnant women.

The possibilities offered by microelectronics for some people to work at home have led to the idea that electronic homework could be an important source of women's employment. It is imagined that women would thus be able to combine work and domestic responsibilities. Traditionally, homeworkers – almost all of whom are women – are among the most exploited of all workers. They are simultaneously subject to exploitation by their employers and to the insistent demands of their own families. With each woman working alone, isolated in her home, the opportunities for organizing with others to battle for better pay and conditions are limited, as is the chance to make contact with other people. For many women, major reasons for getting a job (however arduous or monotonous) include the separate identity that a job outside the home can bring and the social contacts gained at the workplace.

For a number of years now, some computer programming has been put out as homework by companies like F International. Xerox have encouraged some of their managers to work from home. In general, the types of electronic homeworking suggested as prototypes for the 'electronic cottage' relate to types of work done by the middle and upper socio-economic classes. University staff seem to have a particular enthusiasm for working from home,[33] and they are able to do so because they largely set and monitor their own performance goals. Electronic homework may be a viable and welcome alternative to the office, but such middle-class lifestyles and types of work are simply not available to the majority of women.

Microelectronics and the jobs women do

In this chapter, we have discussed part of the considerable body of evidence about the effects of microelectronics on employment in relation to women's jobs. An earlier and much more detailed review of microelectronics and women's employment in Britain systematically related case material and studies to the parts of the economy in which women tend to work.[34] Table 10.3 summarizes the results of that review, and suggests that the effects of the increasing use of microelectronics are fairly uniform in all industrial sectors, involving a loss of women's jobs. There is a systematic relationship between the adoption of microelectronics, job losses for women who work low in organizational hierarchies and the creation of new, technical jobs which are generally taken up by men.

It is difficult to imagine how microelectronics technology can, in itself, be sexist. On the other hand, we know that the organization of our society is exactly that. Modern industrial capitalism is very dynamic – it involves continuous changes in technologies, markets and employment. Crudely, the further individuals can rise in the hierarchies typical of industrial capitalist society, the more insulated they become from the unpleasant effects of the ebb and flow of industrial fortunes, precisely because rising in these hierarchies involves gaining power over those below. In so far as technology is one of the tools at the disposal of people in these hierarchies, it will necessarily be used by those with power in such a way as to maintain the subordination of those without power. The corollary of this is that new job opportunities will tend to appear at a level higher up the hierarchy than that at which job losses occur, and this is exactly the pattern of change which appears with the adoption of microelectronics technology. The new job opportunities are effectively appropriated by men, through their greater access

Table 10.3 Anticipated effects of microelectronics on women's jobs in Britain

Industry/occupation	% of women's employment	Anticipated employment effects
Engineering – production	4.0	Reduction in assembly and similar work
Food, drink, tobacco – production	2.0	No data
Clothing and footwear – production	2.5	No data
Textiles – production	2.0	Further decline
Paper, printing and publishing – production	1.0	Some reduction probable in paper and paper products. Increase possible in printing and publishing
Chemicals – production	0.5	Some reduction in low-level jobs
Rubber and plastics – production	<0.25	Some reduction probable
Office occupations	36.0	Some reduction probable. Large reductions often forecast, but not yet achieved.
Banking and insurance*	1.0	Stabilising after growth; some decline possible.
Distributive trades*	11.5	Decline
Catering occupations	17.0	No data
Public administration*	1.5	Mostly dependent on public policy. Some evidence of decline.
Professional and scientific services ('caring professions')	14.5	Mostly dependent on public policy.

*Excluding women in office and catering occupations

Source: SPRU Women and Technology Studies, *Microelectronics and Women's Employment in Britain*, Occasional Paper no. 17, Brighton Science Policy Research Unit, 1982.

to technological training and knowledge, thus reinforcing male domination of employment hierarchies.

The type of jobs women do and their position in industrial hierarchies reflect:

- women's relative disadvantages in labour markets because of domestic responsibilities;
- discrimination against women in labour markets;
- the socialization of young women which encourages them to behave as 'pre-married' individuals whose career expectations are limited by anticipated domestic responsibilities;
- the orientation of girls' education away from technical subjects.

In combination, these factors mean that women's labour tends overwhelmingly to be marginal – both in the sense that women are used to fill (often temporary) gaps low in the structure of organizations, and in the sense of their being seen as unimportant.

Discrimination against women at work continues, despite legislative attempts to stamp it out. However we doubt that even the effective removal of discrimination from labour markets would in itself substantially improve women's position. Attaining power in modern organizations involves competition between individuals, and women are severely disadvantaged, as well as discriminated against, in this competitive process. This remains true even when the traditional form of working-class solidarity – trade union organization – is involved. Trades unions, including those whose membership is overwhelmingly female, are also male-dominated hierarchies. They tend to reflect the interests of their men members – often in preference to, and sometimes in opposition to, those of their women members.

The disadvantaged position of women in working life and the peculiar vulnerability of women's work to some of the disadvantages of microelectronics cannot be rectified simply by tinkering with labour-market mechanisms in the style of equal opportunities legislation. This does not tackle the underlying cause of the problem. At best, equal-opportunity laws can allow some individual women who (perhaps for reasons of class) can escape the burdens of domestic responsibility and socialization to compete with men on men's terms. While it is hardly possible to legislate patriarchy away, possibilities exist which would help to shift the balance of advantage in employment away from men a little.

Working women's low wages could be improved through minimum wage legislation designed to equalize rates of pay between 'female' and 'male' occupations, at least at the bottom end of the pay scale. A US-style programme of positive action could be initiated in order to move women out of existing work ghettos. A recent report from the Manpower Services Commission argued that organizations should give women more opportunities through career planning, proper training, informal support networks and more flexible working arrangements. Training for women should include confidence building and assertiveness skills, and for men 'more efficient, sensitive, sympathetic, and co-operative management styles'.[35] Social back-up services – especially in the form of proper childcare facilities – could also be more widely provided. Many of these things should be integrated into government social policy. Most individual companies are unlikely to provide them without compulsion because they would unilaterally raise their costs relative to those of their competitors.

However, policies aimed at improving the material conditions of women's working lives and, therefore, improving women's opportunities in labour markets, need to be accompanied by changes in ideas about women's roles in society. Ideas and expectations themselves contribute powerfully to determining the type of jobs that women do. Making it more possible for women to work in the range and types of jobs available to men will not, of itself, improve matters unless there is a widespread belief that women have a right to do so. More positive efforts can be made to encourage girls to take up technical training and work and to ensure that types of training are provided which are conducive to girls' and women's learning needs: as we saw in chapters 2 and 3, being the token female apprentice in a male-dominated engineering shop can be a very intimidating experience.

We are not concerned here to make romantic pleas for a free choice of meaningful career options for individual middle-class women – though there is no reason why they should be denied such options. Rather, we have tried to identify some of the constraints on women's working lives which are built into the structure of our patriarchal form of capitalism. These constraints result from the deep-rooted sexual division of labour in society and the pervasive, competitive hierarchies of male dominance. Only when we have found effective means of overcoming these constraints will women *en masse* be free from the pernicious effects of a segregated working existence – not the least of which are vulnerability to the impact of technological change and a lack of control over the choice and design of technologies.

11. Word processing: new opportunities for women office workers?

Elena Softley

In the UK, 40 per cent of all employed women are office workers. The proportion is similar in other Western industrialized countries, making office work the largest category of women's employment in these countries. The newer forms of the so-called information technologies – word processing, data processing and telecommunications – promise job losses and organizational changes in this work. In particular, word processing threatens the most female-dominated of all jobs – secretarial and typing work.

It has been argued that technological development is a liberating force for women, increasing employment opportunities and making working conditions both cleaner and safer. Engels, for example, thought that through technological change and greater participation in the labour force, women would overcome their subordination. But when women enter the labour force they are confined to a narrow range of industries, in which they are segregated into low-paid, low-status work with minimal job security and few career prospects. This occupational segregation is particularly evident in the office. According to the 1971 UK census, women comprise 63 per cent of clerks, 83 per cent of telephone operators and 99 per cent of typists, shorthand writers and secretaries, but only 18.5 per cent of managers and administrators and 10 per cent of higher professionals.

The office provides a prime target for the introduction of labour-saving technology because, despite the increased use of machinery in recent years, it remains highly labour intensive. Capital investment per head in offices is about one-tenth of that in manufacturing. Recent estimates cited in the financial press and offered at office automation conferences have tended to suggest that office costs are rising by 12 to 15 per cent per year, faster than any other business cost, and labour costs alone account for over half of this total. Pressures to cut costs therefore force many managers to consider new technology as a way of making savings.

Although secretarial and typing labour represents only a small proportion of office costs, it is in this area that new micro-electronic technology in the form of word processing has its most immediate effect. Word-processing machinery is being advertised as a way of raising office productivity by increased efficiency of typing and reduced labour costs. This chapter examines the introduction of word processing technology and its effects on this important area of women's work.

What is a word processor?

A word processor consists of five components: a keyboard, a display device, archival storage, a printer and a microcomputer. The keyboard is similar to a typewriter keyboard, except that it has a few extra control or instruction keys. When text is typed on the keyboard it appears on the display device, which may be a visual display unit (VDU) – a modified form of television screen – or a single line which shows the last few words that have been typed. Archival storage usually consists of magnetic disks on which standard text, completed work and work in progress may be kept, either as a record or for future revision. The printer produces documents which are indistinguishable from typed ones at up to 55 characters per second – far faster than any human typist. The microcomputer controls the whole machine. Some 'shared logic' word processors share a single micro- or minicomputer between several keyboards instead of having a microcomputer for each one.

The major functions of a word processor are editing, storage and printing. Text typed onto the screen can be corrected and revised. Words that have been spelt wrongly can easily be amended by overtyping corrections, and words, sentences or paragraphs can be inserted, deleted or repositioned by pressing appropriate instruction keys. When the text has been edited and the typist is satisfied that it is correct, it can be printed while new material is being introduced at the keyboard.

The separation of keyboarding from printing and the speed at which corrections, alterations and insertions can be made increase the productivity of typists considerably. The actual extent of any productivity increases depends on the type of work being done, with routine redrafting of long documents and preparation of documents from standard text providing the largest increases.

This increased productivity allows companies to reduce the numbers of typists, secretaries and clerical workers as automation is usually accompanied by a reorganization of these functions. In general, the use of word processors in large typing pools or word-processor centres is likely to result in greater job loss than their use by individual secretaries scattered throughout a company.

As with other forms of automation, the advantages of word processing are not confined to cost savings through labour displacement. Increased efficiency can also be achieved by tighter management supervision of work, speeding up the workflow and automatic work-monitoring techniques.

Nonetheless, word processing cannot be treated as just another piece of new technology. It affects a specifically female area of work, and for this reason the impact of any job loss or reorganization is likely to be subtly, though significantly, different from that in traditionally male areas of work. Patriarchal relations are particularly obvious (if very personal) in office work and so, before considering in detail how word processing affects women, we must understand both why certain office jobs have become 'women's work' and the role technical change has played in this division.

Women in the office

There are at present nearly one million typists, secretaries and personal assistants in the UK, representing about 25 per cent of the clerical workforce. Although women form a majority of clerical workers today, this has not always been the case. Clerical work in the nineteenth century was largely a male preserve, an offshoot of the exclusively male managerial function. Since that time, there has been an enormous growth in the scale and complexity of business, with a corresponding increase in the amount of clerical work and the number of clerical workers. In 1851 clerical workers represented 0.8 per cent of all employed persons; in 1961 this proportion had reached 13 per cent.

As the scale of clerical work grew it was accompanied by the rationalization of clerical tasks, the influx of women and the use of office machinery.

By the end of the nineteenth century, suitable female labour was readily available owing to an increasing proportion of single women in the population and greater provision of education for girls.

Increasingly women were able to find work in offices. In 1891 women made up 5 per cent of the waged workforce, mostly as domestic servants, nurses and primary-school teachers, or in the clothing and textile industries and the sweated trades. By 1911 this proportion had grown to 17 per cent, largely because of the employment opportunities opened up to women in the clerical sector.

But women's entry into the office did not go unquestioned. In magazines, for example, women were caricatured as too stupid or careless to be efficient office workers, and great concern was expressed about the moral dangers to women entering offices and the 'unfeminine' nature of their duties.[1]

Ultimately, however, two factors ensured that it was women, and not men, who flooded into the new clerical sector.

The first factor was that women provided cheap labour, working long hours in squalid, ill-ventilated, unheated attics and basements for far less pay than their male counterparts would accept. Second, the introduction of the typewriter, from the 1870s onward, opened up an area of work which, because of its newness, was not already identified with men. Thus, women could find employment without competing directly with men.

From the outset, typing was a female occupation. Indeed, early machines were often hired out complete with a female 'typewriter', later known as a 'typist'. Women were encouraged to type on the grounds that their 'natural dexterity' made them better able to operate the machines than men. Great savings could be made with the use of a typewriter, but the use of a female typist at lower wages than a male clerk was a crucial part of this money-saving package.

The early typists tended to assume a professional and middle-class identity. However, as education was increasingly extended to the working class, and more business colleges and schools provided typing courses, typing ceased to be the preserve of well-educated, refined middle-class women. Such women increasingly turned to shorthand writing as a way of earning their living. Shorthand, though having a history stretching back to Roman times, began to be widely used by male clerks in the early nineteenth century for taking notes of evidence and Parliamentary debates. Yet, by 1888 the *Englishwoman's Review* was drawing attention to the appropriateness of shorthand writing as a career for educated women:

> It is well known that a number of public men and journalists employ lady secretaries, and now political dames and leaders of fashion engage ladies to report drawing room meetings or write out invitations from shorthand notes.[2]

It was at about this time that demand for female clerks with a knowledge of both shorthand and typing began. Although large numbers of women acquired both skills, a gulf was established between the middle-class 'lady' secretaries and the mass of typists who increasingly worked in large typing pools.

Despite continued and often impassioned outbursts by male writers and journalists against the employment of women in the office, their numbers continued to grow. Both world wars encouraged this growth. The 1951 census showed that female clerks outnumbered males by 1.4 million to 990,000. By then the lines of segregation between the sexes had been firmly drawn: 96 per cent of shorthand typists were women.

Female secretarial workers have become a highly stratified group. There is a large gap between the personal secretary and the copy typist in terms of pay, and status. Typing is commonly seen as a way to gain access to secretarial jobs. Yet in her recent study of the office secretary Rosalie Silverstone found that 'mobility into the secretarial ranks was becoming increasingly rare'.[3] Personal secretary grades were being filled by women graduates or by women with high educational qualifications and usually a middle-class background, thus restricting the mobility of working-class women, who remained at the lowest levels of the hierarchy.

Secretaries have a far closer relationship with the men they work for than do typists. In addition to typing and administrative work, a secretary is expected to plan her boss's diary, make appointments and reservations for him, act as hostess to his visitors, tidy his office, water the office plants, and so on. These tasks are not part of an economically rational division of labour, but involve the secretary in a capacity best described as personal servant or office wife to her boss. This role both reinforces a wider gender hierarchy in which women are subordinate to men and explains why secretaries are almost invariably women:

> The perfect secretary is not only required to maintain high standards of proficiency as a human word processor, but is expected to evolve a relation with her employer where she must act out roles of wife and mother and where deference is the key to success but not to promotion.[4]

A secretary derives her status from her boss, who in turn derives additional status from having a secretary. While she may develop some knowledge of and interest in company matters, she is rarely expected to act independently of her boss but instead to seek emotional, non-economic rewards such as flattery and praise for her work. It is this aspect of secretarial work that led women workers in the United States to campaign for pay increases with the slogan 'Raises, Not Roses!'[5]

Sexual harassment of women in offices is a common experience, only now being given serious attention by trades unions in the UK. The incidence of such harassment well illustrates how patriarchal relations subordinate and oppress women. Because the secretarial role is primarily 'office wifely' rather than economically rational, some male bosses perceive that they are buying sexual availability along with secretarial labour. In many ways secretaries have to sell their femininity as a part of their labour power by conforming to a middle-class norm of femininity in their dress, manner and speech. This conformity is somewhat less pronounced with typists.

A typist's work is more standardized and routine than a secretary's. Typists usually follow strict procedures for completing their work and, apart from collecting paper or forms, have little reason to leave their desks. The structure of the typing pool is hierarchical and supervision is formal, supervisors being responsible for monitoring individual as well as overall productivity. Material to be typed is usually brought to the typing pool and distributed among typists by the supervisor, so personal contact between typists and authors is minimal. The use of the latest centralized dictation systems and automated messenger trolleys means that few outsiders need ever set foot inside the typing pool.

This recent rationalization of work within the typing pool has led to the suggestion that a typist's work has been degraded and now resembles unskilled factory work. While there is a clear trend in this direction, several important differences between typing and assembly-line work remain. Typists generally have better working conditions than factory workers (though health hazards in the office have been largely ignored). Work flow may be monitored, but the pace of work in a typing pool is not directly controlled as it is on an assembly line, where pace is determined by the speed at which the line moves. Fluctuations in work flow allow secretaries and typists some control over their work and some moments free from the immediate demands of work. Another difference is the relation of the worker to the finished product. A typist will usually produce a completed piece of work, though someone else will have drafted the letter or document. In factory work, the 'detail' division of labour is so advanced that each worker makes only part of the finished product. Therefore, although typing is rationalized and supervised, typists do exercise an element of control over their work. Finally, both secretaries and typists benefit from what has been called the 'social office':

> those little jobs which women are expected to perform just because they are women: such as making the tea, watering the plants, organising leaving/wedding/birthday presents, going out of the office on errands for the boss, all of which, while on the one hand reinforcing their ideological role as 'office wife', can be used to create space and time away from the routine of typing.[6]

However, it is just this area of control that word processors are likely to weaken. The following section of this chapter shows both how word processing is being used to intensify work and reduce employment opportunities and the ways in which it alters social relations in the office. Much of the evidence is derived from my own research involving a survey of companies in the USA and the UK which have introduced word processing.

Word processing and the reorganization of office work

Manufacturers claim that word processing frees secretaries from routine typing tasks, allowing them to spend more time on administrative and semi-managerial functions. In the USA during the 1970s, the introduction of word processing was often accompanied by a division of secretarial work into 'correspondence' and 'administrative' components. 'Correspondence secretaries', as word-processor operators began to be called, worked in the word-processing centre and were responsible for all keyboarding. Their work was not much different from a typist's in a typing pool. 'Administrative secretaries' carried out the remaining secretarial functions such as filing, telephone and reception work.

Susan Vinnicombe[7] argues that by splitting secretarial work into its 'administrative' and 'correspondence' components, companies were able to use word processors either to reduce the overall number of secretaries or to expand the role of the administrative secretaries so that they took over many of the lower-order managerial tasks. In practice, the number of secretaries is usually reduced, and administrative secretaries rarely end up doing managerial work. Where word processors were introduced into a typing pool, the work of administrative secretaries remained relatively unchanged, but they were often grouped together, shared a larger number of bosses and their total number was reduced. Thus the extra time generated, for administrative secretaries, by the shift of typing to the word-processing centre was taken up with more routine work rather than managerial work. One manager in the US survey went so far as to say: 'Calling a secretary an administrative secretary is just a con. It is not a route into management.' Similarly, a survey by the Equal Pay and Opportunities Campaign found 'very few examples of word processors freeing women to do non-routine work'.[8]

Promotion into management is unlikely; the established patriarchal mechanisms which tend to keep women out of the positions of authority are not dispelled by word processing. Secretaries are, in any case, not part of the main office hierarchy and career progression, but exist as a watertight compartment, identifiable collectively by the fact that they are female and individually by their relation to their immediate bosses. Secretaries actually hold their positions because men benefit from their roles as office wives, servants and status symbols.

In the UK, by 1983, word processing had generally been introduced into typing pools rather than secretarial offices, and thus had not had much impact on the work of secretaries, except in the prestigious offices of multinational corporations based in London. In small and medium-sized companies the quantity of repetitive typing work carried out by personal secretaries does not usually justify the purchase of a word processor. Nevertheless, as word processors begin to be used as computer terminals and for electronic mail, secretaries will be more likely to have access to them. At the same time, however, this trend may be offset by the increasing use of desk-top terminals by managers, which reduces the need for secretaries to act as intermediate information handlers.

What, then, is the impact of word processors on typists as opposed to secretaries? Before a company buys a word processor it will often undertake a work study which entails a detailed accounting of work in the typing pool. Average speeds for typing various documents are calculated to assess whether word processing would increase productivity. If the decision to purchase is made, the work is reorganized and standardized so that it becomes suitable for word processors.

The degree to which typists lose control over their work is related to the level of standardization achieved and the level of work monitoring implemented. Standardization also facilitates greater fragmentation of tasks. Often, work can be transferred from one typist's terminal to another, with different typists working on parts of the same document, thereby increasing the division of labour. Automatic monitoring of work can frequently be done by the machine, which records the numbers of keystrokes or documents completed, allowing a typist's productivity to be measured. This kind of control tends to sap morale and may produce a managerial rationale for even closer supervision.

Although word processing does eliminate many routine tasks, such as correcting a word that has been misspelt several times, this elimination of routine also increases the intensity of work. Eighty per cent of operators surveyed said their workload had increased, and 66 per cent felt the pace and pressure of work had risen. Often, once it was known that word processors were being used, authors would flood the typing pool with extra work, repeatedly sending the same piece back for revision.

Despite this intensification of work, word processing may provide some benefits to typists – at least in the short term. For instance, 72 per cent of the operators I questioned derived more satisfaction from their work after word processing was introduced. None were less satisfied, although it is possible that any women who were dissatisfied may already have left the company. Benefits such as pay bonuses, an improved working environment in the form of redecorated offices and better lighting, and increased feelings of status through working with new equipment all contributed to satisfaction. Several managers interviewed said that the 'novelty effect' of working with new machines facilitated the introduction of word processing, although this later wore off.

One frequently cited problem is associated with the visual display screens attached to some word processors. These can give rise to health and safety problems, such as eye strain, back complaints, headaches and migraine through incorrect adjustment of the screen, poor lighting, too small characters or bad seating. Owing to the wide variety of screens in use and the low level of unionization among clerical workers, insufficient attention is often paid to the changes required in seating and lighting arrangements and the stress arising from prolonged use of a VDU.

Word-processor operators tend to be paid slightly more than typists, though usually on the same scale. Yet these pay increases may simply reflect the initial shortage of experienced operators. As more typists gain experience on word processors and when in-house training schemes become more common, these pay differentials may well be eroded. Without either union pressure for regrading or job evaluation schemes free from sex bias lasting pay increases cannot be guaranteed.

Word processor operators will also lose some traditional typing skills. Centralized dictation has already reduced the need for shorthand, and as more documents conform to standard formats very little manual adjustment by the typist or operator will be necessary. Layout skills will be virtually redundant. The VDU, as well as showing text as it is typed or being recalled from memory, can show information such as the page width, page length, tabulator settings, line spacing and pitch, and display a series of prompts for the operator. Thus, not only does the program controlling the machine determine the range of functions a word processor may perform, but also, by guiding the operator through screen prompts, it determines the degree to which an operator's work follows a specified sequence. Although in some companies I visited operators were doing data-processing work such as invoicing or making up pay slips, the type of mathematical programs embodied in the word processors reduced this work to form-filling.

Limited training for operators ensures that word processors are used almost exclusively as typewriter substitutes and that operators do not have an opportunity to learn new skills such as archiving. Most training is provided by manufacturers in the form of two- or three-day familiarization courses covering only the most basic operational aspects of their word processors. (This may be compared to the situation at the beginning of the century when typewriter manufacturers were responsible for training typists. It was only later that secretarial colleges and examinations appeared.)

Forms of control in the office which have traditionally derived from male dominance and female subservience are gradually being superseded by more obvious forms of control such as work measurement. Yet, it should not be ignored that new working practices such as work monitoring accompanying the introduction of word processors have not always been passively accepted. Some secretaries and typists have sabotaged the work-measurement capacity of the machine by finding ways to 'fool' it. Other tactics include more specifically 'feminine' forms of resistance, such as feigning ignorance of the cause of typewriter or word processor malfunctions in order to snatch a break while waiting for the male technician to arrive. Although, as Jane Barker and Hazel Downing have emphasized, such tactics are an important means of regaining some control at an individual level,[10] they may be something of a mixed blessing for women in general. Any response which strengthens men's belief that women are technologically illiterate is likely to reinforce that illiteracy, reducing the likelihood of women entering such jobs as maintenance. As it is, the manufacturers have an interest in keeping operators (and employers) mystified about the workings of the machines, since after-sales service is highly profitable.

The resistance to management strategies for the implementation of word processing will perhaps in the long term be more effective for women if it results through collective action. Until now typists have lost the opportunity to raise issues of regrading, pay and employment. This is not through any fault of their own, rather it is due to the difficulty of a subordinate section of the workforce being able to find the strength, either outside or within unions, to force a reappraisal of these issues.

Employment effects of word processors
The relationship between technical change and employment is complex, depending on factors such as industrial sector, size of firms and the level of unionization. My own research suggests, however, that even taking these factors into account, the widespread use of microelectronic technology is likely to cause considerable job losses in offices. The International Federation of Commercial, Clerical and Technical employees has estimated that technical change in offices will lead to the displacement of 20 to 25 per cent of clerical staff in Western Europe, or about five million people.[11] A US study of 278 companies using word processing found that 50 per cent of companies had reduced secretarial and typing staff, and 30 per cent had substantially expanded their workload without staff increases.[12] In Germany, Siemens estimated that by 1990 around 40 per cent of current office work would be carried out by computers. German trades unions have calculated that this will mean the loss of two million typing and clerical jobs in that country alone.

UK government studies have consistently played down the labour-displacing effects of new office technology,[13] reminding us that the 'computerization equals massive job loss' scare of the 1960s proved to be unfounded. This optimistic government position is based on two expectations: that the diffusion of word processing will be slow, and that new jobs will be created to compensate for job losses.

Incompatibility of equipment, low levels of management awareness and reluctance to invest in capital equipment during a recession do hinder the diffusion of word processing. Nevertheless the UK word-processing market is currently expanding at 28 per cent per year. At the end of 1982, there were estimated to be 40,000 screen-based word processors in the UK and 350,000 in the USA. Undoubtedly factors such as high office labour costs, low capital investment in offices, the falling cost of equipment, its relative ease of introduction, public-sector spending cuts and the aggressive marketing strategies adopted by word-processor manufacturers will all encourage the diffusion of this technology.

There are many documented examples of job loss as a result of word processing, and my own research revealed more. Among the 18 UK companies I visited, seven reported job reductions of around 60 per cent. All of these 7 companies had adopted centralized installations whereby the word processors had been introduced into a central typing pool. No company reported an increase in typists. In the 11 companies in which typing staff had remained constant, seven used fewer than four word processors, while six had substantially increased their workload without hiring extra staff. Of course, maintaining typing-staff levels does not mean that labour savings are not achieved in other parts of the company. There is already evidence to suggest that many other clerical jobs are lost as a direct result of the introduction of word processing.[14]

All the job losses in the companies surveyed were achieved through 'natural wastage'. The high turnover of secretarial and typing staff makes this an easy way for companies to achieve job reductions. Trades unions have attempted to maintain existing staff levels through 'new technology agreements', but have often had to settle for a 'no redundancy' promise to existing staff. 'No redundancy' clauses do not prevent job loss through natural wastage which effectively transfers unemployment to future women job seekers.

Although unions have been trying to reach agreements with managements over word processing, I found little evidence of any success in my study. Relatively low levels of unionization in the office sector do make it easier for management to introduce word processing. Only two companies of the 18 visited in the UK had involved typists in the process of introducing word processors. Where consultation did take place, it was little more than an informal meeting to explain what management had already decided. In some companies, typists did not find out about the word processors until after their delivery. Unions were most likely to be involved with health and safety aspects of VDU work, and this often led to management arranging eye tests for prospective operators. Certain unions left negotiation to individual branches, which sometimes meant that typists were not properly consulted before agreements were reached.

The expectation that new jobs will be created is something of an act of faith. Usually any new functions in word-processing sales, consultancy, systems analysis and work measurement, are taken on by existing personnel. Furthermore, these few jobs are not ones for which women (especially secretaries and typists) usually have relevant training. Jobs in marketing and customer support are also unlikely to be available to the majority of women:

> Of course the jobs created do not absorb women at an equal rate as men, since there are more male than female sales representatives, and although customer support staff are predominantly female, approximately 3 sales jobs were created for every 2 in customer support. This shift in the balance of opportunities for men and women, with a decrease in the availability of typing jobs (traditionally held by women) and an increase in sales jobs (predominantly taken by men) is an example of a trend which we expect to become more pronounced in the future, partly because more of the new jobs will be skilled and at present more men than women have the required skills.[15]

Women's office employment is also under threat from another direction. By separating the productive and the servicing functions of secretarial work, word processing may open up new areas of work which are not so strongly identified with women. Technically, word processing is merging with data processing and telecommunications. The increasing use of word processors which communicate with each other by telephone line and the use of data-processing packages on word processors are examples of this convergence. Eventually, data- and word-processing work may all be done at the same terminal, and a new type of job – 'information processing' – will then emerge. Will such new jobs necessarily be considered women's work?

Two recent developments indicate that this is unlikely. The first is the increase in male word-processor operators in the USA, which indicates a loosening of the traditional association of keyboarding with women. The second is the fact that schools are now teaching computer skills, so experience at a keyboard will become as common for boys as it has been for girls. As the links with computing grow, keyboarding may no longer be regarded as a purely female skill. A member of the Industrial Society, a British employers' organization aiming to improve standards of industrial training and practice has pointed out: 'Once the sadly devalued name of secretary is renamed as information assistant the job would probably become more attractive to men.'

Word processors are often portrayed in glowing terms promising to give typists more control over their work, eliminate boring routine jobs, cut costs, increase productivity and efficiency and produce better-quality documents. In practice, word processing has brought greater standardization and fragmentation of typing tasks, increased managerial control, reduced personal contact among typists and a reduction in the total number of secretarial as well as typing jobs. Personal secretaries, however, are unlikely to experience changes in the way their work is organized unless they are relocated to a word-processing centre. Word processing and the accompanying rationalization of work have in many ways sharpened the differentiation between personal secretaries and typists or word-processor operators.

There has been little indication to date that word processing will reduce sex segregation in the office. Indeed, there are signs that it may reinforce this segregation. Until now word processors have been used mainly as replacement typewriters, and word processing has remained women's work. Yet women's exclusion from computing design and maintenance suggests that the technology and its control will remain identified with men. The use of increasingly sophisticated terminals combining text and data processing with communications may mean that women will lose their current domination of keyboarding employment. Further, in the absence of appropriate education and training, not only are women likely to be squeezed out of traditionally female areas of employment, but they will also be unable to take advantage of any new job opportunities created by office automation.

It is women's concentration in clerical work that makes them so vulnerable to office automation. Both clerical and women's overall unemployment are already rising faster than male unemployment, despite the fact that much female unemployment remains hidden because of women's dual role in domestic and waged work. Despite this very real threat to their employment, the introduction of word processing does offer an important opportunity for women to come to grips with their position not only as workers in a capitalist economy, but also as women workers who, because of their dual role in domestic and waged work and the strength of sex segregation in the labour force, are most vulnerable to the costs of this new technology.

Behind the rhetoric which often surrounds the introduction of word processing lies some indication of how this technology could be used. Word processing need not inevitably lead to deskilling, fragmentation and the intensification of work. Janine Morgall[9] has listed some of the ways word processors could be used to benefit women: increased productivity could help to reduce working hours and allow part-time working for women and men; decentralized word processing could lead to better working conditions, and proper training could encourage women to seek more interesting jobs in related areas. In principle, word processing could indeed be used to broaden the range of activities in which secretaries and typists engage. The point is that word processing is not generally used in this way. In the UK, unions have been somewhat lax in pushing for regrading and no job loss following the introduction of word processors. One way of beginning to solve this problem would be the establishment of, and participation of secretaries and typists in, local and/or company committees set up to evaluate all aspects of the new technology, and in training programmes specifically designed to break down gender divisions in the office.

Perhaps the most far-reaching implication of word processing and related equipment is the extension of computer networks into the home and the possibility of widespread homeworking via a terminal. But will this form of homeworking be any different from the other highly exploitative forms of homeworking performed by women? Secretaries and typists already have some of the skills that will become vital in the automated office and they should be offered the opportunity to build on these skills rather than being pushed back into the home.

12. Women and computers

Anne Lloyd and Liz Newell

This chapter is about the work and experience of women involved with computing. The first person to do any work which we would now recognize as computer programming was a woman: Lady Ada Lovelace. A gifted mathematician, Lady Lovelace met Charles Babbage early in the nineteenth century and was fascinated by the mechanical computers he was trying to build. She devised a system for programming them, and wrote the only accounts of how they worked.

Babbage's machines were limited in their capabilities by the fact that they were mechanical. Modern computers depend on electronic components, which are faster and more versatile. One of the first electronic computers, ENIAC – Electronic Numerical Integrator and Calculator – was built in the United States during the Second World War to calculate firing tables for the military.[1] Programming was not thought to be important or difficult and was allocated to a group of female clerks who became known as the ENIAC Girls. They spent their time crawling through the mass of wires and electronic valves (tubes) which made up the computer, literally rewiring it for each new program. More recent computers store and interpret programmed instructions without the need for rewiring.

Since the times of Lady Lovelace and the ENIAC Girls, computing has become an industry and programming has become a predominantly male occupation. Men crowded in after the war, and there are now precious few women in the higher-paid and more interesting jobs in the industry. Many of the issues we write about in this chapter are therefore common to other areas of work in which women are an underpaid minority. Despite this, there is a widely held view that computing, as a young and flourishing industry, promises greater opportunities for all.

Unfortunately, very little research has been done about women in computing, so we are unable to explore trends or make many comparisons in statistical detail. We have drawn heavily on our own experiences in computer programming and on those other women in computing, without whose help it would have been impossible to write this chapter. This experience is valuable because, while dry statistics might identify the existence of discrimination against women, they do not explain how sexism operates in practice. But there is another reason for the specifically personal nature of our account. We and the other women whose experiences are reflected in this chapter came together primarily because we were concerned about the impact of computers on our lives. In particular, we were concerned about the possibility that new computing technology could be used to consign women once again to the home – either through job losses in offices and other areas in which women predominate, or through the creation of new opportunities for home-working.

Many people take the present forms and uses of computers for granted, and assume that we have to adapt to them. We want to challenge this view, because it implicitly allows those who control technology also to control our lives. We would like to see computer power applied to all our needs and to levelling imbalances in society, rather than seeing it squandered (as it is at present) on private profit, military projects and glamorous gadgetry of dubious social value. However, the fact that we work within the computer industry does not allow us simply to press a magic button and change the shape of computer technology: this is a project in which we all need to be involved. We are concerned that the number of women entering the computer industry should rise and that women generally should find ways of increasing their confidence in dealing with technology. Without this confidence, it is not possible to democratize the social processes which shape both technology and our lives.

Before considering the prospects for change, we discuss some of the factors which contribute to the lack of women in higher positions in computing. We also share some examples of the subtler forms of sexism women experience working with computers. We start, however, with a brief outline of the structure of computing today and the role of women within that structure.

Where have all the women gone?

There is an increasingly strict hierarchy among computing jobs. At the bottom are the people – almost invariably women – who perform keyboard operations in the process of preparing data for computer input. Next are computer operators, who deal with the day-to-day operation of computer machinery. Above them in status are computer programmers, who write the instructions (programs) which make computers perform their many functions. Programmers tend to work under the supervision of systems analysts, who liaise with computer users and design computer systems to meet their needs. Finally, the data processing manager – who need not be a technical person – is in overall control of the computer installation.

Within each job there are subdivisions such as chief operator, junior programmer, and so on. While people may progress among these subdivisions – say, from programmer to chief programmer – there is no necessary or natural progression up the larger hierarchy. In particular, the women who work in data preparation are most unlikely to progress in this way, and they probably comprise the majority of women in computing work. A smaller number of women work in programming, but few do so at higher levels. The areas in which women are scarce are operating – which normally involves shiftwork – and the highly paid jobs: data processing management, systems analysis and computer maintenance (usually done by men working for the computer manufacturer rather than the organization using the computer).

Women's (re)entry into programming is itself a relatively new occurrence. Philip Kraft and Steven Dubnoff recently conducted a survey in the USA of people working in jobs connected with programming or software work. Nearly a quarter of their 677 respondents were women. This proportion is high, compared with other scientific, technical and engineering fields (bar the 'feminine' professions like nursing), although it is still substantially below the overall proportion of women in the US workforce. In the two years covered by the survey, roughly equal numbers of women and men had started working in software. However, a higher proportion of the women questioned had entered during the last five years,[2] and the survey revealed sharp differences between the types of jobs entered by women and men.

The content and image of programming have changed considerably in the last 15 years or so. Kraft and Dubnoff found that the structure of software work was changing fundamentally, and that specific tasks within software work were being fragmented into distinct, nominally specialist jobs. They concluded that this has created an unprecedented level of stratification among software workers, this being based on pay and responsibility. The underlying trend seems to be towards a polarization between routine and analytical types of work and between managers and managed, with the middle ranks of managers being squeezed out (to be replaced, ironically, by machines of their own making). Generally, when new and more highly paid jobs are created, these are filled by men; women tend to enter the areas left behind. 'Software work has replicated the sexual (and racial) divisions that characterise older occupations. . . . Women seem to have been recruited to fill the openings at the bottom' – that is the 'relatively routine, relatively poorly paid jobs' in software. Ten per cent of the men in the survey were senior managers, compared to only 3 per cent of the women. According to Kraft and Dubnoff, one reason for this is that women with responsibility for decision-making in management tend to supervise other women while men are more likely to supervise other men. 'The status of managers reflects the status of the people they manage.'[3]

Status and pay somehow seem to 'follow' men. Women are not only concentrated in the lowest-paid software jobs but tend also to be in the worst-paying industries – notably finance, real estate and communications. Even within the same industries, specializations and organizational levels, women in the survey were paid less well than men. Kraft and Dugnoff found the best-paid respondents to be those involved with purchasing and other traditionally managerial roles. At senior management level, the average earnings were over 80 per cent higher than even middle managers. The few women at senior management levels were, on average, paid less than male middle managers. Averaging all the software jobs examined, Kraft and Dubnoff concluded that 'It is a $5000 a year liability to be a woman in software . . . the field is not characterised by just random pay discrepancies but by systematic pay discrimination against women.'[4] Overall, the mean earnings of the women respondents in 1981 were 70 per cent of the men's, or 85 per cent when corrected for work experience, hours and education. This is, of course, a substantially smaller difference than the average for the USA, where women's (uncorrected) earnings are 59 per cent of men's, but in a situation where 'the key to financial success is not to specialise and not to get too technical', and where 'the generalists tend to be men whilst the specialists tend to be women',[5] the prospects for women do not look good.

Programming has come full circle. In the beginning it was left to clerical workers. Then, for a long time, it was considered technical and highly demanding. Now it is returning to the realm of routine clerical work. In an earlier study, Philip Kraft attributed this reduced status and the increasingly conventional structures through which programming is managed to the deskilling of programming[6].

Traditionally, the jobs that women do are considered less skilled than men's jobs and are given lower status. As the Kraft and Dubnoff survey indicates, the better-paid and higher-status jobs in software do not necessarily demand greater technical skills than others. Some aspects of programming have become easier over the years, but it is interesting that the new and reduced image of programming coincides with the (re)entry of women.

We seem to be in Catch-22 situation: women are allowed into jobs which men come to see as unimportant or unglamorous and which they leave behind for more prestigious and better-paid positions further up the hierarchy, but our very entry into those jobs reduces their status. If this logic is allowed to operate, women can never break out from low-prestige and generally badly paid work.

Barriers to entry . . . training

After 1945, women working throughout the economy found they were no longer regarded as 'suitable' for the technical jobs they had done during the war. In computing, it was realized that programming was interesting and technically demanding work; the technical aspects of the work were increasingly stressed, and a scientific background was soon seen as necessary to entry. This effectively barred women from the field. As we have seen in chapters 2 and 3, the scientific and technical sides of the education system are biased in favour of boys, giving them the knowledge, practical skills and grasp of technical vocabulary and concepts needed to build up and maintain their confidence in an increasingly technical world.

The increasing power, cheapness and portability of computers has encouraged computer education in secondary and more recently even in primary schools. In our experience, however, this has done little to overcome the technological inhibitions of many girls. In Britain, government computer-education policy amounts to little more than subsidizing the purchase of one microcomputer per school. Since this means sharing a single keyboard among several hundred children, it is clear that this policy is of limited educational value. School computer clubs are attended predominantly by boys. When girls do attend, they are rarely able to compete with the boys for access to the limited number of keyboards available. The attitude of many computing teachers is also disturbing; they constantly refer to their pupils as 'the boys' – as if it is accepted that there will be no girls in their classes.

School microcomputers are generally found in the mathematics department: it is assumed that computing requires a high level of numeracy and that computer applications are necessary mathematical. In fact, many jobs in computing require minimal mathematical ability – programs frequently contain nothing more mathematical than the addition of two numbers. Work at the British National Computing Centre has shown that those with linguistic skills are in fact likely to be better at programming than those with mathematical skills.[7] Yet employers increasingly favour applicants who have a scientific or computer science qualification, even for jobs such as programming where such a background is largely irrelevant.

. . . the image of computing

Women are educated to believe that technology is not their domain and are therefore justified in feeling they are treading on forbidden territory if they want to find out about it. This message is reflected strongly in the computing press. Recently, some of the British literature has improved slightly, with some magazines providing space for discussing women's issues. For the most part, however, the images of women and men portrayed in the computing press (especially in advertising) are far from encouraging. Images of women are often purely decorative, sometimes pornographic, but rarely positive. The women are usually good-looking (in the way women are supposed to look in our society) while the men are nondescript. In pictures of mixed-sex groupings, women are usually portrayed doing clerical work or in passive roles while men are the managers, experts or otherwise in control. Such sexual stereotypes are frequently acted out at the major computer exhibitions. Some firms employ women solely in order to attract men to their stands, their minimal clothing contrasting strikingly with that of the well-covered, besuited men who do the 'real' selling.

Work in the computer industry does not hold a very positive image for women. Indeed, the very words 'technical', 'scientific', 'machine' and 'computing' convey male images: the people we envisage in connection with them are men. The language used in the computer literature is also discriminatory. The constant use of 'he' and the use of male names such as FRED or JOE for sample programs patently assume a male readership. It can scarcely be argued that 'he' is meant to include 'she', because 'she' is used when a woman is obviously referred to (for example, when describing a low-status worker such as a data-preparation clerk) but not when referring to a programmer or someone with higher status. In this respect, computer literature does not differ from other kinds of professional literature.

The words used to describe different aspects of computing involve a more subtle form of stereotyping. The term 'hardware' refers to the tangible machines and 'software' to the intangible programs put into them. Our society values hardness and softness differently. Hard is seen as good, strong, difficult and male (hard facts, hard-headed, hard science – meaning physics and chemistry), while soft is inferior, weak, easy and female (soft touch, soft-soap, soft science – meaning biology, psychology, and so forth). Much of women's traditional work is associated with 'soft' school subjects, with people's feelings, and with support and maintenance roles. It is software work that women are now finding their way back into. Work on the hardware remains an almost exclusively male domain.

. . . and its jargon

In computing, as elsewhere, jargon acts as a shorthand language to describe specialized concepts. It also provides a bond between people who use it – an 'in' group. Naturally, people who invent new computer terminology try to use expressions which are self-explanatory, but often the new terms turn out to be undescriptive or alien. Unintelligible names hinder comprehension by the lay person or the novice (and, of course, by the non-technical boss). Because of the rapidly changing nature of computer technology, new names are continuously being invented. Manufacturers also frequently rename the same equipment or process, giving each their own special name. So, within one company using several computers, a concept often has a different name according to the particular computer to which it relates.

Naming is very important because it can be used to confer ownership rights on the namer. Thus, power over computing processes and techniques can be appropriated by manufacturers and computing departments. Within companies which use computers, computer staff tend to use naming to maintain a position of power relative to other departments.

Jargon has become so widespread in the computer industry that it is a source of joking and games among computer personnel. Some wits have gone so far as to write computer programs to produce random jargon phrases that sound superficially meaningful. These are called 'buzz-word generators' – 'buzz-word' being, of course, computer jargon for 'jargon'. Unfortunately, jargon can be pernicious as well as humorous. The jargon used in computing helps to create mystique and to make knowledge about computers less accessible: it makes computing seem more difficult than it really is. As a result, only a confident élite can gain access to further information. (In order to know what to ask about, you have already to understand and use quite a lot of jargon.) Women are used to not asking questions because replies are often phrased in terms which women lacking a technical background cannot understand, or which are deliberately made difficult in order to reinforce the power of the explainer.

Because women do not generally have confidence in their ability to deal with technological concepts, the extensive use of jargon in the computer industry is a particular obstacle for them. In general, those trained in scientific or mathematical fields are more used to using numbers and symbols to express meaning than those whose education has been more oriented towards words, as women's education usually is. Perhaps it is no accident that COBOL – the most English-like of the common programming languages – is generally sneered at by scientifically or technologically educated programmers. COBOL is also the only commonly used programming language to have been introduced by a woman – Captain Grace Hopper of the US Navy.

Women in computing – what is it like?

It is perhaps not surprising that the idea of women taking anything other than a subsidiary or support role in computing is thought of as strange: it is out of line with the roles assigned to women in society. Women who do step out of their designated role and into the computing industry are often greeted with surprise, dismay and incomprehension. We ourselves have often been the objects of comments such as: 'You don't look like a computer person'; 'Isn't that rather an odd thing for you to do?'; 'What do you do, type things in?' and – spoken with utter disbelief – 'Heavens, you must be brainy!'

Naturally, working in computing is a different experience for women and men. Women who get past the barriers surrounding the industry have their working conditions made more difficult by the fact that there are so few other women around and by the pervasive air of male camaraderie which, by definition, excludes them and often serves to keep women under control. One place where this can be observed is the pub. In our experience, men who work in computing often drink at lunchtime and after work, with the pub rather than the canteen as the normal meeting place at mid-day. Women who accompany the men to the pub often do so with misgivings. They may have more pressing things to do, such as buying food for themselves or their familes, or they may simply not want to drink alcohol at lunchtime and have to justify this to the men. They may also want a break from the computer talk that predominates in the bar as at work. The men tend to stick to common ground: computer talk is a 'safe' subject – probably the only one they are prepared to discuss with each other.

This is an important trap for women in computing. If they choose not to join in, they risk not only the tenuous terms of their acceptability to their male colleagues but also possibly some inside information about work that could be discussed only in the informal atmosphere of the pub. Especially among systems analysts and programmers, who rarely belong to trades unions, the lunchtime drink often fills the role of a union meeting in other occupations. To miss it is potentially to miss out professionally.

The female equivalent of the pub is the women's toilet! Each place provides a relatively safe haven in which to moan about work, perhaps to plot against the boss and escape for a moment the pressure of being at work. In our view, it is no accident that computing workers have chosen a very gender-specific, masculine place – the pub – to serve this function. Because women are left out of the process of 'choosing' this venue, it remains difficult for them to break into the charmed circle of camaraderie among co-workers.

Women who work in computing do so on terms which have been laid down by men. Because men generally hold the positions of power in the industry it is they who define what is desirable and acceptable. The personal qualities required are those usually associated with men – hard-headedness, single-mindedness, ambition, toughness – attributes employers demand in many other areas of work. A plus-point which women find very difficult to achieve is having a wife at home! Working late at the office is a prerequisite for promotion, and jobs rarely allow time off to look after sick children. As in other jobs, the possibility of having to care for children is seen as a reason for not employing women rather than as an argument for nursery facilities. Women who complain about the lack of childcare facilities or about their low status as women within the organization become identified as troublemakers. Women are more acceptable if they share their male colleagues' attitude of silence and acceptance on these issues.

Even success in computing can be problematic for women. Any woman who succeeds in entering an area not normally open to women can be subject to tokenism which, paradoxically, has the effect of reducing other women's opportunities. The presence of a token woman in an otherwise all-male preserve is taken as evidence that women can get into the area if they have the required determination and ability. This then gives the employer an excuse for not making positive attempts to employ other women. Alternatively, tokenism can lead to the portrayal of successful women as exceptions. Marie Curie, for example, is often referred to in a way which suggests that her greatness is something of which other women are not capable!

Nonetheless, being seen to be 'as good as the men' is potentially one of the more appealing rewards of doing well in computing – although women who seek male-defined status also risk alienating themselves from other women. Women employed in computing, however, are rarely allowed to forget that they are women first and workers second. Putting aside the frequency of sexist banter and jokes which get in the way of the female worker's being seen as a person in her own right, she is often expected to act out specifically feminine roles. Thus, women are expected not only to make the coffee and so on, but also to become 'team mothers', taking on responsibility for the emotional well-being of the workforce. This is, of course, a vital managerial role, but when performed by women as an adjunct to their specified responsibilities it is not usually acknowledged with either pay or status.

Should women compute?
So far we have painted a pretty bleak picture of what it is like for women working in computing. So why bother? Why do women get involved at all?

For the majority of women involved – those doing data-entry work – computing is one way to exploit keyboard skills, though often in jobs which are rather dull. We are fortunate enough to work in systems and programming. For us, and for many of the other women we have spoken to, a major reason for doing this kind of work is that it can be fun. We enjoy both the precision and logical thinking necessary, and the feeling of achievement on completing a piece of technical work. Given a series of problems to solve and a framework in which to solve them, coming up with answers is a matter of mind over machine. Some of the more responsible jobs in computing are very creative. We believe many other women are capable of, and would enjoy, this type of work in computing.

There is, however, one final aspect of our experience at work which we would like to share – partly because it is yet another area of difference between women and men and partly because it suggests another strong reason for getting more women into computing. The technical side of computing can be addictive – so much so that some people seem to relate only to the machines and the technology, at the expense of human relations. The result can be deeply alienating. With the advent of personal computers, the 'micro in the attic' syndrome is creating a new generation of 'computer widows'. One man recently explained to us that he no longer has to stay late at the office in order to shut himself away from his family – the home computer now serves this purpose very well.

He is not a freak.[8] Many men appear to find interacting with computers more satisfying than talking to people. They seem to prefer what they know and can control. Joe Weizenbaum, professor of computing at the Massachusetts Institute of Technology, who has been working with computers since the start of the 1950s, describes the syndrome:

> Wherever computer centres have become established . . . bright young men of dishevelled appearance, often with sunken glowing eyes, can be seen sitting at computer consoles, their arms tensed and waiting to fire their fingers, already poised to strike, at the buttons and keys on which their attention seems to be as riveted as a gambler's on the rolling dice. When not so transfixed, they often sit at tables strewn with computer printouts over which they pore like possessed students of a cabalistic text. They work until they nearly drop, twenty, thirty hours at a time. Their food, if they arrange it, is brought to them: coffee, Cokes, sandwiches; if possible, they sleep on cots near the computer. But only for a few hours – then back to the console or the printouts. Their rumpled clothes, their unwashed and unshaven faces, and their uncombed hair all testify that they are oblivious to their bodies and to the world in which they move. They exist, at least when so engaged, only through and for the computers. These are computer bums, compulsive programmers. They are an international phenomenon.[9]

Weizenbaum argues that these 'computer bums' represent one extreme of the set of ways in which scientists and technologists more generally interact with the world: they try to control it. We feel this obsession with control is less likely to develop in women than in men: women's lifestyles and socialization do not generally allow them to forget or sacrifice personal responsibilities and attachments in quite the same way. In our experience, women who work with computers, while not immune to this addiction, are far less prone to it.

Where do we go from here?

It is difficult for women to gain the technical confidence and experience needed to get on in computing. We would like to see a programme of positive discrimination adopted in technological education – at the very least there should be a recognition that sexism exists and that teachers' attitudes need to change.

What is required in computer education is a basic awareness of what computers are, what they can and cannot do, and the likely social effects of applying them in different ways and in different environments. Unfortunately, the lay person often imagines there is a need to know how to write computer programs in order to use computers. This is tantamount to thinking that you need a course in electronics to be able to use a washing machine!

One way in which women can more easily learn about technology is with other women, in a non-competitive and stress-free environment. We would like to see more women's technology centres and self-help groups set up to provide a meaningful opportunity for women to learn in this way. We also think that it is very important for women to understand the computing industry from first-hand experience. Without this informed standpoint, computer technology can seem completely inaccessible.

Certainly there is a contradiction for us, as feminists, in working within an industry that serves to reinforce the economic and social power of men over women, but until male power in society disappears this kind of contradiction must be confronted. The increasing importance of computers means that computer knowledge is a key technical skill. Decision-making and management will require familiarity with computing. If women lack this, they will be still further excluded from power and decision-making in society.

This prospect is of particular concern. As long as it is men who hold the responsible jobs, computing will continue to move in directions which can serve only to reinforce men's social and economic power over women. Decisions will be made without the experience of women's lives and needs at first hand, and crucial issues concerning our lives will be overlooked. One small example of this is the Point of Sale terminals now used in many large shops. Whoever designed these computerized tills surely never considered the stress caused by the irritating electronic noises they make. Most cashiers in these shops are, of course, women.

Women are less likely than men to omit the human element in decisions which affect our lives, if only because they are less likely to be addicted to the technical aspects of the job. In addition, the verbal skills which women tend to be good at are sorely needed to help break down the barriers surrounding computer technology. Unless these skills are valued more, many people will become more alienated from the technology and computers will become even less accessible.

We think that computer technology could and should be part of a transformed scientific and technological practice in the future. If our experience has taught us anything it is that women working inside and outside the industry have a vital part to play in that project. We agree with Rita Arditti when she says that:

> The task that seems of primary importance, both for women and men, is to convert science from what it is today, a social institution with a conservative function and defensive stand, into a liberating and healthy activity: science with a soul which would respect and love its objects of study and stress harmony and communication with the rest of the universe. When science fulfils its potential and becomes a tool for human liberation we will not have to worry about women 'fitting in', because we will probably be at the forefront of that 'new' science.[10]

Notes and References

Introduction

1. Brighton Women and Science Group, *Alice Through the Microscope: The Power of Science over Women's Lives*, London: Virago 1980.
2. Kurt Vonnegut, *Player Piano* (1951), London: Panther 1975.
3. Karl Marx and Friedrich Engels, *The Communist Manifesto* (transl. Samuel Moore 1888), Middlesex: Penguin 1967, p. 83.
4. Harry Braverman, *Labour and Monopoly Capital: The Degradation of Work in the Twentieth Century*, New York: Monthly Review Press 1974.
5. J.D. Bernal, *Science in History* vol. 2, *The Scientific and Industrial Revolutions* (1954), Middlesex: Penguin 1969.
6. See British Society for Social Responsibility in Science, 9 Poland Street, London WC1, and its publication *Science for People*.
7. Erik Arnold, Lynda Birke and Wendy Faulkner, 'Women and microelectronics: the case of word processors', *Women's Studies International Quarterly*, vol. 4, no. 3, 1981, pp. 321–40.
8. Brian Easlea, *Fathering the Unthinkable; Masculinity, Scientists and the Nuclear Arms Race*, London: Pluto Press 1982; Cynthia Enloe, *Does Khaki Become You? The Military and Women's Lives*, London: Pluto Press 1983; W. Chapkis (ed.), *Loaded Questions: Women in the Military*, Amsterdam and Washington D.C.: Transnational Institute 1981.
9. Jalna Hanmer and Pat Allen, 'Reproductive Engineering: The Final Solution?' in Brighton Women and Science Group, *Alice Through the Microscope*, pp. 208–27. Rita Arditti, Renate Duelli Klein and Shelley Minden (eds.), *Test Tube Babies: What Future for Motherhood?* London: Pandora Press 1984.
10. Diane Elson and Ruth Pearson, 'Nimble fingers make cheap workers: an analysis of women's employment in third world manufacturing', *Feminist Review*, no. 7, 1981, pp. 87–107.

Chapter 1

1. UN Report, 1980.
2. Heidi Hartmann, 'The unhappy marriage of marxism and feminism: towards a more progressive union' in Lydia Sargent (ed.), *The Unhappy Marriage of Marxism and Feminism: A Debate on Class and Patriarchy*, London: Pluto Press 1981, pp. 14–15.
3. Frederick Engels, 'Preface to the first edition', *The Origins of the Family, Private Property and the State*, New York: International Publishers 1972, pp. 71–72.
4. see Lydia Sargent, *The Unhappy Marriage*, *op. cit.*
   Annette Kuhn and Ann Marie Wolpe (eds.), *Feminism and Materialism: Women and Modes of Production*, London: Routledge & Kegan Paul 1976;
   R. Reiter (ed.), *Towards an Anthropology of Women*, New York: Monthly Review Press 1975.
5. Margaret Mead, *Male and Female*, Harmondsworth: Penguin 1962, pp. 157–58.
6. Ruth Wallsgrove, 'The masculine face of science' in Brighton Women and Science Group, *Alice Through the Microscope: The Power of Science over Women's Lives*, London: Virago 1980, p. 236.
7. Sandra Harding, 'What is the real material base of patriarchy and capital?' in Lydia Sargent, *The Unhappy Marriage, op. cit.*, p. 152.
8. *ibid.*
9. H. Oldenberg and F. Bacon quoted from Brian Easlea, *Science and Sexual Oppression*, London: George Weidenfeld & Nicolson 1981, ch. 3.
10. J. Glanville and F. Bacon quoted from Brian Easlea, *Science and Sexual Oppression, op. cit.*; see also Brian Easlea, *Witch-hunting, Magic and the New Philosophy: An Introduction to the Debates of the Scientific Revolution 1450–1750*, Brighton: Harvester Press 1980.
11. Lynn White Jr. 'The historical roots of our ecological crisis', *Science*, vol. 155, 1967, p. 1205.
12. *Witches, Midwives and Nurses: A History of Women Healers*, London: Writers and Readers Publishing Co-operative 1973, p. 30.
13. Robert K. Merton, *Science, Technology and Society in Seventeenth Century England* (1938), New York: Harper and Row 1970, pp. 112–36;
    R.H. Tawney, *Religion and the Rise of Capitalism* (1926), Harmondsworth: Penguin 1980.
14. J.D. Bernal, *Science in History* vol. 2, *The Scientific and Industrial Revolutions* (1954), Middlesex: Penguin 1969.
15. *ibid.*, p. 530.

16. *ibid.*, p. 418.
17. see Brian Easlea, *Fathering the Unthinkable: Masculinity, Scientists and the Nuclear Arms Race*, London: Pluto Press 1983.
18. Lynn White, 'The historical roots of our ecological crisis', *op. cit.*
19. J. Glanville, quoted from Brian Easlea, *Science and Sexual Oppression, op. cit.*, ch. 3.
20. see Barbara Ehrenreich and Deirdre English, *For Her Own Good: 150 Years of the Experts' Advice to Women*, London: Pluto Press 1979.
21. see Karl Marx, *Capital* vol. I (1887), Harmondsworth: Penguin 1976.
22. see Elizabeth Fisher, *Women's Creation: Sexual Evolution and the Shaping of Society* (1979), London: Wildwood 1980;
Sheila Lewenhak, *Women and Work*, Glasgow: Collins/Fontana 1980.
23. Ann Oakley, *Housewife*, Harmondsworth: Penguin 1976, pp. 18–22.
24. *ibid.*, chs. 2 and 3.
25. Gerry Toner, 'The Weaver and the Factory Maid' (mimeo, unpublished), Brighton: 1983.
26. Adam Smith, *The Wealth of Nations* (1776), Harmondsworth: Penguin 1970, p. 112.
27. see S.A. Marglin, 'What do bosses do?' in A. Gorz (ed.), *The Division of Labour: The Labour Process and Class Struggle in Modern Capitalism*, Brighton: Harvester Press 1976;
Maxine Berg (ed.), *Technology and Toil*, London: CSE Books 1980.
28. Charles Babbage, *On the Economy of Machinery and Manufactures*, 4th edn. (1835), New York: Augustus M. Kelly 1971, pp. 175–76.
29. Andrew Ure quoted from Marx, *Capital* vol I, p. 437.
30. Nathan Rosenberg, *Perspectives on Technology*, Cambridge: Cambridge University Press 1976, p. 120.
31. see David F. Noble, *America by Design: Science, Technology and the Rise of Corporate Capitalism* (1977), Oxford: Oxford University Press 1979.
32. F.W. Taylor, *Scientific Management* (1947), Westport, Connecticut: Greenwood Press 1972.
33. Harry Braverman, *Labour and Monopoly Capital: The Degradation of Work in the Twentieth Century*, New York: Monthly Review Press 1974, pp. 11–19.
34. Ann Oakley, *Housewife, op. cit.*, p. 37.
35. see Cynthia Cockburn, *Brothers: Male Dominance and Technological Change*, London: Pluto Press 1983.
36. Anne Phillips and Barbara Taylor, 'Sex and Skill: Notes Towards a Feminist Economics', *Feminist Review* no. 6, 1980, pp. 79–88.

37. Census data from Ann Oakley, *Housewife*, *op. cit.*, ch. 3.
38. Hilary Land, 'The Family Wage', *Feminist Review* no. 6, 1980, pp. 55–78.
39. Ann Oakley, *Housewife*, *op. cit.*, ch. 3.
40. Diane Elson and Ruth Pearson, 'Nimble hands make cheap workers: an analysis of women's employment in third world export manufacturing', *Feminist Review* no. 7, 1981, pp. 87–107.
41. see Rita Arditti, 'Feminism and Science' in Rita Arditti, Pat Brennan and Stet Cavrak, *Science and Liberation*, Boston: South End Press, 1980; reprinted in Elizabeth Whitelegg and others (eds.), *The Changing Experience of Women*, Oxford: Martin Robertson 1982.

Chapter 2

1. *Acknowledgements* John Irvine, Ian Miles, Mandy Snell and the editors gave helpful comments on an earlier draft of this chapter. Gary Wersky generously shared some of his work on the history of engineering with me. The Imperial College Archivist, Mrs. J. Pingree, was very patient and introduced me to Hertha Ayrton's biography, and her assistant, Mrs. M. Felton, found the cartoon. Without the Imperial College Women in Science and Technology Group the survey would never have been completed.
2. J.A. Gray, 'A biological basis for the sex differences in achievement in science?', in A. Kelly (ed.), *The Missing Half*, Manchester: Manchester University Press 1981;
G. Weiner, 'Sex differences in mathematic performance: a review of research and possible action', in R. Deem (ed.), *Schooling for Women's Work*, London: Routledge & Kegan Paul 1980.
3. C. Hutt, 'Neuroendocrinological, behavioural and intellectual aspects of sexual differentiation in human development' in C. Ounsted and D.C. Taylor (eds.), *Gender Differences: Their Ontogeny and Significance*, Edinburgh and London: Churchill Livingston 1972.
4. A.W.H. Buffery and J.A. Gray, 'Sex differences in the development of spatial and linguistic skills' in Ounsted and Taylor, *Gender Differences*, *op. cit.*
J.A. Gray and A.W.H. Buffery, 'Sex differences in emotional and cognitive behaviour including man: adaptive and neural bases', *Acta Psychologica* vol. 35, 1971, pp. 89–111;
J. Levy, 'Lateral specialisation of the human brain: Behavioural manifestations and possible evolutionary basis' in J.A. Kiger (ed.), *The Biology of Behaviour*, Corvallis, Oregon: Oregon State University Press 1972;

S.F. Witelson, 'Sex and the single hemisphere: Specialisation of the right hemisphere for spatial processing', *Science* vol. 193, 1976, pp. 425–27.

5. J.A. Gray in A. Kelly, *The Missing Half, op. cit.*;
R.E. Stafford, 'Sex differences in spatial visualisation as evidence of sex-linked inheritance', *Perceptual and Motor Skills* vol. 13, 1961, p. 428;
D.M. Broverman, E.L. Klaiber, Y. Kobayashi and W. Vogel, 'Roles of activation and inhibition in sex differences in cognitive abilities', *Psychological Review* vol. 75, 1968, pp. 23–50.

6. J.L.M. Dawson, 'Effects of sex hormones on cognitive style in rats and men', *Behaviour Genetics* vol. 2, 1972, pp. 21–42;
M.M. Tanner, *On Becoming Human*, Cambridge: Cambridge University Press 1981.

7. On the laterality arguments see H. Fairweather, 'Sex Differences in Cognition', *Cognition* vol. 4, 1976, pp. 231–80;
H. Fairweather, 'Sex differences: little reason for females to play midfield' in J.G. Beaumont (ed.), *Divided Visual Field Studies of Cerebral Organisation*, London and New York: Academic Press 1982;
J.C. Marshall, 'Some problems and paradoxes associated with recent accounts of hemisphere specialisation', *Neuropsychologia* vol. 11, 1973, pp. 463–69;
G. Siann, *Sex Differences in Spatial Ability in Children: Its Bearing on Theories Accounting for Sex Differences in Spatial Ability in Adults*, Unpublished PhD thesis, University of Edinburgh 1977.
On the genetic arguments see: T.J. Bouchard and M.G. McGee, 'Sex differences in human spatial ability: Not an x-linked recessive gene effect', *Social Biology* vol. 24, 1977, pp. 332–35;
J.C. Defries, R.C. Johnson, A.R. Kuse, G.E. McClearn, J. Polovina, S.G. Vanderberg and J.R. Wilson, 'Familial resemblance for specific cognitive abilities', *Behaviour Genetics* vol. 9, 1979, pp. 23–43;
T. Williams, 'Family resemblances in Abilities: The Wechster Scales', *Behaviour Genetics* vol. 5, 1975, pp. 405–09.
On the hormonal arguments see: J. Archer, 'Biological explanations of psychological sex differences' in B.B. Lloyd and J. Archer (eds.), *Exploring Sex Differences*, London and New York: Academic Press 1976;
M.B. Parlee, 'Comments on "Poles of activation and inhibition in sex differences in cognitive abilities", by D.M. Broverman, E.L. Klaiber, Y. Kobayashi and W. Vogel', *Psychological Review* vol. 79, 1972, pp. 180–84;
G. Singer and R.B. Montgomery, 'Comment on "Roles of activation and inhibition in sex differences in cognitive abilities"',

Psychological Review vol. 76, 1969, pp. 325–27.
For an overall critique see: R. Blier, *Science and Gender*, New York: Pergamon Press 1984;
M. Lowe, 'The dialectic of biology and culture' in M. Lowe and R. Hubbard (eds.), *Woman's Nature*, New York: Pergamon Press 1983;
R. Hubbard and M. Lowe (eds.), *Genes and Gender II*, New York: Gordian Press 1979.

8. J.W. Berry, 'Temne and Eskimo perceptual skills', *International Journal of Psychology* vol. 1, 1966, pp. 207–29.

9. B.B. Lloyd, 'Social responsibility and research on sex differences' in Lloyd and Archer, *Exploring Sex Differences*;
S.L. Star, 'The politics of right and left: sex differences in hemisphere brain asymmetry' in R. Hubbard, M.S. Henefin and B. Freid (eds.), *Women Look at Biology Looking at Women*, Cambridge Massachusetts: Schenkman Publishing 1976.

10. On confidence and mathematics see J. Genshaft and M. Hirst, 'The effectiveness of self-instructional training to enhance maths achievement in women', *Cognitive Therapy and Research* vol. 4, no. 1, 1980, pp. 91–97;
E. Fennema, 'Women and girls in mathematics: equity in mathematics education', *Educational Studies in Mathematics* vol. 10, no. 4, 1979, pp. 389–401;
E. Fennema and J. Sherman, 'Sex-related difference in mathematics achievement, spatial visualisation and affective factors', *American Educational Research Journal* vol. 14, no. 1, 1977, pp. 51–71.
On socialization and spatial skills see J.W. Berry, 'Temne and Eskimo perceptual skills, *op. cit.*;
P. Macarthur, 'Sex differences in field dependence for the Eskimo', *International Journal of Psychology* vol. 2, 1967, pp. 135–40;
E.E. Maccoby, 'Feminine intellect and the demands of science', *Impact of Science on Society* vol. XX, 1970, pp. 13–28.

11. For a further discussion of women and mathematics see
S.A. Burnett, D.M. Lane and L.M. Dralt, 'Spatial visualisation and sex differences in quantitative abilities', *Intelligence* vol. 3, 1979, pp. 345–54;
E. Fennema and J. Sherman, 'Sex-related difference in mathematics achievement, spatial visualisation and affective factors';
L.H. Fox, L. Brody and D. Tobin (eds.), *Women and the Mathematical Mystique*, Baltimore and London: The Johns Hopkins University Press 1980;
J.L. Meece, J.E. Parsons, C.M. Kaczala, S.B. Goff and R. Futterman, 'Sex differences in math achievements: Toward a model

of academic choice', *Psychological Bulletin* vol. 91, no. 3, 1982, pp. 324–48;

J.A. Sherman, 'Effects of biological factors on sex-related differences in mathematics achievement' in *Women and Mathematics:Perspectives for Change*, NIE Papers in Education and Work, 1977, no. 8.

For a fuller critique and an account of why the biological arguments remain popular despite severe criticism see D. Griffiths and E. Saraga, 'Sex differences in cognitive abilities: a sterile field of enquiry?' in O. Hartnett, G. Boden and M. Fuller (eds.), *Sex Role Stereotyping*, London: Tavistock 1979;

D. Griffiths and E. Saraga, 'Biological theories on women', *Science for People* no. 43–44, 1979, pp. 8–12;

E. Saraga and D. Griffiths, 'Biological inevitabilities or political choice? The future for girls in science' in A. Kelly, *The Missing Half, op. cit.*

12. M. Alic, 'Women and Technology in Ancient Alexandria: Maria and Hypatic', *Women's Studies International Quarterly* vol. 4, no. 3, 1981, pp. 305–12;

    H.J. Mozans, *Woman in Science* (1913), Cambridge, Massachusetts and London: MIT Press 1974;

    A. Stanley, 'Daughters of Isis, daughters of Demeter: When women sowed and reaped', *Women's Studies International Quarterly* vol. 4, no. 3, 1981, pp. 289–304.

13. E. Power, *Medieval Women*, Cambridge: Cambridge University Press, 1975.

14. S.A. Marglin, 'What do bosses do? The origins and functions of hierarchy in capitalist production', *Review of Radical Political Economics* vol. 6, 1974, pp. 60–112.

15. I. Pinchbeck, *Women Workers and the Industrial Revolution* (1930), London: Virago Press 1981, p. 148.

16. *ibid.*, p. 304.

17. Alice Clark, *Working Life of Women in the Seventeenth Century*, Routledge & Kegan Paul: London and Boston 1982 (originally published in 1919).

18. H.J. Mozans, *op. cit.*, p. 347.

19. *ibid.*, pp. 351–52.

20. D.S.L. Cardwell, *The Organisation of Science in England*, Heinemann: London 1972 (revised edition);

    S. Delamont, 'The contradiction of ladies' education', in S. Delamont and L. Duffin (eds.) *The Nineteenth Century Woman*, Croom Helm: London 1978;

    M.J. Wiener, *English Culture and the Decline of the Industrial Spirit*, Cambridge University Press: Cambridge 1981.

21. E. Sharpe, *Hertha Ayrton: A Memoir*, Edward Arnold: London 1926, pp. 150–51.
22. R. Messenger, *The Doors of Opportunity*, Femina Books Ltd: London 1967;
    M. Sanderson, *Research and the Firm in British Industry*, Routledge & Kegan Paul: London 1972.
23. A. Oakley, *Sex, Gender and Society*, Temple Smith: London 1972.
24. B. Easlea, *Science and Sexual Oppression*, Weidenfield & Nicolson: London 1981;
    B. Easlea, *Fathering the Unthinkable: Masculinity, Scientists and the Nuclear Arms Race*, London: Pluto Press 1983.
25. *15 to 18: A report . . .* (The Crowther Report), Central Advisory Council for Education (England), 1959;
    Half Our Future (The Newsome Report), Central Advisory Council for Education (England), 1963.
26. E.M. Byrne, 'Inequality in education – discriminal resource-allocation in schools?', *Educational Review* vol. 27, no. 3, 1975, pp. 179–91;
    S. Delamont, *Sex Roles and the School*, London: Methuen 1980.
27. H. Weinreich-Haste, 'The image of science' in A. Kelly, *The Missing Half*, *op. cit.*
28. B. Smail, J. Whyte and A. Kelly, *Girls into Science and Technology: The First Two Years*, Paper presented to the International Conference on Girls and Science and Technology: Veldhovern, Holland, 1981.
29. J. Harding, 'Sex differences in science examinations' in A. Kelly, *The Missing Half*, *op. cit.*
30. UCCA, *Annual Reports.*
31. M.B. Omerod, 'Factors differentially affecting the science subject preferences, choices and attitudes of girls and boys' in A. Kelly, *The Missing Half*, *op. cit.*
32. C.S. Dweck and E.S. Bush, 'Sex differences in learned helplessness: I Differential debilitation with peer and adult evaluators', *Developmental Psychology* vol. 12, no. I, 1976, pp. 147–56;
    C.S. Dweck, W. Davidson, S. Nelson and B. Enna, 'Sex differences in learned helplessness: II The contingencies of evaluative feedback in the classroom; III An experimental analysis', *Developmental Psychology* vol. 14, no. 3, 1978, pp. 268–76.
33. Genshaft and Hirst, 'The effectiveness of self-instructed training to enhance maths achievement in women'; Fennema and Sherman, 'Sex-related differences in mathematics achievement, spatial visualisation and affective factors', *op. cit.*
34. G.K. Baruch, 'Sex-role attitudes of fifth grade girls' in J. Stacey, S. Bereaud and J. Daniels (eds.), *And Jill Came Tumbling After: Sexism*

in American Education, New York: Dell 1974; M.S. Horner, 'Femininity and successful achievement: a basic inconsistency' in M.H. Garskof (ed.), *Roles Women Play*, California: Brooks/Cole 1971;

M. Komorovsky, 'Cultural contradictions and sex roles: The masculine case' in J. Huber (eds.), *Changing Women in a Changing Society*, Chicago: Chicago University Press 1982.

35. H. Zuckerman and J.R. Cole, 'Women in American Science', *Minerva* vol. 13, 1975, pp. 82–102.

36. C. Cooper and M. Davidson, *High Pressure: Working Lives of Women Managers*, London: Fontana 1982.

Chapter 3

1. M. Finniston (Chair), *Engineering Our Future: Report of the Committee of Inquiry into the Engineering Profession*, Cmnd 7794, London: HMSO 1980.

2. Martin J. Wiener, *English Culture and the Decline of the Industrial Spirit, 1850–1980*, Cambridge: Cambridge University Press 1981.

3. Nuala Swords-Isherwood, 'British Management Compared' in Keith Pavitt (ed.), *Technical Innovation and British Economic Performance*, London: Macmillan 1980, pp. 88–99.

4. Equal Opportunities Commission, *Submission to the Committee of Enquiry into the Engineering Profession*, Manchester: Equal Opportunities Commission 1978.

5. H.I. Connor, A.R. Fidgett, C.R. Laidlaw, R.E. Laslett and E.B. Sinclair, *Women in Engineering*, Engineering Industry Training Board Occasional Paper No 11, Watford: EITB 1984.

6. *ibid.*, especially Table C6.

7. *ibid.*, especially Section 6; also P. Brayshaw and C.J. Laidlaw, *Women in Engineering*, RP/4/79, Watford: Engineering Industry Training Board 1979.

8. Department of Education and Science, *Statistics on Education* vol. 2, London: HMSO 1979.

9. *Universities Central Council on Admissions*, University Statistics vol. 1, 1980, DES Statistics of Education, vol. 6, 1979.

10. *Blueprint*, Newspaper of the Engineering Industry Training Board, February 1981.

11. Michael Perry Carter, *Into Work*, Harmondsworth: Penguin 1966.

12. Manpower Services Commission, *Special Programmes, Special Needs: Women and Girls*, London: Manpower Services Commission, November 1979.

13. A. Hinds, *Camera Week*, December 1980.

14. Interview.
15. N. Swords, *Feminism and the Female School Leaver*, MA Thesis, University of Sussex, 1970.
16. M. Finniston, *Engineering Our Future*, *op. cit.*
17. A. Hinds, *Camera Week*, *op. cit.*
18. V. Walsh, J. Townsend, P. Senker and C. Huggett, *Technological Change and Skilled Manpower Needs in the Plastics Processing Industry*, Brighton: Science Policy Research Unit, University of Sussex, Occasional Paper No. 11 1980.
19. Quoted by Counter Information Services, *Women Under Attack*, Report 15, London: Counter Information Services 1976.
20. General Household Survey 1978, 1979, Labour Force Survey 1979.
21. V. Walsh and others, *Technological Change and Skilled Manpower Needs*, *op. cit.*
22. Institution of Civil Engineers, *Report of Working Party on the Role of Women in Engineering*, London: Institution of Civil Engineers 1969.
23. C. Cooper and M. Davidson, *High Pressure: Working Lives of Women Managers*, London: Fontana 1982.
24. A. Coote, *Equal at Work? Women in Men's Jobs*, Glasgow: Collins 1979.
25. *Engineering Today*, 13 November 1978.
26. Sadie Robarts, *Positive Action for Women*, London: National Council for Civil Liberties 1981; see also D. Susan Bullivard, 'Women in Engineering – Some Findings of a Study Tour to the USA' in Equal Opportunities Commission Research Bulletin no. 9, *Women in Engineering*, Manchester: Equal Opportunities Commission 1983.

Chapter 4

1. *Acknowledgements* No piece of work is ever conceived or executed in isolation. I would like to thank the following women for their help with this chapter – Marge Bere, Gina Catteral, Lesley Doyal, Julie Newman and Sue Plummer – also, Erik Arnold, John Krige, Ian Miles and Mike Porteous.
2. Barbara Ehrenreich and Deirdre English, *For Her Own Good: 150 Years of the Experts' Advice to Women* (1978), London: Pluto Press 1979, p. 29. This book is an outstanding piece of feminist research and comment; and provided much of the inspiration and material for this article. Chapters 2 and 3 are strongly recommended for anyone wishing to know more about the fate of women healers in the industrialized world.

3. *ibid.*, pp. 30–35.
4. Barbara Ehrenreich and Deirdre English, *Witches, Midwives and Nurses: A History of Women Healers*, London: Writers and Readers Publishing Co-operative 1973, pp. 22–28.
5. *ibid.*, p. 35; see also pp. 28–37.
6. W. Duncan Reekie and Michael H. Weber, *Profits, Politics and Drugs*, London: Macmillan Press 1979, ch. 1.
7. Heinrich Kramer and Jacob Sprenger, *Malleus Maleficarum: The Hammer of Witches*, Pennethorne Hughes (ed.), Montague Summers (trans.), London: The Folio Society 1968, p. 218.
8. From Ursula Gilbert, 'Midwifery as a Deviant Occupation in America', unpublished paper 1975, quoted in B. Ehrenreich and D. English, *For Her Own Good, op. cit.*, p. 86.
9. See Margaret Connor Versluysen, 'Midwives, medical men and poor women labouring of child: Lying-in hospitals in eighteenth century London', in Helen Roberts (ed.), *Women, Health and Reproduction*, London: Routledge & Kegan Paul 1981.
10. Manningham, 1744, quoted in M.C. Versluysen, *ibid.*, p. 31. (original emphasis).
11. Elizabeth Nihill, *A Treatise on the Art of Midwifery*, London 1760, quoted in Versluysen, *ibid.* For more information on other protagnists in the battle see also Datha Clapper Brack, 'Displaced – the midwife by the male physician', in R. Hubbard, M.S.Henefin and B. Freid (eds.), *Women Look at Biology Looking at Women*, Cambridge, Massachusetts: Schenkman Publishing Co. 1979.
12. From Ann H. Sablosky, 'The Power of the Forceps: A Study of the Development of Midwifery in the United States', Masters Thesis, Graduate School of Social Work and Social Research, Bryn Mawr College, May 1975, quoted in B. Ehrenreich and D. English, *For Her Own Good, op. cit.*, p. 85.
13. See M.P.M. Richards, 'Innovation in medical practice: Obstetricians and the induction of labour in Britain', *Social Science and Medicine* vol. 9, 1975.
14. See Lesley Doyal with Imogen Pennell, *The Political Economy of Health*, London: Pluto Press 1979, pp. 30–32.
15. See B. Ehrenreich and D. English, *For Her Own Good, op. cit.*, pp. 42–52.
16. *ibid.*, p. 62; see also pp. 62–84.
17. *ibid.*, p. 29; see also pp. 29–35.
18. Susan B. Blum, 'Women, witches and herbals', *The Morris Arboretum Bulletin* vol. 25, September 1974, quoted in B. Ehrenreich and D. English, *For Her Own Good, op. cit.*, p. 32.
19. See B. Ehrenreich and D. English, *ibid.*, pp. 35–42.

20. *ibid.*, p. 40.
21. See M.C. Versluysen, 'Midwives, medical men and poor labouring women', *op. cit.*, and M.P.M. Richards, 'Innovation in medical practice', *op. cit.*
22. See L. Doyal, *The Political Economy of Health*, *op. cit.*, p. 12; also pp. 27–36.
23. See B. Ehrenreich and D. English, *For Her Own Good*, *op. cit.*, pp. 52–61.
24. Quoted in Edythe Lutzker, *Women Gain a Place in Medicine*, New York: McGraw Hill 1969, p. 48 (my emphasis).
25. *ibid.*, p. 135.
26. B. Ehrenreich and D. English, *Witches, Midwives and Nurses*, *op. cit.*, pp. 52–59.
27. See L. Doyal, *The Political Economy of Health*, *op. cit.*, ch. 5.
28. *ibid.*, p. 236.
29. See Gail Young, 'A woman in medicine: Reflections from the inside' in H. Roberts, *Women, Health and Reproduction*, *op. cit.*
30. See E. Lutzker, *Women Gain a Place in Medicine*, *op. cit.* and L. Doyal, *The Political Economy of Health*, *op. cit.*
31. L. Doyal, *ibid.*, pp. 201 and 205.
32. Stephen Fulder and Robin Munro, *The Status of Complementary Medicine in the United Kingdom*, Threshold Foundation, London (cited in the *Guardian*, 7 April 1982, p. 17).
33. See Hilary Standing, '"Sickness is a woman's business?": Reflections on the attribution of illness' in Brighton Women and Science Group (eds.), *Alice Through the Microscope: The Power of Science over Women's Live*, London: Virago Press 1980; B. Ehrenreich and D. English, *For Her Own Good*, *op. cit.*, chs. 4–8; Michele Barrett and Helen Roberts, 'Doctors and their patients: the social control of women in general practice' in Carol Stuart and Barry Smart (eds.), *Women, Sexuality and Social Control*, London: Routledge & Kegan Paul 1978; and Doyal, *The Political Economy of Health*, *op. cit.*, ch. 6.
34. See, for example, Mayra Buvinić and Joanne Leslie, 'Health care for women in Latin America and the Caribbean', *Studies in Family Planning* vol. 12, no. 3, March 1981; also Kathleen Newland, *The Sisterhood of Man: The Impact of Women's Changing Roles on Social and Economic Life Around the World*, New York: W.W. Norton 1979.

Chapter 5

1. The research was commissioned and funded by the Community Medicine Department of a health district. Confidentiality was

assured the women who took part, and so there is no identifying detail of them or the area.

2. For the purposes of this chapter, the discussion of data is limited to the use of technology in pregnancy, labour and birth.

3. L. Doyal, *The Political Economy of Health*, London: Pluto Press 1979, p. 235.

4. 1963 figures from DHSS, *On the State of the Public Health for 1964*, London: HMSO 1964, p. 88; 1969 to 1978 figures from DHSS, *On the State of the Public Health for 1979*, London: HMSO 1979, p. 83; and 1927 to 1946 figures from J. Lewis, *The Politics of Motherhood*, London: Croom Helm 1980, p. 120.

5. DHSS, *Perinatal and Neonatal Mortality*, London: HMSO 1980, p. 31.

6. For a full account of the development of child and maternal health care in the inter-war years, see J. Lewis, *The Politics of Motherhood*, op. cit.

7. See B. Ehrenreich and D. English, *Witches, Midwives and Nurses*, London: Writers and Readers Publishing Co-operative 1973; and *For Her Own Good*, London: Pluto Press 1979, for a full discussion of this process.

8. S. Kitzinger, *Women as Mothers*, London: Fontana/Collins 1978, p. 154.

9. See P. Townsend and N. Davidson, *Inequalities in Health: The Black Report*, London: Penguin 1982.

10. There are notorious problems associated with the social class definitions of women. My work used, as convention dictates, the occupational category of the husband, according to the Registrar General's classification.

11. See A. Oakley, *From Here to Maternity*, Oxford: Martin Robertson 1980 and *Women Confined*, Oxford: Martin Robertson 1980; also M. Barrett and H. Roberts, 'Doctors and their patients: The social control of women in general practice' in C. Smart and B. Smart (eds.), *Women, Sexuality and Social Control*, London: Routledge & Kegan Paul 1978.

12. See National Childbirth Trust, *Pregnancy and Parenthood*, London: Oxford University Press 1980 and M. Tew, 'Is home a safer place?' *Health and Social Service Journal*, 30 May 1980.

13. See M.F.M. Richards, 'Innovation in medical practice: Obstetricians and the induction of labour in Britain', *Social Science and Medicine* vol. 9, London: Pergamon Press 1975, pp. 595–602.

14. S. Kitzinger, *Women as Mothers*, op. cit., p. 162.

15. National Childbirth Trust, *Pregnancy and Parenthood*, op. cit., p. 217.

16. S. Firestone, *The Dialectic of Sex*, British edition, London: The Women's Press 1979, p. 193.
17. See H. Rose and J. Hanmer, 'Women's liberation, reproduction and the technological fix' in D.L. Barker and S. Allen (eds.), *Sexual Divisions and Society: Process and Change*, London: Tavistock 1976 and J. Hanmer and P. Allen, 'Reproductive engineering: The final solution?' in Brighton Women and Science Group (eds.), *Alice Through the Microscope*, London: Virago Press 1980.
18. Boston Women's Health Collective, *Our Bodies Ourselves*, British edition by A. Phillips and J. Rakusen, London: Penguin 1979, p. 561.
19. See K. Gardner, 'Well-woman clinics: A positive approach to women's health', in H. Roberts (ed.), *Women, Health and Reproduction*, London: Routledge & Kegan Paul 1981. In 'Domino' deliveries women in labour are attended in their own homes by community midwives. The actual delivery takes place in hospital, and the hospital stay is kept to a minimum.
20. DHSS, *Perinatal and Neonatal Mortality*, op. cit., p. 71.
21. B. Ehrenreich and D. English, *Complaints and Disorders*, London: Writers and Readers Publishing Co-operative 1973, p. 88.
22. A. Rich, *Of Woman Born*, London: Virago Press 1977, p. 285.

Chapter 6

1. See, for example, E.A. Wrigley, *Population and History*, London: Weidenfeld & Nicolson 1969.
2. Vivien Walsh, 'Contraception: The Growth of a Technology' in Brighton Women and Science Group, *Alice Through the Microscope: The Power of Science Over Women's Lives*, London: Virago 1980, pp. 187–207.
3. 'Survey of the United States' use of population control in Latin America', *Science for the People* vol. 5, no. 2, pp. 4–8.
4. Mahmood Mamdani, *The Myth of Population Control: Caste and Class in an Indian Village*, New York and London: Monthly Review Press 1972.
5. African National Congress Women's Section (External Mission), 'Population Control in South Africa' in *ICASC Newsletter*, London: International Contraception, Abortion and Sterilisation Campaign – Women Decide! no. 6, 1981, p. 1.
6. Mahmood Mamdani, *The Myth of Population Control*, op. cit.
7. *International Planned Parenthood Federation Plan 1982–84*, London: IPPF November 1980.
8. Mayra Buvinić and Joanne Leslie, 'Health Care for Women in

Latin America and the Caribbean', *Studies in Family Planning* vol. 12, no. 3, March 1981, pp. 112–15.

9. For examples of the effects of technical change on women in factory work, see *Women and Work: ISIS International Bulletin* no. 10, Winter 1978–79, especially 'Women Workers in Asia', pp. 4–5; 'South Korea: Textile Workers Fighting For Their Rights', pp. 6–12, and 'One Boss – One Struggle: Electronics in Southeast Asia', p. 16.

10. *Ninth Annual Report: World Health Organization Special Programme of Research, Development and Research Training in Human Reproduction*, Geneva: WHO 1980, pp. 43–44 and 100–01.

11. Bonnie Mass, *Population Target: The Political Economy of Population Control in Latin America*, Toronto: Lawg 1976.

12. Mark Dowie, 'The Corporate Crime of the Century'; Barbara Ehrenreich and others, 'The Charge: Gynocide, The Accused: the US Government' and David Weir and others, 'The Boomerange Crime', San Francisco: *Mother Jones* Reprint Service November 1979.

13. An organization called Health Action International was formed in 1981 to press for a World Health Organization code of practice on drugs, drug companies and drug dumping. HAI may be contacted c/o International Organization of Consumers Unions, P.O. Box 1045, Penang, Malasia. In Britain, contact Social Audit, 9 Poland Street, London W1.

14. Dalkon Shield Association (London), 'The Dalkon Shield Story', *ICASC Newsletter*, London: International Contraception, Abortion and Sterilisation Campaign – Women Decide! no. 2, 1980, p. 4.

15. WHO, *Ninth Annual Report*, p. 29.

16. Samuel Coleman, 'The Cultural Context of Condom Use in Japan', *Studies in Family Planning* vol. 12, no. 1, January 1981, pp. 28–39.

17. Ruth Holly, 'Population Control in Colombia', *ICASC Co-ordination Report*, London: International Contraception, Abortion and Sterilisation Campaign – Women Decide! June 1982.

18. WHO Task Force on Sequelae of Abortion, 'Health and Economic Effects of Illegal Abortion: Preliminary Findings from an International Study' in G.I. Zatuchni and others, *Pregnancy Termination: Procedures, Safety and New Developments*, London: Harper & Row 1979, pp. 361–69.

19. Mirjana Morokvasić, 'Sexuality and the Control of Procreation', in Kate Young and others (eds.), *Of Marriage and the Market*, London: CSE Books 1981, pp. 127–43.

20. Samuel Coleman, 'The Cultural Context of Condom Use in Japan', *op. cit.*
21. WHO, Ninth Annual Report, p. 32.
22. Contact, Women's Reproductive Rights Information Centre (WRRIC), at 52–54 Featherstone Street, London EC1, Britain.

Further Reading

Marge Berer, *Who Needs Depo-Provera?*, Community Rights Project 1984 (available from WRRIC).

Peter Huntingford, a paper on sterilization given to the *Symposium on Family Planning and Poverty*, organized by the Doctors and Overpopulation Group: London 4 May 1979 (available from WRRIC).

Dianna Melrose, *Bitter Pills: Medicines and the Third World Poor*, London: Oxfam 1982.

Jill Rakusen, 'Depo-Provera: The extent of the problem, a case study in the Politics of Birth Control', in Helen Roberts (ed.), *Women, Health and Reproduction*, London: Routledge & Kegan Paul 1981, pp. 75–108.

Nawal el Saadawi, *The Hidden Face of Eve: Women in the Arab World*, London: Zed Press 1980; for relevant excerpts see *ICASC Newsletter*, London: International Contraception, Abortion and Sterilisation Campaign – Women Decide! no. 4/5, 1981, p. 8.

Population Control (manuscript), 1984, available from the Institute for Food and Development Policy, 1885 Mission Street, California, USA 94103.

NET-OEN: The Other Injectable, 1984, available from War on Want, 467 Caledonian Road, London N7, Britain.

Annual Reports: World Health Organization Special Programme of Research, Development and Research Training in Human Reproduction, Geneva: WHO.

Population Reports, published bi-monthly, Population Information Program of the Johns Hopkins University, 624 North Broadway, Baltimore, Maryland, USA (supported by the US Agency for International Development).

Chapter 7

1. Barbara Ehrenreich and Deirdre English, *For Her Own Good: 150 Years of the Experts' Advice to Women*, Pluto Press 1979, p. 128.
2. Alice Clark, *The Working Life of Women in the Seventeenth Century* (1919), London: Frank Cass 1968, p. 5.

3. Phyllis Deane, *The First Industrial Revolution*, Cambridge: Cambridge University Press 1965, pp. 147–48.
4. Wanda F. Neff, *Victorian Working Women: An Historical and Literary Study of Women in British Industries and Professions 1832–1850* (1929), London: Frank Cass 1966, p. 53.
5. 'Workhouse Visiting' in Rev. F.D. Maurice (ed.), *Lectures to Ladies on Practical Subjects*, Cambridge: Macmillan 1885, cited in Sandra Burman (ed.), *Fit Work for Women*, London: Croom Helm 1979, pp. 40–41.
6. Theresa McBride, *The Domestic Revolution: The Modernisation of Domestic Service in England and France 1820–1920*, London: Croom Helm 1976, p. 83.
7. Carol Dyhouse, *Girls Growing Up in Late Victorian and Edwardian England*, London: Routledge & Kegan Paul 1981, p. 82.
8. W.F. Neff, *Victorian Working Women*, op. cit., pp. 46–50.
9. Fay Pierce, *Atlantic Monthly*, quoted in Susan Strasser, *Never Done: A History of American Housework*, New York: Pantheon 1981, p. 196.
10. Fannie Perry Gay, *Woman's Journal*, 12 November 1889, p. 365 quoted in B. Ehrenreich and D. English, *For Her Own Good*, op. cit., p. 130.
11. S. Strasser, *Never Done*, op. cit., p. 185.
12. E.P. Thompson, *The Making of the English Working Class*, Harmondsworth: Penguin 1967, p. 60.
13. Cited in Catherine Hall, 'The Early Formation of Victorian Domestic Ideology' in S. Burman, *Fit Work for Women*, op. cit., p. 34.
14. B. Ehrenreich and D. English, *For Her Own Good*, op. cit., p. 128.
15. C. Dyhouse, *Girls Growing Up*, op. cit., pp. 4–5.
16. Anne Somers, 'A Home From Home – Women's Philanthropic Work in the Nineteenth Century' in S. Burman, *Fit Work for Women*, op. cit., p. 34.
17. Ailsa Yoxall, *A History of the Teaching of Domestic Economy*, Bath: Cedric Chivers undated (circa 1914), reprinted 1965.
18. Isabella Beeton, *Beeton's Book of Household Management*, London: S.O. Beeton 1861, p. 38.
19. Catherine E. Beecher and Harriet Beecher Stowe, *The American Woman's Home: or, Principles of Domestic Science*, New York: J.B. Ford and Co 1869, p. i.
20. S. Strasser, *Never Done*, op. cit., p. 186.
21. Isabel F. Hyams, 'The Louisa May Alcott Club', *Proceedings of the Second Annual Conference on Home Economics*, Lake Placid, New York, 1900, p. 18, quoted in B. Ehrenreich and D. English, *For Her Own Good*, op. cit., p. 158.
22. C. Dyhouse, *Girls Growing Up*, op. cit., p. 81.

23. *ibid.*, p. 82.
24. *ibid.*, pp. 83–4.
25. *ibid.*, pp. 91–2; 162–4.
26. cited in C. Dyhouse, *ibid.*, p. 168.

Chapter 8

1. Nona Glazer-Malbin, 'Housework', *Signs* vol. 1, no. 4, 1976, pp. 905–22.
2. Heidi Hartmann, *Capitalism and Women's Work in the Home, 1900–1930*, PhD Dissertation, Yale University, 1974.
3. Anthony Byers, *Centenary of Service: A History of Electricity in the Home*, London: Electricity Council 1981, pp. 82–83.
4. Lloyd A. Fallers, 'A Note on the "Trickle Effect"', 1954, cited in Perry Bliss (ed.), *Marketing and the Behavioural Sciences*, Boston, Massachusetts: Allyn and Bacon, 1963, pp. 208–16.
5. L. Needleman, 'The Demand for Domestic Appliances,' *National Institute Economic Review* 12 (November 1960), 24–44, p. 38.
6. Barbara Ehrenreich and Deirdre English, *For Her Own Good: 150 Years of the Experts' Advice to Women*, London: Pluto Press 1979, p. 162.
7. A. Byers, *Centenary of Service, op. cit.*, p. 11.
8. Susan Strasser, *Never Done: A History of American Housework*, New York: Pantheon 1981, p. 79.
9. J.I. Gershuny and G.S. Thomas, *Changing Patterns of Time Use, UK 1961–1975*, SPRU Occasional Paper Number 13, Brighton: Science Policy Research Unit, 1981;
   J. Robinson, *Changes in the American Use of Time: 1965–1975*, Communications Research Center, Cleveland State University, August 1977;
   W.P. Knulst, *Een Week Tijd*, Sociaal en Cultureel Planbureau, Grevenhage (Netherlands), 1977.
10. Joann Vanek, 'Time Spent In Housework', *Scientific American* vol. 231, November 1974, pp. 116–20, reprinted in Alice H. Amsden (ed.), *The Economics of Women and Work*, Harmondsworth: Penguin 1980, pp. 82–90.
11. John P. Robinson and Philip E. Converse, 'Social Change Reflected in the Use of Time' in Angus Campbell and Philip E. Converse (eds.), *The Human Meaning of Social Change*, New York: Russell Sage Foundation 1972, pp. 17–86.
12. Jonathan Gershuny, *Social Innovation and the Division of Labour*, Oxford: Oxford University Press 1983, p. 152.
13. J.I. Gershuny, 'Changing Use of Time in the United Kingdom:

1937–1975, the Self-Service Era', *Studies of Broadcasting* no. 19, Nippon Hoso Kyokai 1983, pp. 71–91.

14. Ann Oakley, *Occupation: Housewife*, Harmondsworth: Penguin 1974, p. 93.

15. Alexander Szalai, 'The situation of women in the light of contemporary time-budget research', proceedings UN Conference of the International Women's Year, Mexico City, 1975.

16. Mary Rowe, 'The length of a housewife's day in 1917', *Journal of Home Economics* (December 1917), reprinted vol. 65, October 1973.

17. Committee on Household Management and Kitchens, *Household Management and Kitchens*, President's Conference on Homebuilding and Home Ownership, Washington, DC: US Government Printing Office 1932, pp. 30–44.

18. Florence Hall and Marguerite Schroeder, 'Time spent on household tasks', *Journal of Home Economics* vol. 62, January 1970, pp. 23–29; M.K. Heiner and N.M. Vedder, 'Studies in distinguishing methods: an attempt to apply methods of job analysis to a household process', *Journal of Home Economics* vol. 22, no. 5, 1930, pp. 393–407; Elaine Weaver, Clarice Bloom and Ilajean Feldmiller, 'A study of hand vs. mechanical dishwashing methods', *Ohio Agricultural Experiment Station Bulletin* no. 772, Kent, Ohio: Ohio Agricultural Experiment Station, May 1956.

19. Mary Rowe, 'The length of a housewife's day', *op. cit.*

20. Maude Wilson, 'Use of time by Oregon farm homemakers', *Oregon Agriculture Experiment Station Bulletin* no. 256, Oregon: Oregon Agriculture Experiment Station 1929.

21. Ann Oakley, *The Sociology of Housework* (1974), London: Martin Robinson 1976.

22. Joseph Spengler, 'Product adding vs. product replacing innovation', *Kyklos* vol. 10, 1957, pp. 249–80; Steffan Linder, *The Harried Leisure Class*, New York: Columbia University Press 1972.

23. Walter McQuade, 'Why nobody is happy about appliances', *Fortune*, May 1972, pp. 180–83 and 272–76.

24. Vance Packard, *The Wastemakers*, New York: David McKay 1960.

25. Victor F. Zonana, 'More foods today are "fresh" from factories and quick to prepare', *Wall Street Journal*, 21 June 1977, pp. 1 and 20; Stuart Ewen, *Captains of Consciousness: Advertising and the Social Roots of the Consumer Culture*, New York: McGraw Hill 1976.

26. Charles Vaugh, 'Growth and future of the fast food industry', *Cornell Hotel and Restaurant Administration Quarterly*, November 1976, p. 18.

27. Lee Flaherty, 'Change in women's status spurs battle of supermarkets vs. fast food chains', *Advertising Age*, 23 May 1977, p. 158.
28. J. Vanek, 'Time Spent in Housework', *op. cit.*
29. Robinson and Converse, 'Social Change Reflected in the Use of Time', p. 44.
30. Myra Marx Feree, 'Working-class jobs: housework and paid work as sources of satisfaction', *Social Problems* no. 23, April 1976, pp. 431–41;
    Lillian Breslow Rubin, *Worlds of Pain: Life in the Working Class Family*, New York: Basic Books 1976.
31. National Center for Health Statistics, *Selected Symptoms of Psychological Distress*, Washington, DC: US Department of Health, Education and Welfare 1970, pp. 30–31.
32. Billye Fogleman, 'Housewife syndrome among Native American women', *Urban Anthropology* vol. 4, no. 2, 1975, p. 184 (abstract).
33. Raymond Bauer and Scott Cunningham, *Studies in the Negro Market*, Cambridge, Massachusetts: Harvard Graduate School of Business Administration, Marketing Science Institute 1970.
34. Katherine Walker and Margaret Woods, *Time Use: A Measure of Household Production of Family Goods and Services*, Washington, DC: Center for the Family, American Home Economics Association 1976.
35. Charles Thrall, *Household technology and the Division of Labour in Families*, PhD dissertation, Harvard University, 1970.
36. J.I. Gershuny, 'The Household Time Economy,' in J. Huber (ed.), *Arbeit Ohne Zukunft*, Berlin: Fischer Alternativ 1984.
37. Charlotte Perkins Gilman, *Women and Economics* (1898), republished New York: Harper & Row 1966.

Chapter 9

1. Many thanks to Felicity Edholm who discussed this article with me, and who was very helpful in disentangling my ideas and prose.
2. A. Whitehead, *A Conceptual Framework for the Analysis of the Effects of Technological Change on Rural Women*, Geneva: International Labour Office World Employment Research Programme 1981.
3. G.J. Van Apeldoorn, *Perspectives on Drought and Famine in Nigeria*, London: George Allen and Unwin, 1981.
4. F. Stewart, *Technology and Underdevelopment*, London: Macmillan 1978.
5. A. Pearse, *The Social and Economic Implications of Large Scale Introduction of New Varieties of Food Grain: Summary of Conclusions*

of the Global Research Project, Report no. 74:4, Geneva: UNRISD 1974.

6. K. Griffin, *The Political Economy of Agrarian Change: An Essay on the Green Revolution*, London: Macmillan 1974.

7. A. Pearse, *The Social and Economic Implications of Large Scale Introduction of New Varieties of Food Grain, op. cit.*

8. B. Agarwal, *Agricultural Modernisation and Third World Women: Some Pointers from the Literature and an Empirical Analysis,* Geneva: International Labour Office World Employment Research Programme 1981.

9. I. Palmer, *The New Rice in Asia: Some Conclusions from Four Country Studies*, Report no. 76:6, Geneva: UNRISTD 1976.

10. I. Palmer, 'Women and Green Revolutions', paper presented to *Conference on the Subordination of Women and the Continuing Development Process* (mimeo) Brighton: Institute of Development Studies 1978.

11. F. McCarthy, *The Status and Conditions of Rural Women in Bangladesh*, Dacca: Ministry of Agriculture, Bangladesh 1978.

12. S. Zeidenstein, *Socioeconomic Implications of HYV Rice Production on Rural Women in Bangladesh* (mimeo), Dacca: Ford Foundation, 1975.

13. J. Ellickson, *Observations from the Field on the Conditions of Rural Women in Bangladesh*, Dacca: Ford Foundation, 1978.

14. A. Phillips and B. Taylor, 'Sex and Skill: Notes Towards a Feminist Economics', *Feminist Review* no. 6, 1980.

15. M. Mackintosh, 'Sexual Contradiction and Labour Conflict on a West African Estate Farm' in K. Young (ed.), *Serving Two Masters*, London: Routledge & Kegan Paul, forthcoming.

16. A. Amsden, *The Economics of Women and Work*, Harmondsworth: Penguin, 1980.

17. M. Mackintosh, 'Sexual Contradiction and Labour Conflict', *op. cit.*

18. D. Elson and R. Pearson, 'Nimble Fingers Make Cheap Workers: An Analysis of Women's Employment in Third World Manufacturing', *Feminist Review* no. 7, 1981.

Chapter 10

1. Shelley Coverman, 'Gender, domestic labour time, and wage inequality', *American Sociological Review* vol. 48, 1983, pp. 623–37.

2. Rachel A. Rosenfeld, 'Sex segregation and sectors: an analysis of gender differences in returns from employer changes', *American Sociological Review* vol. 48, 1983, pp. 637–55.

3. Patricia A. Roos, 'Marriage and women's occupational attainment in cross-cultural perspective', *American Sociological Review* vol. 48, 1983, pp. 852–64.

4. *ibid.*
5. Office of Population and Census, *General Household Survey*, London: HMSO 1981.
6. Office of Population and Census, *General Household Survey*, London: HMSO 1980.
7. P. Elias and B. Main, *Women's Working Lives: Evidence from the National Training Survey*, Warwick: Institute of Employment 1982.
8. J. Hurstfield, *The Part-Time Trap*, London: Low Pay Unit 1978.
9. Equal Opportunities Commission, *The Fact About Women is . . .*, Manchester: Equal Opportunities Commission 1983.
10. Department of Health and Social Security, *Two Parent Families and Their Needs*, London: HMSO 1971.
11. A. Hunt, *A Survey of Women's Employment*, London: HMSO 1968.
12. C.L. Hulin, 'Job satisfaction and turnover in a female clerical population', *Journal of Applied Psychology* vol. 50 (4), 1966, pp. 280–5 R. Wild and A.B. Hill, *Women in the Factory: A Study of Job Satisfaction and Labour Turnover*, London: Institute of Personnel Management 1970.
13. New Earnings Survey, *Department of Employment Gazette*, 1978.
14. C. Hakim, *Occupational Segregation*, Research Paper no. 19, London: Department of Employment 1979.
15. Tom Forester, *The Microelectronics Revolution*, Oxford: Basil Blackwell 1980.
16. Ernest Braun and Stuart Macdonald, *Revolution in Miniature* 2nd edn., Cambridge; Cambridge University Press 1982.
17. Christopher Freeman, John Clark and Luc Soete, *Unemployment and Technological Innovation: A study of Long Waves and Economic Development*, London: Frances Pinter 1983;
    SPRU Women and Technology Studies, *Microelectronics and Women's Employment in Britain*, Occasional Paper no. 17, Brighton: Science Policy Research Unit 1982;
    Ursula Huws, *Your Job in the '80s: A Woman's Guide to New Technology*, London: Pluto Press 1982.
18. E. Mumford and O. Banks, *The Computer and the Clerk*, London: Routledge & Kegan Paul 1967.
19. Ursula Huws, *op. cit.*
20. *Financial Times*, 1979 in SPRU Women and Technology Studies, *Microelectronics and Women's Employment in Britain, op. cit.*
21. Colin Hines, *The Chips are Down*, London: Earth Resources 1978.
22. Catriona Llewellyn, 'Occupational mobility and the use of the comparative method' in Helen Roberts (ed.), *Doing Feminist Research*, London; Routledge & Kegan Paul 1971.
23. *Department of Employment Gazette*, February 1983.

24. L.S. Palmer, *Technical Change and Employment in banking* (diss.) Brighton: Science Policy Research Unit, University of Sussex 1980.
25. SPRU Women and Technology Studies, *Microelectronics and Women's Employment in Britain*.
26. *Financial Times*, 6 April 1978.
27. Ursula Huws, *op. cit.*
28. SPRU Women and Technology Studies, *Microelectronics and Women's Employment in Britain*, *op. cit.*
29. Carpet Industry Training Board, *Report on Employment and Training Opportunities for Women in the Carpet Industry*, London: Carpet Industry Training Board 1979.
30. *ibid*.
31. Heidi Hartmann, 'The unhappy marriage of marxism and feminism: towards a more progressive union', *Capital and Class* no. 8, 1979, pp. 1–33.
32. Cynthia Cockburn, *Brothers: Male Dominance and Technological Change*, London: Pluto Press 1983.
33. See, for example, Murray Turoff and Starr Roxanne Hiltz, 'Working at home or living in the office', *Information Processing*, R.E.A. Mason (ed.), Amsterdam, North-Holland, 1983.
34. SPRU Women and Technology Studies, *Microelectronics and Women's Employment in Britain*, *op. cit.*
35. Manpower Services Commission, *Women Managers: Their Problems and What Can Be Done To Help Them*, London: Manpower Services Commission 1983.

Chapter 11

1. Mary Kathleen Benet, *The Secretarial Ghetto*, New York: McGraw Hill 1973;
   Alan Delgado, *The Enormous File: A Social History of the Office*, London: John Murray 1979.
2. *Englishwoman's Review* no. 184, September 1888, p. 424.
3. Rosalie Silverstone, *The Office Secretary* (diss.), University of London, 1974, p. 302.
4. Fiona McNally, *Women for Hire: A Study of the Female Office Worker*, London: Macmillan 1979, p. 59.
5. Judith Gregory, *Race Against Time*, 1224 Huron Road, Cleveland Ohio 44115: 9 to 5 National Association of Working Women (undated).
6. Jane Barker and Hazel Downing, 'Word processing and the transformation of patriarchal relations of control in the office', *Capital and Class*, vol. 10, Spring 1980, p. 84.

7. Susan Vinnicombe, *Secretaries, Management and Organisations*, London: Heinemann 1980.

8. Equal Pay and Opportunities Campaign, *Women and Word Processors*, London: EPOC, October 1980.

9. Janine Morgall, 'Typing our way to freedom: is it true that new office technology can liberate women?' in Elizabeth Whitley and others (eds.), *The Changing Experience of Women*, Oxford: Martin Robertson 1982, pp. 121–35.

10. Jane Barker and Hazel Downing, 'Word processing and the transformation of patriarchal relations of control in the office', *Capital and Class* vol. 10, Spring 1980, p. 83.

11. European Trade Union Institute, *The Impact of Microelectronics on Employment in Western Europe in the 1980s*, Brussels: ETUI 1979, p. 101.

12. Deutsch, Shea and Evans, *Word Processing and Employment*, New York: Deutsch Shea and Evans 1975.

13. Central Policy Review Staff, *Social and Employment Implications of Microelectronics*, London: National Economic Development Council (mimeo) 1978;
J. Sleigh, B. Boatwright, P. Irwin and R. Stanyon, *The Manpower Implications of Micro-Electronic Technology*, London: HMSO 1979.

14. Emma Bird, *Information Technology in the Office: The Impact on Women's Jobs*, Manchester: Equal Opportunities Commission 1980, p. 42.

15. *ibid.*, pp. 56–58.

Chapter 12

1. Philip Kraft, *Programmers and Managers: The Routinisation of Computer Programming in the United States*, New York: Springer Verlag 1977, pp. 23–26.

2. Philip Kraft and Steve Dubnoff, 'Software for women means a lower status', *Computing*, 9 February 1984; Philip Kraft and Steve Dubnoff, 'A loss of weight from the middle', *Computing*, 16 February 1984.

3. Philip Kraft and Steve Dubnoff, 'Software for women means a lower status', *op. cit.*

4. *ibid.*

5. Philip Kraft and Steve Dubnoff, 'A loss of weight from the middle', *op. cit.*

6. Philip Kraft, *Programmers and Managers*, *op. cit.*, p. 106.

7. *Electronic Times*, 11 October 1979.

8. Sherry Turkle, 'The Subjective Computer: A Study in the Psychology of Personal Computation', *Social Studies of Science* vol. 12, 1982, pp. 173–205.
9. Joseph Weizenbaum, *Computer Power and Human Reason: From Judgement to Calculation* (1976), Harmondsworth: Penguin, 1984, p. 116.
10. Rita Arditti, 'Women in science: women drink water while men drink wine', *Science for the People*, March 1976.

SCIENCE AND TECHNOLOGY REPORT

Edited by Jon Turney

Developments in science and technology alter our lives, affect relations between countries, and determine the strategy of transnational corporations. The 170 articles in *Science and Technology Report* assess the state of science and technology, and locate sci-tech innovations within a wider social and political context. The key issues covered include: geothermal energy; electronic money; cable cities; computer-aided design; R&D policy in the major countries; technology transfers; the role of women in science; the effect of science and technology on employment and leisure.

  Science and Technology Report is the reference book for anyone who wants to know about the latest developments in science and technology. With its suggestions for further reading and its directory of useful organizations, it is an essential guide to the sci-tech world.

512 pages
0 86104 761 3   £8.95

MORE THAN THE PARTS
BIOLOGY AND POLITICS
Edited by Lynda Birke and Jonathan Silvertown

Arguments based on biological science have been used to bolster a variety of right-wing policies and prejudices. Feminism is opposed on the grounds that male domination is a product of male biology; racism is justified with the argument that we have a dislike of strangers wired into our genes; elitism on the grounds that differences in intelligence are innate; the arms race on the basis that competition is natural and desirable.

More than the Parts looks at the ideology and practices of the life sciences. It points to a new approach which recognizes that our 'biology' is not static and pregiven, but may itself be transformed in interaction with our environment.

Written by working biologists and social scientists to make important issues and debates accessible to a non-specialist audience.

256 pages
0 86104 607 2   £7.95 **paperback**

FATHERING THE UNTHINKABLE
MASCULINITY, SCIENTISTS AND THE NUCLEAR ARMS RACE
BRIAN EASLEA

Why does the arms race continue? Why do military-industrial-scientific complexes have an insatiable demand for new weapons systems?

Brian Easlea argues that th_re is a deeper underlying reason than profit. The arms race is the insane, but inevitable, outcome of science performed in a world where men wage war against the 'feminine' values, women and 'female' nature.

240 pages. Index
0 86104 391 X   £5.95

THE POLITICAL ECONOMY OF HEALTH

LESLEY DOYAL with IMOGEN PENNELL

The Political Economy of Health shows that ill-health is largely a product of the social and economic organization of society; that medical practice and research are strongly influenced by their roles in maintaining a healthy labour force, and in socializing and controlling people; and that the medical field provides a large and growing arena for the accumulation of capital.

'Readable and well researched . . . Altogether a stimulating book and a worthy contribution to current debates on the politics of health.' *Lancet*
'The best book on health and health care that I have read for a long time.' *Nursing Mirror*

360 pages. Index
0 86104 074 0   £4.95 paperback

PARTIAL PROGRESS

DAVID ALBURY and JOSEPH SCHWARTZ

Did the Davy miners' lamp really improve safety in the pits? Does automation and mechanization lead to more interesting, satisfying work? This book shows how the work of scientists and technologists is neither inherently beneficial nor morally neutral.

215 pages
0 86104 385 5   £4.95 paperback